ENCOUNTERING MOROCCO

PUBLIC CULTURES OF THE MIDDLE EAST AND NORTH AFRICA
Paul Silverstein, Susan Slyomovics, and Ted Swedenburg, editors

ENCOUNTERING MOROCCO

FIELDWORK AND CULTURAL UNDERSTANDING

Edited by
DAVID CRAWFORD AND
RACHEL NEWCOMB

INDIANA UNIVERSITY PRESS
Bloomington & Indianapolis

This book is a publication of

Indiana University Press
Office of Scholarly Publishing
Herman B Wells Library 350
1320 East Tenth Street
Bloomington, Indiana 47405 USA

iupress.indiana.edu

Telephone orders   800-842-6796
Fax orders   812-855-7931

Library of Congress Cataloging-in-Publication Data

Encountering Morocco : fieldwork and cultural understanding / edited by
David Crawford and Rachel Newcomb.
     pages cm. — (Public cultures of the Middle East and North Africa)
   Includes bibliographical references and index.
   ISBN 978-0-253-00904-3 (cloth : alk. paper) — ISBN 978-0-253-
00911-1 (pbk. : alk. paper) — ISBN 978-0-253-00919-7 (electronic book)
1. Anthropology—Fieldwork—Morocco. 2. Anthropologists—Morocco.
3. Morocco—Social life and customs. 4. Intercultural communication—
Morocco. I. Crawford, David, [date] II. Newcomb, Rachel, [date] III. Series:
Public cultures of the Middle East and North Africa.
   GN649.M65E54 2013
   306.0964—dc23
                                                    2012047778

1 2 3 4 5 18 17 16 15 14 13

To Jamila, Noureddine, and Sofia —R.N.

To Hillary, for acumen, inspiration,
and the babies —D.C.

CONTENTS

ACKNOWLEDGMENTS

A version of chapter 4 previously appeared in *Anthropological Quarterly* and is being reprinted with permission. The anecdotes in chapter 3 appeared in *In and Out of Morocco,* by David A. McMurray, and are used by permission of the University of Minnesota Press.

ENCOUNTERING MOROCCO

Introduction

DAVID CRAWFORD AND RACHEL NEWCOMB

This book introduces readers to Morocco by showing how anthropologists have come to understand it. Each essay takes us into a specific part of the country through the unique voice of the writer. Each delivers a very local story, a vignette of how a particular individual has done fieldwork in a specific context. And each stands as a personal meditation on cross-cultural understanding, the way that one person came to appreciate an alien social world. Together the chapters build a richly textured portrait of the Kingdom of Morocco—a key site in the development of the discipline of anthropology.

As the essays show, ethnographic knowledge unfolds over time through fieldwork. Fieldwork, as anthropologists generally understand it, is built on intimate and often unstructured encounters with various kinds of interlocutors in one or more local contexts. Many different methods may be employed during the fieldwork experience, but participant observation—living among the people being studied—is cultural anthropology's primary research method. Anthropologists attempt to grasp other cultures by living in them for long periods of time. This type of research reveals the daily struggles that underpin larger social processes, and thus offers a vision of how everyday life is connected to larger social, cultural, and political dynamics. Anthropological fieldwork offers a perspective that is impossible to convey at the pace of a television news program or in the space of a guidebook. In an era of global transformation—with Twitter posts and YouTube videos, Occupy Wall Street, and the Arab

Spring—traditional anthropological fieldwork continues to provide uniquely grounded and original insights.

ON FIELDWORK

Anthropologists have not always done what we now call fieldwork. As students learn in their introductory classes, so-called armchair anthropology held sway during the early years of the discipline, in the middle of the nineteenth century. Scholars like E. B. Tylor relied on the accounts of travelers, colonial officials, and missionaries as well as reports from military expeditions to understand the world beyond Europe. This was an era when European society was rapidly expanding, and vast swathes of the planet came to be dominated by Britain, France, and other colonial powers. These powers wanted—indeed, they needed—to understand the places they hoped to control. The curiosity of scholars converged with the interests of powerful states, and the appraisal of subjugated peoples slowly emerged as a legitimate field of study. Scholars like Tylor came to be respected for their knowledge of small-scale, non-European societies, and they worked to establish the intellectual and organizational foundations of anthropology as a formal discipline. These early anthropologists synthesized what was then understood about non-European peoples into a broadly comparative perspective called unilineal cultural evolution—the idea that each culture evolved over time along a singular civilizational trajectory. For Tylor, "progress" depended on human rationality and each society's ability to overcome "the fetters" of its habitual cultural behavior. Arguably this perspective persists in our contemporary era—for instance, in development discourses, in which poor countries are instructed to evolve or progress to be like richer ones.

However, the reliance on secondhand data quickly came to be seen as inadequate, and by the beginning of the twentieth century trips to "the field" for the purpose of conducting research were becoming the norm. These trips were meant to permit increasingly well-trained, professional anthropologists to gather accurate, scientific information about specific cultures. Perhaps the best known of these scholars was Bronislaw Malinowski, who spent much of the period around World War I virtually exiled in the Trobriand Islands, near Papua New Guinea. Though Malinowski had been teaching in London, he was Polish by birth and therefore a subject of one of England's wartime enemies, the Austro-Hungarian Empire. Malinowski did not want to return to Poland, so he arranged to banish himself to the south Pacific. He set up a tent on a beach among the Trobriand Island natives he hoped to study and spent much of his time doing what he called participant observation, by which he meant living and participating in the society that he hoped to understand. Subsequent work, and Malinowski's own diaries, showed that his idealized account of anthropological fieldwork was somewhat different from his own practice, but nonetheless basic standards had been set.

Observations by themselves were not good enough, according to Malinowski; one needed to take an active part in the everyday lives of those one hoped to comprehend. The years that Malinowski spent in the Trobriand Islands had the effect of setting the bar very high for time spent in the field. Even today when anthropologists "do fieldwork," they typically stay many months—if not years—learning the local language, eating local food, and living as much like the study population as possible. As we will see in this volume, some anthropologists become part of the society they set out to study. This is a key difference between anthropological fieldwork and other sorts of knowledge production.

This long-term engagement was important for deep cultural understanding, for gaining "the native's point of view"—which Malinowski claimed was the "final goal" of the research (Malinowski 1984 [1922], 25). This extended exposure to their subjects gave rise to a notable sense of empathy among most fieldworkers and worked to dignify local practices by making them an accepted object of scholarly inquiry. Malinowski and others began to make the case that customs and behavior considered odd or even perverse from an outsider's perspective nonetheless functioned to solve real problems. In this way a discipline born of colonial power and privilege began to change.

Anthropology started to question the ideology of Western cultural superiority even while it relied on Western political power to secure access to "the field."

At about the same time, at the very end of the nineteenth century, the German-born Franz Boas created the first anthropology program in the United States, at Columbia University in New York City. Boas, too, emphasized fieldwork, and he began his own among the Eskimo of Canada in 1883. He trained many of the first generation of American anthropologists, including such celebrated women as Margaret Mead and Zora Neale Hurston. Boas took a different approach to cultural understanding than Tylor or Malinowski, and his American students tended to work "at home," with Native Americans or minority communities, rather than in foreign lands. Sometimes conceptualized as "salvage anthropology," this investigation of cultures thought to be on the edge of extinction gave rise to a uniquely American perspective. Because Native American groups had been militarily decimated, and the remnants were typically confined to reservations, studying the function of indigenous American customs did not seem sensible. However, studying the resilient culture was still possible. Myths, beliefs, and native worldviews remained distinct and vibrant despite military defeat, and thus culture became the American anthropologists' focus. There emerged a split between British social anthropology and American cultural anthropology. Culture as an object of study has since become dominant in anthropology.

Boas emphasized the emotional and habitual underpinnings of culture, and he was less interested in specific scientific rationales for a cultural practice than the process by which a cultural trait was borrowed from one society and incorporated into another. Boas believed that culture is sui generis, that cultures have their own dynamics that cannot be reduced to exogenous causes. He also thought that a great deal of empirical data needed to be collected before anthropologists started to generalize about laws or dynamics that cut across cultures. Unlike Malinowski, who focused on function, Boas wanted his students to research the specificities of a particular cultural configuration, and especially the historical process by which it had reached its current form. Unlike Tylor and other early cultural evolutionists, Boas strongly asserted the dignity and particularity of each culture in its unique historical formulation. He fought against the idea of ranking people as "more" or "less" civilized, and he was actively anti-racist. Boas promoted the notion of cultural relativism, the idea that each culture must be seen in its own terms. And he insisted on the professional, direct engagement of anthropologists with the people under consideration—whether these people were subcultures at home or whole societies abroad.

From here anthropological perspectives began to multiply. Some scholars took a positivist, scientific approach, arguing that anthropology should be a science like any other. Others adopted a more humanistic perspective, making the case that human action is fundamentally different from other sorts of phenomena. Because people act in ways that are shaped by culture and history rather than purely biological motivations, studying human beings requires researchers to grapple with native understandings of the world, their sense of right and wrong, and their own definition of normal or natural. From this perspective, the *meaning* of behavior becomes comprehensible only through interpersonal engagement. This was famously made clear by Clifford Geertz, who used the distinction between an involuntary twitch of the eye and a deliberate wink to make a key point about human culture (1973, 6). A wink is meaningful but a twitch is not, despite the fact that the act itself is the same. A wink is communicative; it is saying something. And the job of anthropology should be to figure out the meanings conveyed rather than merely note the observable twitches.

This conversational, or dialogical, approach is dominant among the authors of this volume. So too is an emphasis on the meaning of social action as opposed to its function. There is much more to say about the ways that cultural anthropologists think about studying culture and engaging people who understand the world differently. Not all of this volume's contributors necessarily agree on the best way to discover what we want to understand, or to understand what we happen to discover. However, despite varying theoretical orientations and some differences of method, we all agree on the value of patient, empathetic, long-term fieldwork. This remains the foundation of our work. Participant observation is still our key mode of engaging the cultural worlds of other people, of fathoming their perspective.

Moreover, for most us, fieldwork is a personally transformative experience. Through fieldwork we learn about ourselves as much as about other people, and we are changed by the process. This aspect of fieldwork had been relatively unexplored in our discipline, but during the 1980s anthropologists began to pay more attention to it. From pioneering texts like Paul Rabinow's *Reflections on Fieldwork in Morocco* (2007 [1977]) to the later turn to what is known as reflexivity, anthropologists came to be more interested in the process of fieldwork itself, especially the question of how our own personal and cultural background inflects what we are able to see and choose to record. Consequently, we began to write somewhat differently and include more personal details about ourselves and our experience, a movement captured by books like James Clifford and George Marcus's *Writing Culture* (1986) and Ruth Behar and Deborah Gordon's *Women Writing Culture* (1995). Anthropological texts became less unself-consciously objectivist, less like a bird's-eye view of a society, and more the story of an engagement between a particular person and a new cultural setting. The chapters in this volume fit squarely within this tradition of self-consciously aware anthropological writing. What they add to it is a collective focus on a specific place, a complex place we help readers understand through the assembled idiosyncrasies of different fieldwork experiences.

Fieldwork has long been a rite of passage, an almost mystical transformation in which the anthropologist ventures to the field and returns older, wiser, and professionally legitimate. The ritual aura remains even when anthropologists research their own societies, the world they come from. We prepare ourselves ahead of time by planning our project, becoming as fluent in the local language as possible (if we are not already), and reading everything there is about the place we want to understand. Then we enter the liminal fieldwork experience, the part emphasized in this volume. We return from research with reams of notes, and from these we produce dissertations, articles, chapters, and possibly books or films. We try to puzzle out and illuminate the lessons we learned during the many months that we did fieldwork. And eventually, some of those materials are assigned to students and perused by other readers, who confront our arguments in a polished, even sanitized, final form.

Only occasionally do readers get a behind-the-scenes look at how we derive our information. What we show in this volume is that anthropological fieldwork can be a difficult, messy, serendipitous, exhilarating, lonely, and confusing experience. In reading the articles and books that anthropologists write, readers may not imagine the individuals who produced the work, or how our experiences with other cultures have changed us. This book attempts to remedy that by offering a look at the fieldwork that is at the heart of cultural anthropology. It provides a sense of how profoundly different fieldwork can be in the same country. We focus on some of the challenging ethical and personal issues that have come up in the course of our long-term engagement with Morocco, topics that range from the mundane to the profound. For instance: How do we speak to people in a foreign land? How do we find things out? How do people perceive us? What counts as knowledge, and how do we produce it? What does friendship mean in another cultural context—or love or parenthood? What if the people don't want us to study them, or want to be studied in a particular way that makes no sense to us? What if they don't understand anthropology or view it with suspicion? How do we handle our own social awkwardness, our loneliness, our ignorance? What happens when the anthropologist is tempted to "go native"—or when he or she does so? None of these questions have easy answers. All of them reveal something of the challenge and rewards of anthropological fieldwork.

IN MOROCCO

Morocco is a wonderful place to do anthropological fieldwork. Extraordinarily diverse, scenic, with a government that is generally hospitable to foreign researchers, Morocco has attracted anthropologists from the United States and Europe since Carleton Coon and Robert Montagne in the early years of the discipline. Along the way a number of key anthropological debates have had their basis in ethnographic research carried out in Morocco, including much of the experimental ethnographic writing that paved the way for a volume like the present one. Anthropological knowledge is not spread evenly around the globe. A few places—Papua New Guinea, India, Mexico, Indonesia, and Morocco among them—have produced far more than their fair share of ethnographic insights. For a relatively small place, Morocco has outsized importance for anthropologists.

Located in the northwest corner of Africa, Morocco is culturally and linguistically tied to the Middle East and Africa as well as to Europe. The northernmost part of the country is only a few miles from Spain, across the Strait of Gibraltar, and indeed the name Gibraltar comes from Tariq ibn Ziad, the first Muslim general to cross the straits into Spain in the year 711 (*Jebel Tariq,* which means Tariq's Mountain, became Gibraltar over time). Before the era of European expansion, Morocco controlled a thriving trade in gold, salt, and slaves across the Sahara. There has been a deep and long-term engagement between Morocco and its northern, eastern, and southern neighbors; today Morocco remains a crossroad of African, Middle Eastern, and European influences.

Morocco is also geographically diverse. In the north of the country the rugged Rif Mountains border the Mediterranean Sea. The Atlantic coastline generally enjoys mild temperatures that extend inland across a wide coastal plain to the Middle and High Atlas Mountains. These high ranges divide the fertile plains from the Sahara Desert; some peaks soar to over 14,000 feet. The snowfall collected in the mountains runs west to form rivers across the coastal plain, and east into the Sahara Desert. These waters sustain agricultural communities on both sides of the mountains. Toward the south of the country is the Anti-Atlas mountain range, lower and drier than the country's other mountains. The Anti-Atlas is generally less well suited to agriculture than other areas of the country, and it has a long history of people migrating to other regions.

The major cities of Morocco include Fes, Marrakech, Rabat, Casablanca, and Agadir. Fes is arguably the cultural heart of the country. It lies in the fertile Sais Plain, between the Rif and Middle Atlas Mountains. Home to one of the world's oldest universities, the medina, or old city, of Fes is one of the great living monuments to Islamic urban design. Marrakech is nearly as ancient. It was founded almost a thousand years ago, near the base of the High Atlas Mountains in the Haouz Plain. Today it has become a popular destination for tourists and a playground for the rich and famous. Rabat is the capital of the country and houses most of its main political institutions. Casablanca is the country's main commercial center and the largest city. It is home to migrants from all over the nation. Agadir had traditionally been a fishing town on the southern coast. It has recently had a surge in popularity with tourists, who are drawn to its beachfront resorts and mild weather.

The most widely spoken language in Morocco is a variety of Arabic known as Darija. People in Algeria and Tunisia speak a similar form of Darija, but the language is not well understood anywhere else. Darija is not taught in school, only learned at home. Many educated Moroccans can also read, write, and converse in Fusha (pronounced "foos-ha"), or Modern Standard Arabic—which, as the name implies, is understood across the Arab world. Modern Standard Arabic is the language of news broadcasts and scholarship. The indigenous language of Morocco is Berber, or Tamazight. This has been spoken for thousands of years and exists in three main varieties: Tarifit in the north, Tamazight in the Middle Atlas Mountains, and Tashelhit in the south. At least 30 percent of Moroccans speak some variety of Berber as their mother tongue. Many Berbers today call themselves Amazigh because the word "Berber" is not indigenous to Morocco. We thus sometimes speak of Amazigh culture or language. Because much of Morocco was a protectorate of France between 1912 and 1956, many Moroccans speak French as a second or third language. Others speak Spanish because the northern zone and the extreme south were both controlled by Spain. Currently many Moroccans study English and other languages in order to do research, work with tourists, or travel abroad.

Socially, Morocco is intriguingly diverse. Most Moroccans are Sunni Muslims of the Maliki *madhab,* or school of Islamic law. However, Morocco follows Islamic laws only in the area of family law (for example, regarding marriage and divorce). Business and criminal law are governed by civil codes similar to those of European countries. While many Moroccans are religiously conservative, Moroccan society is friendly, open, and tolerant. Jews historically played an important role in the country, but its sizable Jewish population has dwindled since the creation of Israel, in 1948. The king of Morocco rules together with an elected legislature. Many people are seeking to expand democracy in the country, but King Mohammed VI has managed to retain control over most important government functions. Morocco has long had a solid relationship with the United States and much of Europe, and this has been one reason foreign anthropologists have found it convenient to do research in the country. In general, Moroccan cities are quite liberal—with bars, clubs, every possible kind of restaurant, and a wide variety of accepted clothing styles. The countryside tends to be much more conservative, and also much poorer.

Morocco is a study in contrasts. Swanky seaside bars in Casablanca and venerable mosques in Fes, modern freeways and urban slums and the mule-plowed fields of rural villages—Moroccans inhabit a dazzling variety of social worlds. The anthropologists of this volume reveal these worlds as they show how anthropological fieldwork can lead us to a sophisticated, prismatic understanding of this intriguing place.

OVERVIEW OF THE CHAPTERS

The organization of the book roughly follows the process of fieldwork as most anthropologists undertake it. The early chapters focus on the process of getting acquainted with the country and navigating some of its surprises, while later ones emphasize the building and nurturing of the relationships that help us find things out. The final few chapters reflect on the terms of engagement and how they change over time, and the last essay, by Kevin Dwyer, places the other chapters in a historical and disciplinary context and shows how they relate to one another thematically.

The first essay, by Charlotte van den Hout, begins with the beginning of her fieldwork, shortly after she arrived in Salé to conduct research in a psychiatric hospital. Salé is an ancient port city just across the river from Rabat, Morocco's political capital. Van den Hout introduces us to one of the first things visitors encounter in the country: the dizzying mix of relevant languages described above. Van den Hout explains how she came to understand that what she wanted to say was necessarily linked to the question of what language she should say it in. This essay reminds us that far from being a transparent vehicle for conveying meaning, languages are meaningful in their own right.

Next, Karen Rignall explores the process of getting set up for fieldwork in the town of Kelaa Mgouna, east of the Atlas Mountains and on the edge of the desert. For Rignall, getting settled included getting her husband situated for his own research and sorting out day care for her two children—then explaining her situation as a mother momentarily separated from her children to the people she was trying to interview. Through this process, her understanding of work was transformed by the very different Moroccan way of dealing with the concept, and she was left struggling with different sorts of professional and personal work that needed to be sorted out before she could proceed with her research. For anthropologists, our "work" has a tendency to blend with our "lives." It tends, in many cases, to *become* our lives, so finding a work-life balance is difficult to achieve, or even imagine. While this may in fact be analogous to the experience of many rural Moroccans, for whom the work of staying alive is life itself, it is unsettling for Americans who assume that work, life, and family are categorically separate spheres.

David McMurray's topic is social class in the northern coastal city of Nador. Class is one of the key social axes that matter in the country, and Moroccan society is notably class-conscious. Everything from language to parenting is finely tuned to one's social class.

One does not simply *have* a class in an objective sense (for example, owning the means of production or selling one's labor); in Morocco, as elsewhere, class is *performed* in culturally specific ways. What is a class-unconscious American to do? McMurray illuminatingly fumbles through his own lifestyle decisions and comes to see how profoundly social class shapes cultural expression in Morocco. He also explores the different ways Western theorists have imagined social class, and how his Moroccan experiences fit (or don't) with these ideas. Nador is noted as a gateway for European products coming into Morocco and for Moroccan workers moving out to Europe. Research at this sort of crossroad helps McMurray to critically examine European theories of social class in a novel context.

Emilio Spadola works in the ancient city of Fes, a place many see as the cultural center of Morocco. He takes us through a crucial early phase of anthropological fieldwork: establishing rapport. This mysterious process is about making friends who are also interlocutors, enjoying people's company while making those same people the vehicles for, or even the objects of, research. For Spadola this process is complicated by the deeply held religious beliefs of Mohammed—his friend, research partner, and teacher in Fes—and by Spadola's own eventual religious conversion. In this essay we are privy to an intimate view of the anthropologist being profoundly transformed by the process of research and coming to learn fundamental lessons about friendship. Spadola taps a theme that stretches back to the origins of the discipline: trying to understand others teaches us vital lessons about ourselves. Anthropological fieldwork helps us to grasp the cultural specificities of another place while revealing the common humanity we share.

Katherine Hoffman touches on this theme, too, as she writes about the difficulty of establishing rapport and the way that dynamics internal to communities restrict researchers and their agendas. Working in the southern Anti-Atlas region, from which many men have emigrated and whose villages are largely populated by women, Hoffman writes about local understandings of legitimate knowledge and how these influence what can be studied. How do anthropologists work with so-called local experts? Who can be such an expert, how is this identity influenced by gender, and what sorts of things should the expert know? How does all of this change over time? In a patriarchal and deeply suspicious atmosphere, how can knowledge be gathered, understood, and published? Hoffman shows how notions of gender, authority, and expert knowledge have transformed during her long-term engagement with southern Berber communities.

Paul Silverstein also tracks the theme of what counts as legitimate knowledge and who produces it. Working with Amazigh activists in the eastern town of Goulmima, Silverstein notes that local intellectuals have appropriated earlier anthropological texts, quizzing the anthropologist on his knowledge of the ethnographic canon. For many years Berbers were repressed by the state, forbidden to use their language, and largely excluded from the official history of the nation. Silverstein shows us how local activists are working to reclaim notions of Berber identity, and the ways that an increasing blurring of the division between home and the field seems to pose new sorts of challenges to the way we conduct our anthropological dialogue. Locals have always instructed anthropologists on what we should study and know. Now they do it with a deep grasp of the history of our discipline, their own international connections, and a clear personal and political stake in the matter.

Rachel Newcomb continues the theme of the possibilities and limits of rapport and raises vexing questions about the relationship between her private life and professional research in Fes. As the wife of a Moroccan and a mother, Newcomb enjoys privileged access to domains most foreigners never see. Yet her movement across social boundaries is hardly unproblematic or ethically straightforward. Newcomb has to navigate conflicting roles as wife, mother, daughter-in-law, and anthropologist as she, like Spadola, contemplates the links between her religious identity, her family, and her research. Her essay reveals the complexity of things we might take for granted about family, femininity, and knowledge.

Jamila Bargach trained as an anthropologist in the United States then returned to her native Morocco to carry out an assessment of a women's shelter in Casablanca. Bargach is confronted by the deep gulf between her formal training (which pushed her to valorize the locals and be attentive to their concerns) and her task of conducting a formal evaluative review for a grant agency. Submitting "the locals" to this sort of scrutiny runs counter to the author's anthropological instincts, and some of what she witnesses makes ethical disengagement impossible. Returning "home" with anthropological training presents a curious set of dilemmas, as does putting anthropological knowledge to work for social change.

Deborah Kapchan writes about her deep and long-lasting encounter with Morocco—first as a student and then as a researcher, wife, and mother. Kapchan explores the role of empathy in cultural understanding and critiques some of the major (male) writers who have purported to engage North African society. She ponders the way that anthropologists come of age professionally through the fieldwork experience, and what that means for the way we present our cultural others. And she illuminates what happens as a field site becomes home, and the performance of everyday life is simultaneously one's job.

David Crawford carries on this reflective theme. Returning to Morocco after marrying and having children, he finds himself transformed in the eyes of his rural friends. While in some ways his family life seems to bring him closer to the Berber farmers with whom he works, he finds that differences in the social organization of parenting present as many challenges as the fact of being a parent might resolve. This is compounded by his younger child's autism. Fatherhood matters in both Morocco and the United States, but not in the same way. How much of this is culture, how much is social class, and how much depends on the specificities of parents and children is difficult to decide.

Finally, Kevin Dwyer reflects on the volume as a whole. As a major contributor to the transformation of the genre of ethnographic writing in his *Moroccan Dialogues* (1982), Dwyer explores the form and substance of the ethnographic chapters by analyzing some common themes running through the essays. In this sophisticated musing on the project as a whole, Dwyer concludes the book by drawing out some of the less obvious connections among the essays and examining their place in the larger anthropological canon.

Long ago Clifford Geertz wrote that "if you want to understand what a science is, you should look in the first instance not at its theories or its findings, and certainly not at what its apologists say about it; you should look at what the practitioners of it do" (1973, 5). We believe that the most fundamental thing that anthropologists *do* is fieldwork. There have been numerous books on the process of doing fieldwork, sometimes in a how-to format and at other times as a more eclectic assemblage of what scholars have done in different places, presenting what has worked or (less frequently) what has not. There have been nearly as many books on Morocco as there have been on fieldwork, and even a few on fieldwork in Morocco. What can this book add?

In this volume we have focused our exploration of fieldwork, the fundamental practice of anthropology, on a single well-studied place: Morocco. This is meant to show what specific anthropological engagements brought together can tell us about a complex society, and also what the collective engagement with a complex society tells us about anthropological practice. We have traced particular routes through Morocco, routes that are at once locally inscribed and broadly revealing. The particular encounters described in these pages illuminate the sensuous diversity of Morocco and the particularities of the process through which fieldwork experience is rendered into anthropological insight. Our hope is that readers have tasted enough to want more, both of Morocco and of anthropology, and that those readers who choose to engage Morocco (or any other place) will do so anthropologically—that is, gently, slowly, and with concern for all that a people and place have to share.

1| Arabic or French?

The Politics of Parole *at a Psychiatric Hospital in Morocco*

CHARLOTTE E. VAN DEN HOUT

It is Thursday morning, and the patients and doctors of the open women's ward at a Moroccan psychiatric hospital are gathering in the lounge for the weekly *ijtimaᶜ*, an hour or so of sharing stories, experiences, and impressions of life at the hospital. As the women take their seats on the couches—made in a traditional design, but with a modern twist—the hum of excited whispers hangs in the air. There's been conflict in the corridors this week, and the patients are expecting the issue to come to a head at today's meeting.

This morning I sit next to Nadia,[1] a woman in her fifties who has been hospitalized for treatment of depression. She's been here for a few weeks now and is clearly doing better. She has rediscovered an appreciation for the company of others, no longer isolating herself in her room. She's gotten back into the habit of applying eye makeup in the morning, and the curl has returned to her short, auburn hair. Over the past few days, she has sought me out on the ward to tell me stories of her past and illness, as well as plans for her future.

She is slightly restless this morning as she listens to her fellow patients' reports. The group's anticipation has been satisfied: the women engaged in conflict have indeed brought their issue to the meeting.

It is a dispute over religious freedom, with one party claiming her right to religious expression (in her case, the recitation of Qurʾanic verses in the ward's corridors) and the other arguing for her right to freedom from religious indoctrination (especially at ten o'clock at night, when she would prefer to be sleeping). With growing emotion, the two women explain their viewpoints to the group. The doctors are barely able to maintain order.

It is a heavy topic for any group of Moroccan women to address on a Thursday morning. Yet it is not the content but the form of the argument that prompts Nadia to lean in and whisper a question into my ear: "Can you follow all this Arabic?"

I smile, make a gesture to imply that I'm getting the gist, and suggest we try to listen. But Nadia isn't done yet. She leans in again, seeking understanding in my eyes.

"I have a really hard time understanding the Arabic," she confesses. "I'm not used to it at all."

And indeed, when it's Nadia's turn to talk, she makes a point of announcing that she would rather speak French. She cannot express herself as freely in Arabic, she explains to the doctor, whose nod indulges Nadia in her request. And so Nadia begins, noticeably changing the tone of the meeting as she informs her audience—in soft, polished French—that she had a good week. A few women shift in their seats, straightening their spines, and a subtle sense of formality seems to have seeped into the room. All disruptions have come to an end; even the bickering group is now silently listening to the cadence of Nadia's French syllables. But then—just like that, in a blink of an eye that completely negates the gravity of her original request—Nadia downshifts back into Arabic, formulating her closing statements in the local dialect.

This curious linguistic shift is something we've all come to expect of Nadia. She identifies herself as a Moroccan woman, and we've all heard her speak her country's brand of Arabic in chats with staff or fellow patients. Nevertheless, she exhibits a distinct and consistent preference for the language of Morocco's former colonizer, and there is a moment in every conversation when she calls explicit attention to that fact.

This behavior throws the anthropologist for a loop. Why would an individual prefer to speak a second language—a language stained with notions of colonial subjugation, no less—rather than her or his native tongue? The basic methodological principles of ethnographic fieldwork assume that a research participant will always prefer to speak the language in which he or she is most comfortable (see, for instance, Briggs 1986), and that this will inevitably be that person's native tongue. In keeping with this assumption, learning that language usually constitutes an essential step in any anthropologist's preparation for the field. Along with qualifying exams and the dissertation proposal defense, it is a rite of passage in the transition from graduate student to legitimate ethnographer. Scholars of Morocco thus devote considerable time and effort to the study of Moroccan Arabic or one of the many Amazigh (or Berber) varieties that are spoken in the country. As an aspiring ethnographer I, too, passed through several of Morocco's language schools before beginning my fieldwork, in the hope of attaining conversational fluency in Arabic.

Nadia's choice, however, suggests that linguistic landscapes and ideologies in Morocco are more complex than this basic methodological assumption would suggest. Indeed, the ethnographic literature characterizes Morocco as a highly heterogeneous and multilingual society. Though Modern Standard Arabic (or Fusha) is the country's official language, daily life is lived mostly in Darija, the local dialect of Arabic, or in one of the various Amazigh dialects. French, the language of Morocco's former colonial ruler, adds further complexity to the mix by maintaining a persistent presence in government circles and civic institutions, and in northern Morocco one might even come across a word or two of Spanish. Each of these languages plays a distinct role in shaping Moroccan cultural identity and social relationships; each of them harbors unique and complex meanings. A number of scholars have provided rich analyses of the way in which individuals navigate this linguistic multiplicity in the everyday reality of their lived experience, and how language is implicated in assertions of identity and belonging (see, for example, Hoffman 2008b; Ennaji 2005; Sadiqi 2002; Mansouri 1997).

In the following pages, I intend to explore what impact this Moroccan brand of linguistic diversity might have on the experience of conducting ethnographic fieldwork. I do so by sharing stories and anecdotes that I collected over the course of my research in a very specific arena of social interaction: the metropolitan psychiatric hospital where Nadia was being treated for depression. This clinical environment set the stage for my dissertation research, a project in which I examine how psychiatric practice interacts with public discourses on modernity and tradition, and analyze how mental illness affects Moroccan women's experience of life in a rapidly changing postcolonial society. I had conceived of this project as primarily medical and psychological in approach, and I had not planned to focus much on questions of language. However, in the course of conversations with different interlocutors, I came to realize that the key words with which women frame their self-reflections—cultural identity, social status, personal relationships, ambitions, education, freedom of expression—often come wrapped in the delicate tissue of a particular linguistic ideology. Understanding these ideologies, then, is a crucial step toward understanding how these women position themselves within their social world. Through the stories I share in this essay, I explore what these ideologies entail for daily interaction at this psychiatric hospital, and what all this might mean for an anthropologist and her efforts at conducting a clinical ethnography. I begin by turning back to Nadia.

Nadia describes herself as a proud Moroccan Muslim. Yet her words and behavior betray an apparent need to separate, or distance, herself from mainstream Moroccan consciousness. In fact, contradiction and juxtaposition weave themselves continuously in and out of her autobiography; they have become the thematic backbone to her story. She was born into a conservative family and raised in Fes, a bastion of tradition, but she was educated at the French mission's schools and walked around her neighborhood's streets in pigtails and short skirts. Her siblings all followed in her father's footsteps by pursuing degrees in theology, but Nadia chose a career in medicine instead. Her sisters have all been unhappily married for more than twenty-five years, while Nadia is a divorcée who has had several long-term boyfriends. And finally, Arabic[2] is the language of her country and her family, but Nadia prefers French, the language of international sophistication and style.

What emerges from Nadia's autobiography of contrast is the carefully constructed image of an autonomous, self-sufficient, educated, and highly disciplined woman who needs neither man nor family to provide her with a sense of purpose. Her amorous relationships are fleeting, the bond with her family constant yet tenuous. She describes herself as modern, Westernized, and independent, three characteristics that she claims set her miles apart from the average Moroccan woman. Her profession—she is a medical doctor and holds a teaching position at one of Morocco's medical schools—seems to personify these fundamental characteristics. It is a role she is proud of and one she has great difficulty relinquishing, despite the fact that on this particular stage she, herself, has now been cast as a patient. Nadia employs extensive psychiatric and psychoanalytic jargon when she explains her own history of illness, offers unsolicited advice to the ward's doctors on how to treat other patients, and is clearly most in her element when she is advising fellow patients on how best to manage a lingering cough, painful joints, or dry skin.

The above description suggests a number of possible explanations for the fact that Nadia prefers to speak French. First, the use of a foreign language may provide an additional way for her to emphasize her separateness and distance—from family, culture, and social expectations. As Nadia explains it, Moroccan culture is the source of her illness. Her depression was born of suffocation, a case of asphyxiation by the insurmountable pressure of cultural mores and taboos. She spent a few years in France, which she remembers as a place of lightness and air, where she hadn't a care in the world to weigh her down. The thick blanket of sadness did not descend on her until she returned to her native land, fifteen years ago. It is possible, then, that her preference for speaking French might simply be driven by the need for "a breath of fresh air" (Fanon 2008, 5). Perhaps speaking Arabic—a language indelibly linked to and thus bound by Moroccan standards of (expressive) propriety—feels to her like breathing air deprived of oxygen. "To speak means being able to use a certain syntax and possessing the morphology of such and such a language, but it means above all assuming a culture and bearing the weight of a civilization" (ibid., 1–2). Might French, then, be her escape hatch from that weight, a seam in the tightly spun fabric of moral codes? A helium balloon that lifts her high beyond the reach of Moroccan gender expectations?

It is likely that French is also, quite simply, a language with which Nadia is by now more comfortable than Arabic. It is no surprise that Nadia is more easily able to express herself in French after an education at Morocco's French schools, earning a medical degree, and a life lived in Morocco's elite social circles. The language of the former colonizer maintains a strong presence in the Moroccan public and institutional sphere, despite persistent societal efforts to combat its influence. In the first decades after independence, the Moroccan government embarked on a process of Moroccanizing the institutional infrastructure of schools, public services, and power that had been left behind by the French. The goal was to unify the newly independent country under a single culture, language, and governmental structure: all posts and positions were to be filled by Moroccan citizens, and French was to be replaced by Modern Standard Arabic (Obdeijn, de Mas, and Hermans 2002).[3] In practice, however, the influence of French proved difficult to eliminate (Howe 2005). The scarcity of well-educated Moroccan citizens made it difficult to do without assistance from France (Pennell 2003), and the country's incredible linguistic diversity made the systematic replacement of French with Arabic difficult. The multiple versions of Arabic in use by Moroccans posed a significant challenge to any substantive Arabization. Moreover, the Modern Standard Arabic that had been chosen as the country's official language was in many ways as foreign to the population as French had been—to speakers of Berber and Darija alike. Finally, the Moroccan elite was reluctant to switch from French to Arabic. This undoubtedly had to do with the fact that, like Nadia, they had been educated in French and were simply less accustomed to speaking Arabic. It also indicates, however, that despite strong currents of nationalism in post-independence Morocco, French remained the language of European—and thus sophisticated, elite—culture, status, and power. By the late 1980s, King Hassan II had conceded that bilingualism should be considered an enrichment to Morocco's culture, rather than a threat (Pennell 2000, 2003), and efforts at Arabization came to a halt. The modern result of this incomplete Moroccanization is a somewhat linguistically bifurcated public sphere in which some institutions are primarily francophone, others use Arabic, and a majority employs them both, albeit at different registers. Public elementary and high schools (as well as some university departments) now teach in Arabic, but private schools and most branches of higher education—including medicine—remain entirely francophone. Both languages maintain a strong presence in the Moroccan media, but French dominates the business sector. And finally, while Arabic might be an important language of informal daily interaction in hospitals, clinics, and government institutions, French is the language of choice for official reports and communications.

The cultural and political meanings associated with French, as briefly mentioned above, provide one last motivation for Nadia's linguistic preference. I suggest that it is in a significant way also her concern with status that drives her persistent choice to speak French. The use of its idioms is not only an escape, but also a way to underscore her identity as an educated authority figure and member of the upper class. Again, I invoke Frantz Fanon's analysis of language in *Black Skin, White Masks:* someone who "possesses a language possesses as an indirect consequence the world expressed and implied by this language" (Fanon 2008, 2). In Morocco, as in Fanon's Antilles, the "world" invoked by French is one of status, civilization, and power. French is not just the language mastered by those who have had the privilege of pursuing a (private) higher education; it is also the language of those with enough status or money to move about in the higher echelons of the Moroccan public sphere—and of those with connections to Europe. In order to explore in more detail how French may be employed in assertions of status and authority, let me turn away from Nadia for an instant and discuss the use of this language in communications among the medical staff at the psychiatric hospital where Nadia has been reduced to the role of patient.

Quite a bit of Darija is spoken in the hospital's corridors, and most patients and clinical staff employ a mixture of French and Arabic in their daily conversations. In classrooms, staff meetings, and medical files, however, French is the only acceptable idiom. French is, in other words, the language of official medical communication. This is somewhat of a logical continuation of the fact that, as mentioned above, physicians receive their training in French. However, attitudes toward the use of this language suggest that its dominance, both in the classroom and in the clinics, is by no means the result of random circumstance. In fact, I suggest that French harbors certain meanings that the hospital staff deem essential for the adequate performance of the role of physician. Before I elaborate further on this idea, let me provide a brief ethnographic vignette that illustrates, if somewhat negatively, this clinical importance of French. In this episode, a psychiatric resident's insufficient knowledge of French was not only vehemently criticized but was also linked to notions of professional incompetence.

Every morning the hospital's professors of psychiatry met their residents in a conference room for their daily staff meeting, at which the doctors read through and discussed the files for patients who had been admitted the day before. These dossiers were usually written up by residents in training, who take primary responsibility for hospital admissions. During these meetings, however, a professor would typically take it upon her- or himself to read these files out loud to the group. And more often than not, the reader would supplement this presentation by pointing out written errors in spelling, grammar, and syntax. On one particular morning, a professor came across a file in which a young resident had referred to a patient's mother as being *vivante,* or alive. The professor announced, with a deep sigh of disappointment, that the appropriate term to use in this case was *en vie.* She continued: "It's as though you never learned French. Your classes in medical school were all in French—how is it that it seems like you speak no French? How could you make a mistake like that? If your French is inadequate, you take extra classes. This file is the work of an amateur."

In fact, both *en vie* and *vivant(e)* mean "alive," in the sense of "not dead." The error was not so much one of grammar as it was one of jargon: the resident had failed to use the term that is customarily employed in these medical files. But by linking a linguistic mix-up to the notion of being an amateur, the professor here directly suggested that a lack of perfect command over French was associated with professional incompetence. This suggestion frequently recurred in discussions between professors and residents. Even residents themselves seemed to have adopted this belief. When discussing colleagues' clinical performance, proficiency in French was often included among the professional skills evaluated.

This suggests that French is more than just a means of communication: something about French seems to be crucial to the practice of psychiatry. Several psychiatrists explained to me that Darija simply does not lend itself well to discourses about mental illness, because of its limited vocabulary for the definition and expression of emotion.[4] But there is more going on here than such simple dismissals of the Moroccan dialect as lacking in sophistication. I suggest that French, as a language particularly associated with power and status, is instrumental in the exercise of medical and psychiatric authority.

It could be said that French facilitates the exercise of what Foucault called the "disciplinary power" of the "asylum" (2006). At this Moroccan hospital, French is the language of diagnosis: it is the language used to classify, describe, and thereby subject patients to the power of medical truth. Furthermore, the use of French in medical files serves to reinforce the inequality of the doctor-patient relationship. The one-way diagnostic gaze of the psychiatrist takes on physical form in these dossiers, which contain the doctor's observations but are not available to the patient. By writing (or speaking) in a language that the patient may not speak, the doctor's knowledge of the patient becomes even less accessible to him or her, which reinforces the doctor's unilateral authority. In addition, the use of French in written files requires a constant translation of the patient's words, which were spoken in Arabic. It thus always brings about a measure of distancing from the patient's immediate, lived experience—a further denial of the patient's own agency and control over the way in which his or her experiences are interpreted.

In a much more fundamental way, however, I believe it is simply the association of French with education—and educatedness, culturedness—that facilitates the exercise of medical power. Medical authority emerges from, and rests on, the image of the doctor as an educated expert: someone who understands what is going on, and knows what to do to remedy the situation. Given the Moroccan association of French with higher education, and with status in general, this language invokes such an image with greater ease than Darija.

The use of French, as the language of power and status, occasionally creates a battleground for authority between patient and doctor. In most cases, doctors adapt their choice of language to the patient's preference. Since the majority of patients speak little or no French, most doctor-patient interactions take place in Darija.[5] However, it is primarily with such patients that French can become a tool in the exercise of disciplinary power. For example, I was often surprised at the seeming lack of confidentiality at the hospital. Doctors would routinely comment on a patient to colleagues (or to me, the anthropologist) in that patient's presence. They would invariably do so in French, however, knowing that the patient would be unable to understand what was said (yet fully aware that he or she is being talked about). French here reinforces the unidirectionality of the doctor-patient relationship: the patient is subject to the doctor's constant gaze but neither knows nor has the power to adjust the observations that the doctor makes.

With patients who do speak French, the struggle for authority can become more overt and direct, as the following anecdote illustrates.[6] The episode took place one late morning at the hospital's addiction ward. A young, petite female doctor in her first year of psychiatric residency brought Mr. Abbas, one of her patients, into the ward's consultation room to see how he was doing. Mr. Abbas was a thin, clean-shaven man in his fifties. He was well-spoken but restless as he answered his doctor's questions. Sitting on the edge of his seat, he kept getting up and walking around the room, as though he was acting out the story he was telling. He was beating around the bush, and the resident repeatedly called him on it: "You're not answering my question," she would tell him.

He was not providing the resident with the information she was looking for. Neither was he speaking her language. While she persistently posed her questions in Moroccan Arabic, he insisted on answering in French, uttering not a word in dialect throughout the meeting. At first I assumed he was doing this for the benefit of the observers in the room: two students in clinical psychology, a psychiatric resident from France, and me. Of course, our presence did affect his conduct. But there was more to Mr. Abbas's performance.

Mr. Abbas was an alcoholic, and he had checked himself into this clinic in order to conquer his addiction. When his doctor introduced us, the observers, during this particular consultation, Mr. Abbas responded with a polite and pleasant *"enchanté"* and proceeded to tell us quite an elaborate autobiographical story. He is a successful lawyer, he told us, well educated and fluent in French. Over the course of the consultation, he talked about his practice, his nice car, and his wife—none of which the resident had asked him about. After he left, his doctor revealed to us that actually Mr. Abbas hadn't worked in three years and his wife had left him. In fact, the life he had just described to us had been completely destroyed by his addiction. What began to emerge at that point was the sad picture of a man dethroned, a man who had lost everything he thought validated his existence, a man who was desperately trying to maintain an image he knew he had already lost.

In the presence of the doctor and the observers—all of whom were young women—Mr. Abbas had felt the need to assert himself as a man of status, to reclaim a measure of respect, and perhaps to avoid confirmation of the powerless role of patient by answering the resident's questions. Speaking French was part of that endeavor: along with his movements and gesticulations, it was a way of illustrating or underlining the image he was trying to present.

For the resident, however, it was essential that Mr. Abbas accept his role of patient and her authority as doctor. This particular doctor was not quite fluent in French (a deficiency for which she was often criticized by her superiors and colleagues, though she was perfectly able to discuss psychiatry in French), and her patient was undoubtedly more proficient than she was. Compelling him to speak Arabic was an attempt to maintain the upper hand, not only by claiming the right to dictate the mode of interaction but also by turning him away from a language that conveys status—a language over which this patient had more command than she.

In other words, language here became a tool for the negotiation of the dynamic balance of power that is inherent in the relationship between patient and doctor. For both of these players, the use of French constituted a claim to status and the assertion of a certain measure of agency. For the patient, this claim was essential in order to hold on to a sense of self-worth in the face of his struggles. The doctor, however, perceived this behavior as a threat to her authority and disciplinary power in this particular setting.

Like Mr. Abbas, Nadia also turned to French as a way of asserting a last modicum of status and authority. It was proof of her education, her social power—and part and parcel of her profession. Nadia employed her explicit rejection of Arabic as a way of distancing herself from the role of patient, a role particularly antithetical to the one from which she derived so much of her self-worth—that of a professor of medicine. But unlike those of Mr. Abbas, Nadia's claims seemed to be accepted by the medical staff. Her doctors accepted her choice of language and predominantly conversed with her in French. Being a fellow physician, Nadia's status perhaps resonated with the psychiatrists in a way that Mr. Abbas's did not. Moreover, many of the psychiatric residents knew her not only as a respected member of their professional world, but as an authority figure who had had a hand in their own education. The confusion of her status as both patient and clinical professor affected their behavior as much as it did hers.

Given the role of French in the assertion and exercise of medical power, I was wary of using this language when I first arrived at the hospital. Remembering that the establishment of psychiatric facilities had been part of what the French considered to be their civilizing mission in North Africa (Keller 2007), that Fanon (1963, 1965) had considered psychiatry to be a particularly violent instrument of colonial subjugation, and that even today these psychiatric institutions apply a Western discipline of medicine to a population that, for the most part, does not ascribe to biomedical "truths," I was worried about what my presence as a European researcher would suggest.[7] Highly concerned about asserting any kind of authority or even agency, I spent my first few weeks at the hospital trying to be as unassertive as possible. I silently observed, worried that simply asking permission to do certain things or gain access to certain places would be an inappropriate assertion of power. I even worried that recruiting individuals for interviews would suggest my complicity in a kind of continued colonial subjugation. I insisted on speaking as much Darija as I could, hoping that I could show, at least linguistically, that I was here to adapt and learn, rather than dictate and determine.

During those first few weeks, however, I slowly began to realize that the reality of power dynamics and language at the hospital was not so black and white. French, I learned, is less the language of subjugation than simply the language of status and legitimacy. What applied to psychiatrists was true for the ethnographer as well: any scholar worth her salt speaks French. Though my developing knowledge of Darija was always met with approval and encouragement, my command of French was constantly tested. In fact, my ability to communicate in this language played a significant role in the hospital administration's determination that I was qualified to conduct research there, and their subsequent decision to authorize my presence on the wards. Likewise, my command of French facilitated acceptance of my presence by clinicians and patients alike. For both groups, my use of French seemed to signal competence, education, and expertise. On the basis of these notions, I was deemed a legitimate researcher.

Indeed, French proved a far more dominant language of interaction in my research than I had anticipated. Both patients and doctors decidedly preferred to speak this language with me. As mentioned above, I resisted at first. I took it as a confirmation of my inescapable status as an outsider, struggling with the connotations of power that came with that status, but also with its slight suggestion of ignorance. For a while I felt like a fraud: an amateur anthropologist who took the easy way out by speaking French with her interlocutors. I worried that my command of Moroccan Arabic was considered inadequate. I felt the need to prove myself, and I spoke as much Arabic as I could—attempts that were met with approval but also with persistent responses in French. I finally gave in and stopped trying to elicit responses in Arabic. I do still believe that my foreignness affected my interlocutors' language preference, but I came to realize that other factors were at play here as well. My interlocutors' choice of French had as much to do with their impression of me as it did with the impression of themselves that they wished to convey. French, I suggest again, is less a language of subjugation than a language of status. Rather than resist its use as a way to resist power, individuals at the hospital (patients and doctors alike) wielded this language as a way to assert their own personal legitimacy.

Like Moroccan linguistic ideologies, the image and status of anthropology is complex. For the doctors and patients at this hospital, my identity as an ethnographer seemed to straddle two worlds at once. Insofar as I was a scholar, researcher, and educated individual who was interested in the world of psychiatry and medicine, I belonged to the realm of French—and my command over this language constituted my entry visa. Anthropology, however, is seen as the study of culture, people, traditions, and superstitions. It invokes the works of Edward Westermarck (1926) and Ernest Gellner (1969)—and all of that belongs solidly to the domain of Darija, a uniquely Moroccan language and thus indelibly tied to all things cultural and traditional. The people who populated this hospital impressed on me on various occasions that one cannot truly acquire an understanding of Moroccan culture if one does not learn to speak the local language. In fact, psychiatrists often suggested that, as an anthropologist, I should not be talking to the educated, upper-class patients who spoke French. They are not the true representatives of Moroccan culture, the hospital's professors would tell me. If I was truly interested in Moroccan psychiatry, I should be speaking to the uneducated, the people who live outside of the major cities. I should ignore the women with depression and look instead for those with hysteria. I should sidestep the ones who had mastered French and talk instead to those who spoke only Darija.

As mentioned above, Darija is the Moroccan dialect of Arabic. It is a form of Arabic weathered by the test of time, foreign influence, and the transformative process of linguistic evolution. Moroccans agree that no dialect is as far removed from standard Arabic as their own—and that, in consequence, it is all but incomprehensible to other speakers of Arabic.[8] Nevertheless, most Moroccans deny their dialect the status of a real language—a sentiment reflected by the late King Hassan II's choice to make Fusha, rather than Darija, the country's official language. Moroccans consider their dialect to be something of a bastard child. It is the language of mundane, daily activity: of bargaining at the market, chatting about the weather, bantering with friends. If one chooses to talk about loftier issues—such as religion, economics, or politics—the vocabulary of Fusha or French seems better suited.

Nevertheless, actual daily usage of the two languages at the psychiatric hospital suggests that there is a flip side to this coin. French may be the language of cosmopolitan modernity while Darija is that of mundane reality—but French can also be characterized as the language of arrogant outsiderness and Darija as that of cultural authenticity. The social and cultural value accorded to Darija is ambiguous and changing. Although it continues to be seen as unsophisticated and even crude, Moroccan society increasingly values its identity as uniquely (and thus authentically) Moroccan. Darija has long been considered a strictly oral language, but several media outlets now make an effort to incorporate more written dialect into their publications. And while foreign television shows once were usually dubbed in Syrian or Modern Standard Arabic, the voice-overs now are in Darija.

Residents at the psychiatric clinic reflected the dual values of these languages. They participated in the continuing dominance of French as a language of authority and considered it to convey a sophistication that Darija did not have. However, there were also times when they expressed frustration with this particular status quo. At these moments, psychiatrists suggested—either explicitly or implicitly— that this linguistic ideology not only complicated their communication with patients but also posed a threat to the authenticity and preservation of Moroccan culture. These sentiments were expressed in their most explicit form one morning over coffee, as a few residents and I discussed a xeroxed copy of the 2010 medical school entrance examination, brought in that morning by one of the hospital's professors as a show-and-tell curiosity. I was struck by the fact that this test of biochemistry, physics, and math was written in Modern Standard Arabic and wondered aloud what may have driven this choice, given that medical school classes are taught in French.

"It makes no sense," Dr. Bensoumane agreed. "We're an Arabic-speaking country, but we study medicine in French. At the hospital, we write up our observations in French. It makes no sense: our patients speak Arabic, we speak Arabic, but we write these observations in French, a foreign language."

His colleague, Dr. Sadqi, agreed. He had a brother-in-law from Denmark, with whom he had once had a similar discussion. "In Denmark," he now reported to us, "they speak Danish. In medical school, the books they use are in English. Doctors write articles in English. But at the hospital, they speak Danish with their patients, and they write up their files in Danish as well."

Dr. Bensoumane turned back to me. "What about Holland?" he asked.

I explained to the group that the case of Holland was similar to that of Denmark. English plays a large role in the world of medicine, but communication with and about patients always takes place in Dutch.

"See?" Dr. Bensoumane demanded, appropriating this fact as evidence to support his case. "In Holland they use Dutch. In Denmark they use Danish. So in Morocco, we should use Arabic."[9]

A young first-year resident, Dr. Loukili, spoke up: "There are so many things that don't translate into French. The other day a patient of mine told me he believes he's the *mehdi el mountadar*.[10] How do you translate that?"

One of her fellow first-year interns nodded in understanding. "You can't," he sighed.

Dr. Bensoumane told us that he once discussed this dominance of French with one of the hospital's professors. The latter had justified it simply by explaining that Morocco is a bilingual country. At this point, Dr. Sadqi scoffed and mumbled, "Well, yes, if you're talking about Arabic and Tamazight."

Dr. Loukili smiled. Sarcastically she asked, "Oh, Morocco is bilingual? Does that mean I can write up my observations in Arabic if I want to?"

"Yeah, right," Dr. Bensoumane responded with a smirk.

He then turned to me. The country's linguistic situation, he argued, simply does not work. Morocco needs to stop according so much importance to French. It's holding the country back: Morocco looks at the world through the lens of France and thus is lagging behind the steady pace of globalization we see elsewhere in the world. Arabic, Dr. Bensoumane concluded, should be the language of national (and hospital) discourse, and English should be used for communication with the outside world.

A few telling points emerge from this conversation. Dr. Bensoumane characterized French as a foreign language, the usage of which often lacks relevance or resonance with the Moroccan cultural environment. Dr. Loukili mentioned the fact that important cultural references are lost in the translation of patients' expressions into French. The suggestion is that French occasions a distancing from the experience of one's patients, and a loss of a certain authenticity. And finally, even the language's status as a vehicle of modernity and globalization is contested. Dr. Bensoumane suggested that, in fact, French is what is keeping Morocco from any real connection to international trends of development and culture. The complete rejection of French here does, perhaps, suggest a notion of resistance against what is in some ways seen as a remnant of colonial power.

In sum, this means that French may constitute a signifier of status and authority, but at the same time it signals a disconnected outsiderness—a threat to Morocco's autonomous sense of national identity. It pollutes notions of cultural authenticity, integrity, and legitimacy. When it is time to assert one's Moroccan identity, people thus often explicitly turn away from French.

Likewise, Nadia's preference for French was seen by some of her fellow patients as a pollution—a threat, even, to the authenticity of the ward's Moroccan identity. The occurrence of French[11] conversations in the ward's corridors elicited occasional comments during the Thursday morning meetings. "It's almost like we're no longer 100 percent Moroccan," a woman remarked one morning, during a time when the presence of a few francophone patients had led to particularly frequent use of French on the ward.

Once in a while, Nadia's French elicited more confrontational reactions. In one such case, the hostility came from Halima, a fellow patient who happened to overhear Nadia in conversation with the parents of a newly admitted young woman. Nadia had eagerly asked the French mother of this young patient where she was from and then began to share her own pleasant memories of time spent in that particular city. Halima had been standing nearby, and now approached to hiss at Nadia, in French:

"Stop bothering these people, they're here for their daughter. They don't want to talk to you!"

Nadia looked at her calmly. "I'm just trying to be friendly, Halima," she explained. "I just want to make them feel welcome."

The parents listened in slightly disconcerted silence as the two women continued their argument. Halima retorted that the parents had no need of a welcoming committee; they'd been living in Morocco for years. Nadia responded that it is always nice to exchange memories of other places, and to hear about familiar cities in France.

Halima, at a loss for a witty retort, responded with an angry look and then grumbled, in the local dialect, "Well, I'm Moroccan, and I'm Muslim. I'm proud of it, and I'm going to speak Arabic."[12]

"But that would be impolite," Nadia responded in French, calm as ever.

"Not at all," Halima corrected, still in the local tongue. "These people live in Morocco; they understand Arabic perfectly." And with that, she walked away.

Nadia turned to the parents and offered them an apologetic smile. Then she looked at me.

"Do you see these Moroccan women?" she sighed. "They're so shortsighted, they don't understand any lifestyle that doesn't resemble their own."

In this interaction, Halima had perceived the use of French as a threat from the outside to Moroccan cultural integrity. Since these parents had been in Morocco for so long, they could no longer simply be seen as guests, and their usage of French was no longer acceptable. Such hostility toward the use of French may arise from sentiments that go deeper than simple cultural pride. Like Mr. Abbas's psychiatrist, Halima (and other patients) may also have rejected Nadia's use of French as a way to resist what they perceived as the other's claim to authority. For a patient who speaks little or no French, the fact that other people speak a language she or he does not understand may further deepen the sense of powerlessness that comes with the experience of mental illness. Unable to participate in conversations or to monitor what is being said, such patients might feel yet further deprived of a voice.

Comments like Halima's above were elicited also, of course, in response to the daily presence of an anthropologist on the ward. My status as an outsider certainly contributed to the dominance of French in conversation and might thus have been interpreted as an additional threat to the authenticity of the ward's Moroccan character. Though patients often clearly preferred to speak French with me, I also picked up on the occasional suggestion that there was no place for a foreign language on a Moroccan hospital ward—suggestions that reinforced my concern with conveying notions of power and outsiderness.

What tended to mitigate this sense of threat, however, was the news that I spoke Arabic. The discovery that I spoke and understood Darija was often eagerly shared among the ward's patients and constituted an essential piece of information whenever they introduced me to a newly admitted woman. My actual speaking skills were hardly ever tested by my interlocutors and thus always remained more theoretical than factual. Nevertheless, my ability to appropriately use phrases like "*inshallah*" (God willing), "*bisahha*" (to your health), and "*llah ysehel*" (may God make it easy on you, may God ease your difficulties) seemed to provide me with a certain legitimacy. While my command of French proved my validity as a scholar, my knowledge of Arabic underscored my status as someone who, if not a true insider, was at least genuinely interested in and capable of learning about the truth of Moroccan culture.

Psychiatrists shared this sentiment. In fact, my speaking Arabic was often cited as a decidedly positive factor in the comparison between me and another foreigner present at the hospital: a psychiatric resident from France, who arrived at the hospital for an elective six-month internship mere days after the start of my fieldwork. At first the Moroccan residents enthusiastically engaged with her. They found her fresh perspective interesting and eagerly displayed their own familiarity with the French psychiatric system. Gradually, however, their interest in her began to decline, and complaints began to emerge about her "superior" attitude. After her departure, the residents reflected on her presence at the hospital. And inevitably, comparisons were made to me—the other foreigner.

"At first," one resident commented one afternoon, "we expected her to get along with us much better. We thought she'd fit in more because she's a psychiatrist like us, and you're an anthropologist. But as it turns out, you're the one who easily fit in."

The psychiatrists offered several explanations for this fact. They mentioned the French resident's tendency to compare Moroccan psychiatry unfavorably to the system she was used to, and what they interpreted as her sense of cultural superiority. But the most commonly cited reason why I had succeeded where she had failed was that "she didn't try to learn Arabic, but you did." This failure was the ultimate sign that she was not interested in truly getting to know Morocco.

In this case, language had trumped education as a vehicle of mutual understanding. The doctors' comments suggest that the simple fact of speaking Arabic (no matter how imperfectly) represents something larger: it signifies a certain openness to and acceptance of the Moroccan cultural environment. Whereas the French resident had ultimately proved herself to be judgmental in her evaluation of the hospital and its world, my speaking Arabic had been taken as a positive sign of comprehension.

What I have tried to show through this series of stories is that each of the languages commonly spoken at this Moroccan hospital has its own very particular set of meanings—meanings that can be positive or negative, depending on the particular context. Darija is considered to be a kind of polluted Arabic, an illegitimate language. It is the idiom of small-town Morocco, of superstitions, of the uneducated. But while Darija can thus be the language of the plebs, it is also the language of the people. Darija is undeniably a vessel of authenticity and of belonging. It is the language of true Moroccan culture, of tradition, and of the country's historical pride. French, in contrast, signals a kind of outsiderness, a possibly haughty or arrogant disconnect from all that is authentically Moroccan; it is a language still stained with hints of colonial power. But once again there is another side to the coin. French is also the vehicle of Morocco's historical, political, and economic ties to the rest of the world. It signals development, power, education, globalization, and modernization.

The importance of learning the local language is an undisputed given in the practice of anthropology. However, our focus on language should not end there. In a post-colonial society like that of Morocco, the persistent presence of the former colonizer's language creates a complex linguistic landscape in which multiple languages interact dynamically, and each is employed in unique ways to index specific social meanings, cultural references, and levels of status. In the interest of approaching one's interlocutors on their level, an ethnographer might shy away from any use of a foreign or colonial language. I initially attempted to avoid the use of French at the clinic, assuming it would send all the wrong signals about claims to power or my openness toward authentic Moroccan experience. But as I have attempted to point out in this essay, dismissing French is to ignore the very real and significant role that this language can play in Moroccans' construction of identity and negotiations of status. French is, quite simply, no less part of the true Moroccan environment than Arabic or Tamazight. Insisting on speaking Arabic can, in some cases, be construed as a denial of the interlocutor's attempts to assert status or identity—and might in that case constitute precisely the kind of subjugation that we were trying to avoid. I refer again to Fanon's *Black Skin, White Masks* (2008), in which he denounces the "White" man's refusal to accept or acknowledge the "Black" man's use of eloquent French. By allowing our interlocutors to choose the language in which they wish to express themselves—even if that is a language in which they are not fluent—we allow them the agency and autonomy to present themselves to us as the people they are, and we allow ourselves the ability to pick up the complexities of cultural meanings, linguistic ideologies, and societal moralities that are conveyed through interpersonal interaction.

NOTES

1. In the interest of privacy, I have changed all names and any other information that may identify the individuals I mention in this chapter.

2. I use the terms "Arabic" and "Darija" interchangeably, as Moroccans do, to refer to the local dialect. When I refer to the modern standard variety of Arabic, I use the terms "Fusha" or "Modern Standard Arabic."

3. Riding on a wave of pan-Arab nationalism emanating from Egypt at the time, the Moroccan government chose to adopt Modern Standard Arabic, rather than the Moroccan dialect (or Berber), as its official national language.

4. For example, the word *mqallaq* is used to mean worried, upset, distraught, and sometimes even angry.

5. For the occasional Berber-speaking patient, this of course still means that he or she must explain personal things in a foreign language. However, it is a sad sign of the uneven distribution of psychiatric services in Morocco that few Berber-speaking individuals are ever hospitalized at this clinic. The Berbers (or *Imazighen,* as they are known in their own language) are more likely to live outside of the major cities, and thus not within reasonable distance of a psychiatric hospital.

6. I wrote about this episode on 12 November 2009 on the weblog I kept while in Morocco, http://bisahha.blogspot.com.

7. Although I live and work in California, I was born and raised in Amsterdam, the Netherlands. The Netherlands has no colonial ties to North Africa, but the country does, of course, have a significant and infamous history as a colonizing power elsewhere in the world. Moreover, the Netherlands today is home to a large Moroccan diaspora that unfortunately suffers considerable discrimination and prejudice in Dutch society.

8. This incomprehensibility seemed to be treated at once as a point of pride and a criticism. It underscored the uniquely Moroccan character of the language but also made that language useless. I was often asked why I invested so much time in learning a language that no one outside of Morocco could speak.

9. When I asked them whether this should then be Darija or Fusha, they responded, to my surprise, that it should be the latter. Darija would not work, they explained, because it is only a dialect and has not been standardized; every region of Morocco has its own version.

10. The *mehdi el mountadar* is an Islamic concept that is similar to the Christian Messiah, but specific to Islamic history.

11. And the occasional English conversation, as well. Patients who spoke English had a distinct preference for speaking that language with me. Like French, I think English signified education and cosmopolitanism and suggested a kind of connection to American (pop) culture. These English conversations would

often turn toward discussions about Hollywood celebrities, American exports such as Coca-Cola, and—inevitably—President George W. Bush and his foreign policy.

12. Halima's nearly automatic connection of her Muslim identity to her Moroccan one hints at one reason why Arabic (particularly Modern Standard Arabic, but also the dialect, I believe) is a continuing source of cultural legitimacy. Arabic is the language of Islamic scripture, the language in which it is believed that God revealed his message to the Prophet Mohammed. With such holy status, the value of Arabic cannot be contested.

2| Time, Children, and Getting Ethnography Done in Southern Morocco

KAREN RIGNALL

When ethnographies assume polished form, the process of selecting a field site usually appears to have been a serendipitous alignment of intellectual commitments and affective attachments. The "arrival narrative" begins to take shape in those first days at the field site. As the narrative becomes fixed in the published ethnography, the anthropologist's cultural connection—that commitment to people and place—becomes naturalized. In retrospect, the relationship can appear inevitable, even foreordained. My choice of field sites had more to do with day care than serendipity.

Perhaps I can admit my pragmatic concerns because my affective attachments had already been established. I had previously lived in the south of Morocco, managing a community-development organization and traveling as much as I could throughout the arid steppe and the green river valleys that wended their way down the jagged topography of the southern High Atlas Mountains. Years later, I designed my dissertation project with the knowledge that I wanted to return to the region. I had seen how migration remittances and livelihood diversification had transformed it in sometimes surprising ways. Rather than withdrawing from agriculture and settling their families in Lyon or Casablanca, many people were reasserting their commitment to the *tamazirt,* the homeland. I wanted to understand how they expressed this commitment, and I developed a research agenda around the reasons people were expanding agriculture into the steppe. This meant that my choice of field sites was to a certain extent decided for me. I needed to go where people were, in fact, converting rangeland for cultivation. But my pre-dissertation research visit, shortened to the bare minimum because I did not want to leave my two toddlers for any longer than necessary, focused less on surveying the extent of rangeland conversion than on finding a site that could satisfy the basic needs of a young family, at least a young, middle-class, American family. We needed day care, a reasonably accessible hospital, and an Internet connection so that my spouse could work—and so that our children could have video calls with their grandparents.

We settled on Kelaa Mgouna, a regional market town nestled at the bottom of the Mgoun Valley. People come here from the mountains and surrounding plateaus to sell produce at the weekly market, buy supplies, take care of official business, visit doctors and relatives, and commute to their jobs in the businesses that have grown up around the one main intersection in town. An old friend directed me to a good preschool, and we would have the medical care and other amenities to secure the well-being of our family—a vibrant weekly market, a comfortable apartment, even a *hammam* (public bath)—on our block. And I would be right next to the rural communities where people were expanding agriculture into the steppe, the communities that form the heart of my research.

I began writing this essay only four months into my fieldwork. The immediacy, at times traumatic, of settling in has compelled me to reflect on how rupture, discomfort, and even failure not only inform my experience of fieldwork, but also challenge my intellectual understanding of anthropology as a discipline. When I arrived, I thought back to Paul Rabinow and his reflections on the same experience that was proving so disconcerting to me. He frankly admitted that he "had gone into anthropology in search of Otherness," but that the shock of actually encountering it forced him to reevaluate cultural categories in ways he had not anticipated (Rabinow 2007 [1977], 29). He also acknowledged that this was emotionally difficult, but I resented him nonetheless for what I perceived as his privilege. As a single man, he had the freedom to wait for his fieldwork to take shape as he adjusted to these experiential shocks. I, on the other hand, felt rushed from the day I arrived. Because I had brought my family with me to the field and we were on a strict one-year schedule, I felt the pressure of having a limited window in which to settle us in and gather all the material necessary for a dissertation. By organizing my field research in terms of a work plan—formally structuring my days as a job—I thought I could make my project manageable. I fashioned myself as a commuter, leaving the house in the morning to work in my field sites and returning in the evening to share a meal and help put the children to bed. While this approach may have facilitated my work-life balance, it also meant that I had much less flexibility than Rabinow to deal with the many shocks of adjustment.

Even before leaving for Morocco, I was conscious that I would not be there "out of time," freed from the practical exigencies of daily life to devote myself to anthropology as an all-consuming vocation. I would be there to do a job, with low pay (albeit higher pay than most of my interlocutors received) and completely undefined working conditions. In this essay, I reflect on this aspect of the fieldwork experience to consider what the practice of ethnography reveals about the nature of work and time, within the discipline of anthropology and our lives more generally. Before beginning fieldwork, I was not particularly worried about encountering otherness in the way Rabinow described. Not only was I familiar with the region, but thirty years of anthropological theorizing since the publication of his reflections had schooled anthropologists in training like me about the problematic nature of ethnography as a dialogic encounter. However, the shocks I experienced unsettled that complacency and led me to question whether anthropology had taken its critique of the ethnographic encounter far enough. When we anthropologists acknowledge fieldwork not only as the dialogic production of knowledge but also as a particular form of work, I think we can do a better job of situating our scholarship and ourselves in the contemporary social order. Since Rabinow wrote his reflections, anthropology has changed significantly, with more kinds of people—women, families, older people, activists, indigenous anthropologists, and others—going to the field. My experience beginning fieldwork in Morocco brought me to the visceral conclusion that the discipline needs to better integrate this diversity of experience, but as my fieldwork went on, I also became more aware of the kinds of privilege that the work we do still entails.

SEPARATING WORK AND LIFE: WORKING WITH AND AROUND CHILDREN

In my first weeks in Morocco, I felt so overwhelmed by the logistics of settling in that I was sure something was wrong. I sent out plaintive e-mail messages looking for sympathy from advisors and experienced anthropologist friends, but their replies generally assumed a tone of amused recognition rather than surprise. Everyone noted that the process of beginning fieldwork is rife with bureaucratic holdups and innumerable hours spent waiting, shopping, and negotiating. But this lost time disappears from ethnographies. While I agree in principle with the idea that everything we experience becomes fodder for ethnography, in reality, not everything holds narrative or analytic interest. Even in our age of critical ethnography, the assumption remains that the ethnographer's whole life in the field is oriented toward anthropology, with little allowance for the quotidian responsibilities of caring for children or maintaining a household. Though there is a tradition of anthropologists taking on jobs as part of their projects, I still sense the expectation that while in the field, anthropologists' exclusive vocation should be their fieldwork—attaching themselves to other people's jobs. When they are not experiencing ethnographically rich moments, anthropologists should be reflecting on and writing about those moments in contemplative solitude.

This expectation persists although many more anthropologists now bring their families to the field. My anecdotal understanding, though, is that the families often trail senior anthropologists whose first terms of engagement with the field were as young, single individuals with more unstructured time to establish relationships. The anthropologists later insert their families into an existing network of social ties. I also know that many people go to the field without bringing their families. This was not an option for me. I returned to graduate school midway through my career, with two small children and an academic spouse whose more senior status limited our mobility. A basic requirement for me when I considered whether or not to return to school was that I have no extended separation from my family. This was easier said than done. Extricating ourselves from our lives in Kentucky to come to southern Morocco felt Herculean. As I watched fellow graduate students pack up their futons and put some boxes in friends' basements a few weeks before leaving for the field, my family and I set to work a year in advance of our departure to secure a leave for my husband, manage bank accounts, renegotiate insurance contracts, and find a real estate management company. We researched preschools, health care, and how to quickly set up a household in rural Morocco. I ran through my fieldwork grant money less than three weeks after arriving in Morocco.

Once we arrived, fieldwork became a distant goal on the horizon as we set about the task of settling the family in. I had brought my family to the field, but my family was not a research tool for my fieldwork. My husband had a book of his own to write—with the help of a not-so-high-speed Internet connection and an assistant to scan books from U.S. research libraries, he needed to spend his year writing on post-colonial literature rather than accompanying me on fieldwork visits up and down the Mgoun Valley. This had very concrete implications for the way I designed my research. With his own job responsibilities to fulfill, my husband could not care for the children as I conducted interviews or harvested wheat with women in the village. We not only needed child care so that we could both work, we also wanted our children to reap the benefits of preschool, especially in Arabic and French. So I structured the daily routine of fieldwork in a way that deliberately excluded my children.

This goes against the grain of more romantic notions about bringing children to rural Morocco. When people in the United States asked me about taking children to the field, I noted how the Moroccan love of children and the emphasis on childbearing as a measure of a woman's success would give me an entrée into the rural communities where I would be conducting my research. All along, I knew that this was a formulaic response and that fieldwork with children would be more complicated. It is true that having a family in Morocco makes me culturally intelligible in important ways, indicating that I have the basic priorities of life straight. But as David Crawford highlights in his essay in this volume, differences in child rearing between the United States and Morocco and the basic challenge of dropping American children into a completely new cultural setting mean that children cannot simply tag along as anthropologists conduct their research. My three-year-old son and five-year-old daughter are fairly well mannered, but they spent one of their first afternoons in a village tossing other visitors' shoes off a second-floor balcony, to the amazement of the children looking on. My son and daughter chatter through meals, asking a constant barrage of questions, while the children of our hosts hover quietly behind their parents. Even if my hosts repeatedly counsel me to let my children be, I am self-conscious about these differences in behavior and the cultural differences in our approaches to parenting.

One Moroccan friend described to me how he was reprimanded by his relatives for pandering too much to his children's needs. The proper way to raise children, he was told, was to give children a piece of bread and a cup of water, send them out of the house, and let them be. Too much attention would spoil them. I would have loved to let my children run free in the village because that would confirm that I am not a "helicopter" parent, hovering over their each and every move. I realized that I had taken parenting style as one measure of how well I had integrated into Moroccan life. Assuming the more relaxed approach of my friends would index successful rapport and lend me greater cultural legitimacy. But I also realized that just let-

ting my children run free would not work. I needed to structure fieldwork like a job in order to make it feasible for me. I cannot conduct
a formal interview if at the same time I have to monitor the children
to ensure that they do not wreak havoc on a weaving loom or dis-
mantle carefully arranged piles of blankets. I chose to situate us in
Kelaa Mgouna rather than immerse the whole family in village life
partly so that my children could attend preschool and free up my day.

The fact that I wrote my children out of fieldwork in order to get
the work done meant that I brought an American separation of work
and life to a context that does not operate according to the same divisions. Especially in the beginning, this separation caused me considerable anxiety. My husband and I spent the first six weeks settling
our family in, making what seemed like endless visits to utility offices, household supply and hardware stores, furniture makers, and
government agencies. We had to drag our children screaming to preschool, where the emphasis on writing exercises and chanting in uni-
son contrasted with their previous Montessori-style experience with
self-driven play and social interaction. Not only did I second-guess
my decision to bring my family along, I began to wonder if I would
ever get my project started. If I had been alone, I could have let some
of these practical issues slide, but I could not dive into research before
my children had adjusted at least a little bit to their new surroundings. Before I could begin my own work, I needed to make sure that
they had a routine, a structured context for them to do the work of
being children.

Sure enough, a couple of weeks later, the children started singing us the Arabic songs they had learned in class, and we no longer
needed to physically carry them in the mornings to prevent them
from trying to escape from school. By now they are also getting used
to being in villages with less supervision, exploring the nooks and
crannies of the large adobe compounds in search of cows and sheep.
I bring them regularly for social visits, understanding that I may not
be able to conduct formal interviews but can gain insights into the
way families here raise their children—and can simply spend time
with friends who have so generously welcomed us into their lives.

My children may not be a tool for my research in any formal way, but I have found a way to integrate them into my life here that allows me and my husband to get our work done, at least most of the time. Given what I know about gendered spaces in southern Morocco, I should have foreseen one difference: my friends constantly ask me to bring the children to the village, but they do not have the same expectation about my husband and usually just inquire briefly and politely about him. He is off the hook for most social visits, able to devote his valuable leave time to writing his own book.

However, my dilemma regarding the role of my children in field-work has not disappeared. Given the separation between my field sites and our home, the time I need—and want—to spend with my family still feels like time I am not doing real anthropology. I struggle with the nagging feeling that I should be in the field more, especially on those weekends when my family and I just take a walk to the river to have a picnic and play in the mud. Nor does my division between work and life map easily onto such divisions here. Men who need to maintain mobility for their livelihoods, whether they are school-teachers with two jobs or livestock traders constantly on the move, do not have to worry about child care, while women rely on extended families or take their children with them to the fields in order to fulfill their double burden of child care and agricultural labor. I am neither completely free of child-care responsibilities, nor immersed in a work environment that includes my children. This means that I make frequent awkward explanations of why I have to, say, return home to pick up the children from school rather than stay through the evening. Sometimes I do stay in the village, but I also want to share child-care responsibilities with my husband—and to see my children at the end of the day. Men ask, "Isn't there someone who can do that for you?" Women ask, "Why don't you bring your children with you?" I leave with an acute sense that my fieldwork suffers from my not having more unstructured time in the village, and I wonder what people think of the way I approach family life.

It took me some time to realize that, my sense of awkwardness aside, people were probably relieved to see me leave so that they could get on with their own work and lives. I had been proud of myself for my pragmatic recognition of ethnography as work, but I eventually understood the lack of reflexivity embedded in my modest critique. Fieldwork may be labor, but it is a fundamentally privileged form of labor. There was so much less at stake for me if I did not get to an interview or missed a wedding than there was for research participants, for whom missed opportunities could deepen livelihood insecurity. Observing the daily hardships of people's lives disrupted my assumption that in separating work and life, *I* was the one immersed in capitalist notions of time-labor discipline, while rural Moroccans seamlessly integrated their diverse livelihoods, child-rearing responsibilities, and thickly layered social obligations. Joining work and life is hardly effortless for women here, while sloughing off family responsibilities is hardly unproblematic for men. As part of their struggle for secure livelihoods, families confront questions of time, balance, and labor in stark and often poignant ways. I had not anticipated this, thinking that the ways Moroccans value children and structure their work would ease the burdens of child rearing, at least in the rural south.

The idea of letting children tend to themselves in the village glosses over the challenges people face in more rural settings. Migration has been a fact of life in the Mgoun Valley for so long that the emotional toll that it takes can be easily normalized. Men have described to me the loneliness and isolation of living in tents on construction sites throughout Morocco. Many try to find construction jobs in the valley so that they can live with their families for a few more months out of the year (though some are happy to be in a more urbane setting, away from the demands of family and community). Katherine Hoffman (2006) has documented the toll on women of men's livelihoods stretched across wider and wider spaces. Women shoulder the responsibility of maintaining the cultural authenticity of the homeland, in part through long, hard workdays that preserve a way of life men regard nostalgically and women consider a burden.[1] I have seen that one of the first projects many rural development associations initiate in the area is a day-care facility. In part, this reflects the notion (promoted by the teachers who tend to lead the associations) that early formal education creates responsible citizens and facilitates children's adjustment to elementary school. But it also reflects the basic reality that providing child care for women in rural communities allows them to meet their increasing labor obligations.

Rabinow used his observations of the "less overtly significant areas of day-to-day activity" to reflect on fieldwork as a rite of passage (2007 [1977], 58). In retrospect, I had taken for granted his deconstruction of ethnography as a form of cultural knowledge when I discounted the importance of that daily activity for my own ethnography. It turns out that the mundane shocks and discomforts of settling my family in offered an instructive lesson about how the dialogic encounter of fieldwork involves the production of work and time as well as knowledge. As I observed the divergent ways that I and my interlocutors balanced work and life, I did not see gaping cultural difference so much as our mutual embeddedness in the contemporary economic and social order. In this order, our divergent positionalities shaped our varying abilities to control the conditions of our work and the nature of the time we devoted to that work.

THE PROBLEM OF TIME

A more critical perspective on fieldwork as labor invariably turned my attention to what Jane Guyer terms "the temporality of lived economies": how contemporary capitalism shapes people's experience of the economic transformation in time as well as space (2007, 411). I had come to southern Morocco with an understanding of how modern processes of differentiation and exclusion had marginalized the region. Everyone—from Moroccan migrants working in France to young women harvesting wheat in the mountains—confronts "modernity's aporias" in the ways they experience poverty or vulnerability (ibid., 417). Although I had taken people's livelihood strategies in this context as my central research problem, I had not fully considered the temporal dimensions of those strategies. It was only when I ran into the challenges of scheduling interviews according to my workday that I became aware of the disjuncture between my experience of capitalist time and that of my Moroccan research participants.

On any given day, the cafés lining the only major intersection of Kelaa Mgouna are full of men drinking tea with the resigned expression of having too much time on their hands. It may be true that the young *chômeurs*, the educated unemployed who tend to occupy café tables for long stretches in Morocco's urban centers, find themselves at a loss for what to do with their time. In Kelaa Mgouna, in contrast, even those who are apparently idle don't seem to actually have enough time. Everyone, from young adolescents to the very elderly, scrambles to juggle their diverse responsibilities. Sometimes this scrambling involves the rush of a medical emergency. At other times, it involves long hours sitting around as nothing apparently happens. I have seen how often research participants are called away to attend to a family crisis or have to take a whole day to retrieve identity papers in their natal district. While I try to maintain my regimented schedule, people have to maintain flexibility so that they can take valuable time away from their work to meet their many social and economic demands. I was frustrated at the intrusions on my fieldwork when various bureaucratic procedures required me to repeatedly search out municipal officials to notarize my signature, but for my Moroccan acquaintances, this searching and waiting means money not earned, fields not planted, and other obligations not met. Many of those men drinking tea in Kelaa are waiting for transport to take provisions they purchased from the weekly market up to their homes in the mountains, while the women waiting in the minibuses are often returning from a doctor's visit that took two or three days out of their work routine.

The need to maintain flexibility can be even more challenging for teachers, office workers, and shopkeepers than for people engaged primarily in agricultural livelihoods. On the one hand, people in those formal occupations have rigid schedules that mirror my own, although the way I have structured my work frequently conflicts with the way they structure theirs. As I cross the footbridge over the

Mgoun River to one of my rural research sites just outside of Kelaa in the morning, I greet a stream of people heading in the opposite direction, to the market or their jobs in town. The village has the surface appearance of a farming community, but it is more peri-urban than rural: people drive the economic activity that Kelaa generates as a regional town and also benefit from it. I have knocked on numerous doors to conduct introductory interviews, only to learn that people are off attending to business in Kelaa, and I realized my arrogance in assuming that people would be free to meet with me on my own terms. Indeed, a good deal of my ethnography of the village must actually be done in Kelaa for the simple reason that the villagers spend so much of their time in town.

On the other hand, people in formal occupations are forced to work around routine as much as anyone else. One acquaintance is constantly rearranging his work schedule as a teacher in a primary school because of his activities as president of an association and leader of the nonprofit community in town. At one point he was urgently called away from one of our interviews by the pasha (the leading municipal authority) for a meeting that turned out to be a planning session for an event months away. This acquaintance explained that this is the way the administration works—without planning or forethought—in an effort to display state power. As he put it, officials hastily convene people simply because they can, even when the meeting could have been scheduled in advance. Friends have had to drop everything to attend day-long workshops organized at the last minute—some, ironically, on themes like "participatory development" and "gender and development." I now understand why my research assistant is so cavalier about pickup times at the preschool both of our children attend. Whereas my husband and I rush to retrieve our children at 5:00, remembering the penalty fees for late pickups at our Kentucky day-care facility, my assistant often swings by thirty to forty-five minutes late. The teachers understand that parents are not masters of their own schedules.

At first, I regarded the time people spend waiting in government offices, attending to family problems, and doing errands on others' behalf as time spent away from their work. In many important ways, it is. People express frustration when they are late planting crops or have to wait for hours on the floor of hallways in the medical center. But they also express a weary patience that indicates they accept this frustration as an inevitable part of their daily lives. Initially, I ascribed their patience to a more relaxed conception of time, a less capitalist kind of time distanced from the "space-time compression" that I experienced as a neoliberal subject in the digital age (Harvey 1990, 15). People's equanimity in the face of unexpected demands and their willingness to take time to socialize amid overwhelming labor obligations seemed like an enviable counterpoint to my own anxieties about my work schedule.

In essence, I had inadvertently reproduced the gap Johannes Fabian described as central to the ethnographic encounter: anthropologists constitute our objects by projecting them into an irretrievable past (Fabian 2002 [1983]). I had assumed my research participants were enacting a traditional conception of time in contrast to my own sensibility, which had been formed through immersion in globalized cultural and economic circuits. Enough afternoons waiting together at utility offices eventually helped me understand their experience of temporality not as an essential cultural difference, but as a response to their different position in these same circuits—an expression of their very contemporary marginalization by the Moroccan state and European labor markets. They have to maintain flexibility in order to cope with insecurity in ways more akin to the capitalist time of the Asian neoliberal free trade zones that Aihwa Ong (2006) describes than to the pre-capitalist time of a mythical rural peasantry.

The temporality of life in the margins has reshaped my perspective on what work and productivity mean to the people involved in my research. They readily complain about the inefficiency and oppression of the government, or the inconveniences of daily life. However, they do not speak about the many activities that ostensibly take them away from their work in terms of lost productivity. I returned to the scholarship I had read on livelihoods and agriculture in Africa to explore why (see especially Berry 1993; Guyer 1992 and

2004). This line of research documents the way people invest in social relationships to navigate unstable political systems and ambiguous land tenure regimes: maintaining diverse relations with peers and patrons, extended families, and powerful officials keeps livelihood options open and secures access to a broader array of productive resources. Sara Berry (1993) argues that while this may reduce agricultural productivity over time because capital is spread across different activities rather than concentrated in intensifying production, it is a key strategy for people who struggle to achieve livelihood security during uncertain times.

This analytic perspective compels me to look for people's "work" in unexpected places and times, including an unplanned trip to the market to get provisions for a wedding and an afternoon spent accompanying a neighbor to a government office to help navigate the bureaucracy. People allocate resources and time across various activities with a deep sense of social obligation and a simultaneously instrumental sense of how these activities contribute to their livelihoods by maintaining networks of reciprocity. My perception of many of the things people do as time spent away from their primary productive activity assumes that one activity is primary and that people distinguish productive from nonproductive activities in formal economic terms. People may not get all their work done in the hours I have marked off as my workday, but they certainly work a lot—for money, subsistence, and the good of people they care about or depend on for their livelihood.

THE COMFORT OF METHODS

Beyond the practical realities of getting the job done, regarding ethnography as work has broadened my theoretical horizons—and forced me to think of methods in more concrete, even mundane, ways. I spent time in an anthropology graduate program in the mid-1990s, and my theoretical training during that period of heated debates emerging from post-modernism, post-structuralism, and critical theory shaped my sense of what constituted good anthropology. Perhaps it

was my infatuation with high theory, but at that time I regarded undue attention to methods—questions of sampling, structuring questionnaires, and data collection strategies—as allegiance to a questionable kind of positivism. Good anthropologists needed an intense
engagement with their field setting and a critical sensibility to interpret what was happening around them. I knew I could not do that
kind of anthropology when I returned to the field with my family
ten years later—because I would not live where I work, I did not feel
I had the luxury of letting participant observation serve as the sole
or even primary framework for my research.

I began designing my methods with a dual concern for my research
questions and the logistical realities of what my life would be like in
Morocco. I returned to some of the methods that had aroused my
suspicion in the 1990s, sensing now that they might be more ame-
nable to a work plan that I could fit into my "working hours." I was
excited to find in the field of political ecology a range of approaches
that both assumes a critical theoretical stance and deploys some of
the formal methodologies developed in the environmental sciences
and related disciplines. Political ecology is a diverse field of inquiry.[2]
I invoke it here to emphasize the fact that it not only gave me a theoretical language for addressing livelihood and environmental issues,
but also showed me how I could critically deploy research tools more
closely identified with positivism in a way that did not offend my former anthropological self.

More pragmatically, designing specific research questions, interview guides, and an extended questionnaire allowed me to envision
doing meaningful work without the level of immersion I would have
considered ideal for fieldwork. I felt comforted, somehow, at the thought
that I could make epistemological choices that were theoretically acceptable to me and could also make research more manageable in
my circumstances. This approach to methods gave me the security
of a plan and a list of things to do, which helped me regain my com-
posure once the shock of settling in had subsided and I was able to
begin my research. But my initial assumption that I needed to adjust
my methods because I do not live where I work, like so many of my

initial assumptions, turned out to be wrong. I do live where I work, because people here live and work in such diverse places and times.

Before I left for Morocco, my advisor offered a piece of parting advice: write every day, no matter what I had done that day. Sometimes, after I finish a day of interviewing and put the children to bed, I am simply too tired. But her advice still resonates with me, helping to loosen the neat separations I set up in my mind between work and life. My sense of the "field" has indeed expanded beyond the set of research questions that structured my dissertation proposal. Even with my more formal methods, I still write many field notes about the rhythm of daily life, my own and others'. My notes chronicle the feeling of a dust storm at the open-air vegetable market, the challenge of figuring out the holiday schedule at our preschool, and the daily pleasures of building our lives in a small Moroccan town. Despite my initial skepticism that this could happen, some of my most important analytic insights have come from these daily encounters. I have learned that my job as an ethnographer is to use whatever tools are at my disposal, whether a formal questionnaire or the shared experience of waiting in line for an official signature, to understand how people's experiences of life and work take shape. I needed the ruptures and discomforts of my fieldwork experience to come to that realization.

NOTES

1. However, as my research develops, I find that the idea of nostalgia does not adequately capture why people in this region continue to invest so much emotionally and economically in agriculture. Subsistence farming and, to an increasing extent, commercial agricultural play an important role in people's livelihood portfolios in communities that have an adequate supply of water, and even in some that do not. Social status is also closely tied to landownership and working the land.

2. See D. Davis 2007, Ilahiane 2004, and Mitchell 2002 for scholarship on the Middle East and North Africa situated in this tradition.

3| Thinking about Class and Status in Morocco

DAVID A. McMURRAY

MY SOCKS

A barber worked directly across the street from the front door of our apartment in the late 1980s in Nador, a gritty boomtown in the Berber north that was exploding with the repatriated wealth of emigrants away in Europe as well as the revenues from goods smuggled in from Spain and hash smuggled out of Morocco.[1] The barber's shop was decorated with posters of stylish men, all of them models advertising various hair care products. He had hired another barber—a poorer man, judging by his attire—to help out during busy times, such as early evening hours and Fridays. He also made the second barber sweep out the shop at night when they closed, about 9:00.

The head barber would lounge in the doorway to his salon between customers. Nothing that we did across the street escaped his eye. He claimed, and I believed him, that he had spent a few months in Germany. His clothing, which could have been labeled at the time "urban Mediterranean," suggested that he knew his way around the local big city of Oujda, perhaps even the national big cities of Fes and Casablanca, for he wore tight-fitting, open-collar shirts unbuttoned to mid-chest. His slacks had no back pockets so they could hug his hips and butt, though they did have immaculate creases down each leg. His sockless feet were planted in polished loafers. His hair, while short, had some gel-like substance in it to make it glisten. He never dressed in traditional Moroccan male attire on Fridays or holy days, which suggested that he wasn't especially religious or especially en-amored of local customs. His trade let everyone know that he wasn't a wealthy man. However, the families in his building would often re-ceive their letters addressed in care of the barber. This was a way the families used to maintain some anonymity, but it also revealed that they trusted him.

Late one afternoon I came out of my front door on the way to the neighborhood baker to get bread for dinner. The barber stopped me. We exchanged the usual pleasantries. When the conversation had begun to wind down and I was getting ready to move on, he said, "Why do you wear socks with your sandals?"

My normal attire in Morocco consisted of an all-purpose sport coat, buttoned-down shirts, khaki pants, and wire-rimmed glasses; in short, nothing too out of the ordinary except, apparently, for when I wore socks under my sandals. By "out of the ordinary," I mean of course for a foreigner from the global north. My clothing choices were not made in imitation of Nadori notions of style, though I was trying to dress in a way that I hoped locals would interpret as conser-vatively respectful. Parenthetically, Michael Taussig (1993, 174–75) has pointed out that in colonized societies, men commonly anchor the mimetic pole while women embody alterity; hence, men around the world wear suit coats and pants in imitation of European attire, while women wear highly specific, local costumes. Perhaps in un-conscious adherence to that rule, my wife wore typically Nadori fe-male clothing in and out of the house and thus held down the alterity pole, while I wore a Sears sport coat made out of cotton and polyes-ter, a reasonable imitation of American—if not exactly European—male attire.

I no doubt cut a ridiculous figure, which the barber could no longer resist commenting on. The first thing I thought to say back to him was, "You don't like them? I think they look distinguished." Then I wanted to say something like: "You never know when you're going to get invited into someone's house and have to take off your shoes. I want to make sure, even when I'm wearing sandals, that I've got something on underneath because my bare feet are always dirty or they smell."

But I didn't say either of those things. I tossed back at him what people often said to me when I inquired about something they either hadn't thought about or thought was too trivial to think about: "It's a tradition in our country" (*taqlid fi bledna*).

"No it's not," he retorted, catching me off guard. "I saw some Germans doing it, too. So tell me the truth, why do you wear them?"

He was smirking at having called me out, at having challenged my little white lie. He waited for my reply. I was flustered. I smiled awkwardly, waved, and said I was in a hurry and we'd talk later.

I went home and thought about what I should have said to the barber. It's not easy analyzing your own identity and the sartorial signifiers that you put on every day to mark who you are. It's much easier to cast a critical eye on others. I tried to think the point through anyway. I first thought about such things marking me as a Westerner. That would explain why the Germans and I chose to wear the same items of clothing. But that wasn't the whole answer because lots of Americans, and probably Germans too, did not wear socks with sandals. I also, of course, did not want to be lumped in with Germans. Like my fellow countrymen who find themselves in Morocco, it bugged me a little initially to know that I was referred to by terms like *Rumi* or *Franji,* which literally signified "European" and were derived from borrowings of European designations into Arabic (*Rumi* from "Rome" or "Roman" and referring, someone told me, to the people from the Eastern Orthodox lands ruled by Constantinople; and *Franji* from "Frank," referring to the European invaders during the crusades) but which were understood more generally to name all foreigners from the global north. I wanted to be counted apart. I was an American from the New World, not someone from the Old World. I wasn't answerable for their colonial crimes. Yet my attire made me indistinguishable from them.

On this same subject, Tobias Jones, a northern European who took up long-term residency in Italy, writes of how easy it is to spot northern Europeans vacationing in a Mediterranean country simply because they are less stylish. He quotes Italo Calvino on the subject:

> goofy and anti-aesthetic groups of Germans, English, Swiss, Dutch, and Belgians . . . men and women with variegated ugliness, with certain trousers at the knees, *with socks in sandals* or with bare feet in shoes, some clothes printed with flowers, underwear which sticks out, some white and red meat, deaf to good taste and harmony. . . . (my emphasis; quoted in Jones 2005, 140–41)

So it would seem that my Berber barber neighbor and the Italian Riviera's Calvino shared a common disgust for my wardrobe choices and a common pity for my lack of "taste." That certainly provides anecdotal evidence for a Mediterranean-wide sense of what constitutes baseline status and prestige markers in the realm of male attire, and it also suggests that the barber was a keen observer of everyday life.

In any case, I eventually moved on from thinking that I was dressing as a Westerner. I found it more plausible to think that class dispositions and social status were the major factors in my dress decisions. Of course, age, which is a subset of status, also influenced me. Socks with sandals would not be worn by a very young man in the United States. But they also probably wouldn't be worn by a working-class male of any age. Given those restrictions, I think that at some level they probably signified to me a certain bookishness, especially when you threw in the wire-rimmed glasses. I think it's fair to say that I was trying for a look that signified a mature, middle-class, Western male with a fair amount of academic prestige. In hindsight, my attempts had been wasted on the barber, and probably on most Moroccans. Since the barber took a fair amount of pride and care in his own self-presentation, he could only cast a dismissive glance my way and scorn what to him were the sloppy sartorial choices I had made. I was no match for his tasteful performance of lower-class male, Mediterranean urbanity. I do thank him, however, for getting me started thinking about cultural markers of class, status, and prestige and how they operate differently in different locales around the world. I like to think that the barber got me interested in the symbolic importance of class-specific tastes as an alternative to the notion that someone's class position rests mainly on an economic relation to the means of production as identified by his or her occupation or income.

I want to shift gears here to consider the application to the Nadori case of theories of status and prestige markers developed elsewhere. The fact that they are not homegrown should give us some pause. The ways Nadoris think about prestige and the ways they represent status and class differences cannot be assumed to run on tracks parallel to their Euro-American counterparts. If there is overlap, it needs to be demonstrated, not taken for granted. Think, as just one of several examples, of the chasm-like differences between distinctions associated with colonizer and colonized societies. Add to that differences between an Arabo-Islamic heritage or an agricultural and resource-extraction economic orientation, on the one hand, and a secular European heritage or an industrial-based economy, on the other hand. However, at the risk of being Eurocentric, I have cast a wide net just to try out the possibility that such foreign approaches can shed some light on the way things work in Morocco.[2] I think I found that they do provide a beginning point for a discussion of lifestyles, aesthetic dispositions, and consumption choices being made by people of different class origins in places like Nador. In any case, I was pleased with some of the results, so much so that I want to share a sample of them. I leave it up to you to decide whether or not they might help to illuminate the ways in which status and class distinctions are marked by Moroccans.

COMPETITIVE PARTIES AND "CHOCOLATE BOY" BACHELOR PADS

The earliest theorist that I have netted and hauled in to illuminate class and status distinctions is Thorstein Veblen, who coined the famous term "conspicuous consumption" in *The Theory of the Leisure Class* (1899). Veblen was writing during the Gilded Age about the increasing emphasis on the accumulation of wealth at the expense of productive activity. In evolutionary terms typical of his day, he describes the move from viewing possessions as evidence of successful foraging, hunting, and fighting skills among barbarians to viewing wealth as conveying honor in its own right, followed by the development of the even more perverse view that inherited wealth bestows even greater honor on the possessor (ibid., 28–30). So as to distance themselves from the lower classes, whose members place value on one's ability to work, the wealthy decline to participate in any form of labor, indulging instead in what Veblen called "conspicuous leisure." The idle rich have developed all sorts of "quasi-scholarly and quasi-artistic" ways of showing that they have spent their time unproductively, according to Veblen. "Knowledge of dead languages and the occult sciences; of correct spelling; of syntax and prosody; of the various forms of domestic music and other household art; of the latest proprieties of dress, furniture, and equipage; of games, sports, and fancy-bred animals, such as dogs and race-horses," and in general all of those bodily movements classified under the heading of "manners and breeding," Veblen points out, attest to one's conspicuous consumption of leisure (45–46). His list is interesting and foreshadows the later work of Paul Fussell (1983) in that Veblen (like Fussell) doesn't do much with his insights on how class markers operate—he just lists them as demonstrations put on by the well-mannered to display how much time they have spent acquiring them.

My reading of Veblen, long after I had left Morocco, put me in mind of the time the sewer pipe in the garage of our apartment in Nador backed up and started leaking. Our landlord, an affable ex-peasant from a nearby village who had emigrated to Germany and saved a tidy sum—tidy enough to build the four-plex in which we both lived—immediately got out a shovel and started to uncover the pipe. He bellowed for his two sons to join him. Unfortunately for our landlord, those two had fled out the front door at the first sign of dirty work. "Honest work," our landlord would have called it. His sons disagreed. They had been brought up in the relative luxury permitted by the remitted wages of the father and so had come to embrace the concept of conspicuous leisure without ever having read Veblen. Manual labor carried with it déclassé connotations. The sons' nails were manicured, while their father's had dirt under them. The boys valued not having to work just as much as their father valued physical labor. As in many other areas of the Arabo-Islamic or Mediterranean world, white—or at least light-colored—clothing; clean, polished shoes; and long nails on the little finger all marked the man of leisure, the man who hired others to do his labor.

Conspicuous consumption refers to the practice of the gentleman of leisure consuming the finest commodities to be found, whether they be food, clothing, shelter, ornaments, or amusements (Veblen 1899, 73). This entails the development of connoisseurship on the part of the gentleman, so that he can discriminate between excellence and mediocrity and then consume the former and avoid the latter. He must also demonstrate an ability to consume in a refined way, showing off for all to see his excess of etiquette. In this his friends and competitors, who form a kind of mutual aid society to further their joint interest in flaunting their opulence, join him. The most common way of doing so is through the holding of feasts. Such costly entertainments allow the guests to help the host consume in quantities far beyond his personal abilities, while also allowing him the opportunity to demonstrate his excess of consumables and mastery of etiquette (ibid., 75).

The big bourgeoisie, the very rich, and the rural notables living in Nador have a less palpable daily impact on the culture of the city than Veblen outlined, perhaps because of their very small numbers and absenteeism. There are, however, some interesting exceptions to this generalization. It was true that the Nadori bourgeoisie refrained from organizing within a political party. But they did pursue their interests in the form of an apolitical pressure group called the Association Socio-Culturelle du Bassin Méditerranéen. They also managed on occasion to control political offices associated with the region. For example, in 1976–77, seven out of eight representatives elected to the Moroccan parliament from Nador were big businessmen (Ouariachi 1980, 335–36). Their primary meeting ground and way of achieving group solidarity and harmony was by means of *zerdas,* which in Nador consisted of sumptuous feasts of several courses that were hosted in round-robin fashion. These were the true forums in Nador where the members of the elite hammered out their common political positions and no doubt, following Veblen, vied with each other publicly to display their wasteful, opulent excess. A wealthy man in our neighborhood in Nador had a *zerda* at which sixty sheep were consumed, a feast that was still talked about years later. Kaïs Ouariachi recounts that the association mentioned above once had a *zerda* of 300 sheep, 1,000 chickens, and 5,000 eggs (ibid., 391–92)! No wonder corrupt businessmen are called *iᶜaddissen n rehram,* or "stomachs of sin" (ibid., 338).

The *zerda* is a fairly recently invented tradition of the Nadori notables, for there was no rural counterpart. Actually, the idea probably was imported from the Arab interior, where it is practiced on a grander scale. The concept had trickled down to the point where members of the petite bourgeoisie were starting to put on these affairs. Veblen remarked on this kind of trickle-down effect, calling it the "coercive influence" of the leisure style of life of the higher over the lower classes (1899, 84).

The promotion of conspicuous consumption was practiced by the offspring of the Nadori wealthy as well. Many of these young men (sometimes derisively called "chocolate boys" by the less wealthy) cultivated a lifestyle of ease by pooling their monthly stipends and renting and equipping bachelor pads. The fathers provided them with enough money to do this, though they never knew about the clandestine flats. The boys then decorated these clubhouses with colored lightbulbs, stereo cassette recorders, and beds on the floor. Most of the time they just gathered to play cards or drink and socialize in these spaces. Everyone's dream was to one day entice a prostitute or out-of-town female shopper up for a party.

The fathers of these chocolate boys were motivated by the desire to see their sons cut a swath in society. I think that the fathers believed their sons were extensions of themselves and thus must be provided with enough spending money to keep up with their wealthy peers. But they also left it up to the young to determine how exactly to measure their peer standing. "My father keeps my pockets full," said one young son of a migrant in front of his admiring friends. He had reason to gloat. He had just beaten the other three boys in a week-long restaurant round-robin contest to see whose pockets were the deepest. The four continued dining out night after night until only he could pay.

I think Veblen would have had no trouble recognizing the displays of wealth being incorporated into the everyday lives of these rich Nadori fathers and sons as examples of conspicuous consumption.

THE GREAT MERCEDES DEBATE

The second theorist's work I want to bring to bear on the discussion of Nadori status and prestige issues is that of the late, infamous French sociologist and semiotician, Jean Baudrillard. What seems pertinent to Nador is Baudrillard's notion that modernity is marked in part by the shift in dominance from internal to external codes of status and prestige. This distinction refers to the possibly global transition from earlier sign systems (gestural and ritual means of marking deference and prestige, modes of address, and so on) that distinguished a so-cial hierarchy (of class, caste, or birth) to the external sign systems of social standing in the contemporary capitalist world. These newer systems subsume the criteria of social discrimination that are inter-nal to caste or class or birth status and that are thus "in the world" (such as proper speech, diction, or accent; and forms of etiquette or norms of politesse) into a more universal and universally recognized status code based on the external relations between objects, activi-ties, and information—in short, a system or code to be "consumed" by systematically manipulating its object-signs (Baudrillard 1988, 19–22). Hierarchies of class, stratum, gender, and age are differentiated more and more in terms of the sign systems of consumption that govern the distinguishing significance of a given object and how it relates to others. Having good versus bad taste in matters of home décor, automobile choice, house styles, clothing, and so forth rests on a Nadori's ability to discern what is considered refined and what is rustic—designated by the term ʿaroubi—and then not mixing the two. More important in Nador was the struggle between emigrants and non-emigrants to specify what those distinguishing signs would be and then to organize them into dominant—that is, legitimate— sign codes or systems. Raymond Jamous, a French ethnographer of the Nador region in the 1960s, provides several examples of some of the older internal codes of the region in his study of the pre-capitalist period of the five-tribe confederacy surrounding the town. He describes their status distinctions based on the social prestige involved in competitive hospitality (1981, 71–73); the recognition of social rank encoded in bride price (ibid., 252–53); and the judicious use of language by the "man of honor" (ibid., 70).[3]

Let me give you an example of an external, object-oriented sign code that seemed to be up for grabs in Nador when I lived there in the late 1980s: bureaucrats complaining that the emigrants had overturned the automotive indexical markers that operated throughout the rest of the country. In other regions, a Renault 4 assembled in Morocco was the cheapest car given to an official for his personal use. The level of car then rose with the bureaucratic level of the driver. In Nador, however, an emigrant or emigrant's family member might own the make of car that elsewhere indexed a high official. Many Nadori emigrants and merchants actually vied with each other to possess the latest model of Mercedes, a make of car associated only with generals and diplomats in the rest of the nation. Even taxis in the north were Mercedes. Public servants resented this undermining of the automotive status index. Yet it was so common that Nador was called *Thamdinth n Mercedes* in Berber (City of Mercedes).

I often wondered if the complaints that wealthier, older Nadori families voiced against the nouveau riche emigrants' inflation of bride prices, car prices, wedding prices, and land prices weren't really just a cry against modernity, especially in its guise as rapid urbanization. With the massive move from many villages to one city, the local histories and local tribal ways of doing things that once determined one's respect and pride of place had been overtaken by the Baudrillardian shift in dominance from internal to external codes of status and prestige. Now the make of your car, not the historical reputation of your family name, determined how you were treated in Nador.

HICKS DON'T JOG

The next theorist I want to enlist is Pierre Bourdieu, the late French sociologist who is famous for, among other things, identifying the distinctive sets of cultural preferences in 1960s France that roughly followed class lines. Bourdieu's emphasis on class position as a cultural as much as an economic phenomenon places his work at the center of any analysis of status and prestige. His signature contributions have been to popularize the notion of "cultural capital," as a set of distinctive skills, knowledges, and practices akin to economic capital in that it acts as a resource on which people draw to further their position in the social hierarchy. Bourdieu took the idea further by identifying cultural capital with the symbolization of social life embodied in the concepts of taste and the lifestyle built from it. Equally important was his analysis of the ways different social origins produce different kinds or quantities of cultural capital, which then become naturalized and thus thought of as the innate characteristics of the elite or the working class. In practice this means marking one's difference and identity—that is, one's class position—in terms of consumption practices based on values, principles, language use, and so forth that flow from class distinctions (Bourdieu 1984, 394). Bourdieu selected clothing, language, education, and cultural discrimination as the arenas in which taste could most easily be read and in which signs of sophistication and moral superiority could be transformed into supposedly natural inclinations of the well-born and well-bred.

The constellation of distinctions most important in assessing consumption preferences and the preferred style of life in Nador (and thus in providing higher social status for those able to live according to these stylistic criteria) revolved around the distinction between *thamdinth* (the city) and *rcampu* (the country). This major distinction encompassed a series of more specific ones, the most important of which was being urbane as opposed to being countrified, that is, ⁽aroubi. The codes of conduct and consumption built on these foundations were shared for the most part by both emigrant and non-emigrant families in the city. The break in this case was between households that had re-established themselves in the city—whether emigrant or not—and those just in from the country who had yet to absorb the dominant sign system used to mark status.

Let me take up each of these distinctions in turn and provide illustrations of how they operated to distinguish respectable Nador residents from the riffraff just in from the country. Many students in public school with recent country origins felt the sting of humiliation when their rural names were read out in class. The names for boys that produced giggles from the city kids included Muhammadi, Mohand (not just a name but also slang for penis), Moh, Fadil, and Haddou. According to schoolteacher friends of mine, girls suffered even more when they were named Mimount, Mimouna, Thmimount, Thraithmas, Louiza, or Hadda instead of Latifa, Samira, Farida, or other names popularized by Egyptian soap opera starlets or singers. (Such negative discriminations based on taste are not so much markers of class boundaries as they are displays of one's cultural competence, because they depend on a certain level of cultural capital while also acting as bases for determining whom one is not attracted to, wants to avoid, or finds boring, thereby reproducing status boundaries.)

Certain mannerisms also marked the country man in the city. For instance, urbane, sophisticated males would hiss or say "psst," but they would never loudly hail their friends by name in public as country bumpkins did. In medium-size and big cities in the country's interior, the effusive, Arabic style of multiple-phrase greetings and leave-takings, sometimes including light pecks on the cheek, was associated with good manners, while the country way was to say less and to say it more haltingly, while giving hearty smacks on the cheek.

Younger girls in secondary school displayed their urbane refinement to each other by speaking in Egyptian Arabic and mimicking the singsong intonation pattern of soap opera starlets. Their elder counterparts might also use French in public; more commonly, they would pepper their speech with French loan words as a mark of their education (the longer someone went to school, the more French he or she would have taken) and sophistication.

Within the realm of interior decoration, the subject matter of wall decorations did not seem to break along class lines: Islamic bric-a-brac and laser posters could show up in the most modest huts as well as the most opulent villas. The main status-distinguishing features were the use of items in frames in wealthier homes, with magazine illustrations taped to walls usually found in poorer homes, and the additional tendency in wealthier homes to display smaller pictures arranged symmetrically on walls in triangular or diamond patterns. This illustrated Bourdieu's (1984, 379) contention that the higher the social status of the household, the more likely every item and space in the home would be thought out in aesthetic terms, not just conventionally decorated.

One more example: as Bourdieu had pointed out for France (ibid., 390), upward mobility and asceticism seemed to go together in Nador. For example, educated, cosmopolitan, white-collar women of the urban, bureaucratic stratum of Nadori society were the only ones who attended aerobics classes and talked about dieting. The few male joggers present in Nador also came from the ranks of the urban, bureaucratic milieu. Children and lower-class males, whether in school or not, preferred soccer and street games—that is, traditionally popular competitive sports whose goal was not bodily perfection.

THE IMPORTANCE OF ROYAL PORTRAITS IN PLUMBING SHOPS

The last theorist I want to take up who might provide some help in analyzing Moroccan status and prestige considerations and the way they dovetail with class relations is Paul Pascon, who wrote an (admittedly slight) discussion of Moroccan culture in terms of intertwined modes of production. He lists four that form the Moroccan social formation: patriarchalism, feudalism, tribalism, and capitalism. Moroccan individuals, according to Pascon, seldom if ever completely master the mix. They constantly make mistakes. It's hard to see how they could do otherwise, he says, because each of the four modes creates its own competing "ideologies, conventions, mores, values, legal systems, technologies, and cognitive systems" (Pascon 1986, 211).

Pascon illustrates his point by providing an amusing example of a peasant in the process of getting a government loan. The peasant seeks out a cousin who works in the ministry to act as intercessor, even though the cousin is a lowly mechanic. The peasant also brings a chicken to the bureaucrat who is arranging the loan, perhaps as a bribe, gift, or payment—or maybe all three. The bureaucrat in turn requires that the near subsistence-level peasant take out fire insurance before he can qualify for the loan, in spite of the fact that the bewildered peasant has no clue how the insurance is supposed to benefit him. He will also have to take the papers back home and get the local village *muqqadim,* or *shaykh,* to co-sign them and thus verify that the peasant is who he says he is. All of these small moments, according to Pascon, spring from the dynamic interplay of capitalist, feudal, and tribal modes of production.

I can think of several anecdotes that might be better explained if they were to be unpacked with Pascon's intertwined modes of production in mind. Often in Nador things came up that seemed to me to be mixing registers. I am thinking, for example, of the fact that the king's picture was obligatory in all public spaces in Nador. This extended even to private shops. For example, one day a plumbing supply shop opened for business but did not put up the king's picture. Within a few weeks of its opening, the police came by and told the owner that something was missing and that he had better rectify the problem. They did not specify the royal portrait, but he knew what they meant. He bought a copy of the king's portrait and displayed it prominently on the wall behind the cash register. I heard this anecdote while visiting the plumbing shop in question with a friend. We had walked by dozens of plumbing shops on the way to this one. I had asked him why we hadn't stopped at one of the others, and he

told me that he made it a rule to shop in the stores of fellow tribes-
men, like the owner of this shop. "Better to be cheated a little by
someone you know than to be cheated a lot by someone you don't
know," he said.

A Pascon-inspired analysis of the above paragraph might point,
first, to the extent of capitalist penetration in Nador, which is so great
that shopping absorbs many hours of the day and important interactions occur in and around places of business. Yet in spite of that,
tribal loyalties still influence some commercial decisions. That, presumably, is an example of the mix of modes of production in Morocco. A mode of production analysis would also of course point to
the more feudal propensity to display in public a portrait of the current king as representative of Makhzenian[4] control over the hinter-
lands (not to mention the regional and occupational preferences for
portraits of the king in business attire or dressed as Commander of
the Faithful in traditional robes). So at least three modes of production may be intertwined in the everyday life swirling around that
little plumbing shop. Pascon sums up the jumble of experience this
way: "If one lives in a composite society, one has a personal tendency
to abide by a set of morals and behavior patterns that are a composite of several value systems" (1986, 213). Pascon might have said that
the decorative decisions and status strategies arrived at by Nadoris
are conditioned by tribal and feudal values as well as by values stemming from the capitalist mode of production. Since Pascon's writing,
the Rif has been massively monetarized, yet many pre-capitalist tendencies remain, suggesting the plausibility of his notion that these
aren't residual traits but characteristics of a heterogeneous social formation.

CLASS DISMISSED

My point is not that anthropological studies of Morocco don't pay attention to detail or ignore class and status relations entirely; it's that
they don't often analyze distinctions of status and prestige in terms
of status markers that form coherent sets of preferences that can

be mapped along class lines. They don't unpack home décor, clothing choices, consumer goods, attitudes, interactions, activities, and so forth as signifiers of class relations—which isn't the only way to think about them, of course, but is a productive way to do so. I have found that many Moroccans are quite conscious of status signifiers and how they are deployed in everyday life and so can provide excellent insight into the workings of the system at the local, regional, and national levels. Thus, when we anthropologists don't avail ourselves of these local experts to explore these markers of class distinctions, we are missing a golden opportunity.

One area that forms an exception to what I am suggesting might be studies of the female body and its marking by tattooing, hair styles, and clothing (especially veils, scarves, gloves, and other accoutrements of modesty). From at least the mid-1970s onward, the ways in which social status, signified by various sartorial choices, plays a role in the creation of gender subjectivity is a well-mined subject. I am thinking here of Rachel Newcomb's book (2009) on the women of Fes. Newcomb has very interesting things to say about the sartorial performance of piety, for instance, as well as the general fetishization of appearances and how important it is for Fassi (meaning "from Fes") women to distinguish themselves in terms of dress and demeanor. But her work remains an exception, I think, in Moroccan studies. Or, perhaps more to the point, most other work seldom surpasses the anecdotal, personal level. Fatima Mernissi's (1995) autobiography of growing up in a harem in Fes provides some valuable anecdotes waiting to be mined for the general patterns they reveal. I am thinking especially of her reminiscences about traditional Moroccan bourgeois forms of female adornment and attitudes about what to wear when in public and in the home.

Susan Ossman's (2002) study of beauty salons in Casablanca adds to this. Her emphasis on differing female Moroccan notions of body image across the twentieth century is potentially very fruitful. I am thinking, for example, of the way she analyzes how bodily heaviness is associated with the country, the last generation, illiteracy, and passivity; while bodily lightness or thinness is associated with female mobility, modernity, urbanity, activity, and even liberation (ibid., 19–20). She cites Bourdieu's influence on her, especially his notion that in order to make sense of personal style we must first form a sense of the common ground of style at the level of social class and social epoch. Personal style is above all a deviation from this norm, which, in the process of deviating, draws attention to its relation to the common style. These are important points. My hesitation about Ossman's work is that she does not set out to demarcate this common ground of style, but wants instead to dwell on the individual deviations from it (ibid., 151). That assessment might be too harsh. Ossman has some very interesting things to say about the ways regional status markers compete with national ones at the same time as internal codes of status and prestige give way to the spread of external status codes based solely on consumption. I am thinking of her example of how Fassi families recognize that they no longer monopolize the nation's commerce but still cling to the notion that only they have good taste when it comes to cuisine. Or take the example she mentions of the Soussi (southern Berber) entrepreneurs, who believe their success is based on their own grave austerity— even as they decorate their nouveau riche palaces with gilded furniture (Ossman 1994, 163–64).

In terms of valuable anecdotal sources waiting to be mined, I think also of the famous Moroccan novel by Leila Abouzeid, *Year of the Elephant*, which has a wonderful scene about rapidly changing class dispositions on the eve of independence. The female narrator is recounting to a friend why her husband, a social-climbing junior bureaucrat in the making, is divorcing her because her more traditional ways of being in the world cause him to see her as something of a liability to his advancement. The reasons for the divorce thus all have to do with changing notions of what constitutes proper style and etiquette at the dawn of this particular new age. As she is recounting to her friend the reasons for her husband's desire to separate, she says: "Fury rises up inside me and I exclaim bitterly; I don't eat with a fork. I don't speak French. I don't sit with men. I don't go out to fancy dinners. Is that enough or shall I continue?" (quoted in Cohen 2004, 61).

Another study very worth mentioning is Shana Cohen's *Searching for a Different Future: The Rise of a Global Middle Class in Morocco* (2004). She is wonderful at discussing various aspects of class formation, job markets, education, and ideological elements, like the rise of individualism, that figure in the creation of class identification. She brings an almost cultural-studies sensitivity to the richness that literature and film can provide to the analysis of class-based cultures. She comes up with some interesting examples, not the least of which is her analysis of the classic novel of Driss Charaibi, *Le Passé Simple,* and its fascinating scenes of class conflict between the wealthy patriarch, who is illiterate and unfamiliar with everything outside his traditional world of business, and thus a rock-solid member of the traditional Moroccan bourgeoisie; and his son, who is French-educated and straining to be free of all filial duties, especially taking over the family business, and who is thus an example of the new middle class with its dependence on educational attainment and government largesse.

In her book, Cohen mentions Bourdieu and his elaborate research project into the study of class dispositions and styles. She even provides a few pages of provocative and very useful examples of how to think about this work in the Moroccan context. But then, to my mind, she does the reverse of Ossman's investigation of individual subjectivity by pulling back too far, to a less intimate, more macro level of analysis. Cohen thus merely scratches the surface of the study of accents, dress, interior décor, and so forth that form the baseline of the style that she claims marks the Moroccan national from the international middle class.

One important exception to my complaints about the absence or the inadequate treatment of markers of class and status distinctions would be a short article from the 1980s by the Palestinian writer Anton Shammas. In this article, Shammas meditates on the differences in photo placement in his grandfather's village house and in contemporary dwellings. He reminds us that the destabilization of Arab culture following the invasion of the Arab world by Westerners and their kitsch took place in stages. He argues that there is a distinction between the attitude toward representation on the part of the older people who lived through the invasion by the West and the younger generations who came of age more recently. The latter live in houses decorated with escapist art or cluttered with juxtapositions of First World and Third World cultural production. More strikingly, all of the art is hung at or near eye level. The older generation, on the other hand, placed its representations on the wall above eye level, at or near the ceiling. Shammas suggests this elevation of decoration was an expression of a now lost sense of honor. He puts it thus: "For honor, generally, implies a certain awe, and things which inspire us with awe are usually placed high. Arab culture regarded the imitation of reality with awe. The transmission of reality via the artistic vision entails for the villager an element of defiance against the supreme power" (1987, 23).

I found that Shammas's Palestinian examples seemed to hold for Nador as well, because none of the houses I visited in and around Nador positioned their pictures near the ceiling. The exception, as might be expected, was the elevated placement of the obligatory photo of the king in places of business. I cannot say when the change to eye-level arrangement of photographs took place, but I imagine, like Shammas, that it was not that long ago, perhaps even as late as the 1970s.

Leaving such exceptions aside, I suspect an older tradition within the anthropology of Morocco is responsible for pushing the analysis of markers of distinction by class and epoch to the margins. Many of the studies that would today be considered as forming the canon of Moroccan anthropology privileged ethnic identity, patron-client relations, religious training, tribal affiliation, patrilineal descent, membership in occupational groups, membership in ascriptive groups (such as race and religion, as opposed to groups whose membership is based on merit), membership in religious brotherhoods, or some combination of these, viewing them as more important than class in determining status distinctions. I don't think that models of social stratification based on the above criteria are sufficient today, if they ever were. I think, instead, that many of those relationships exist alongside of class relations and, often as not, in subordination to them or embedded in them. In addition, there has long been a tendency to study status distinctions in terms of roles played by individuals while ignoring the wealth of other kinds of markers, material or otherwise. But regardless of the model used to explain the system that reproduces them, markers of status distinctions can still be analyzed in their relational detail in productive ways. I am thinking of the way Bourdieu draws dichotomies that distinguish working-class from elite ways of living in the world, with the overarching, all-encompassing one being the distinction between the urgency, necessity, and function that are characteristic of the working-class relationship to the material world and the distance, detachment, and abstraction that underlie the relationship to reality lived by the bourgeoisie. This simple distinction constitutes the core of all others and strikes me as being a useful beginning point for a discussion of lifestyles, aesthetic dispositions, and consumption choices made by people of different class origins in places like Nador, Morocco. I also like to think, though I am probably stretching things here a bit, that the barber across the street was making just this distinction by pointing out a wasteful, functionless extravagance on my part. My socks in sandals served no role that he could discern; rather, they represented the bourgeois triumph of form over function, which of course was no triumph at all to his way of thinking because they looked ridiculous and attracted dirt.

NOTES

1. The period being described here is the late 1980s. The anecdotes discussed appeared in an earlier version in chapter 4 of McMurray (2001) and are included here with the permission of the University of Minnesota Press. I realize that more recent developments, including the greater penetration of social

media into Morocco and the appearance of new migrant destinations such as Italy, have altered some of the objects that form the codes of status and prestige; nonetheless, I think the general points being made here still stand.

2. Actually, my net isn't all that widely cast. For instance, the greatest influence on this kind of investigation probably would be Max Weber (1978 [1968]), who goes unremarked on in this essay. His authority did more than anything else to expand the analysis of social-class stratification beyond Marx's emphasis on property possession and into the realm of status groups formed on the basis of noneconomic things, such as shared lifestyles, reputation, status considerations, and shared values. It was only a short, lateral move for someone slightly less influential, like Lloyd Warner in the next generation, to include a consideration of clothing, housing, neighborhood, transportation, speech, and other things governed by one's "taste" that then figure into the relative respect and deference paid to the individual and the group that is formed around the consumption of these most important indicators of status (Warner, Meeker, and Eells 1949). The other catch that my net missed was a good example of a Moroccan analyst doing this kind of work. Fatima Mernissi, Zakya Daoud, and Hinde Taarji may have written as insiders about the status and prestige markers at play in Moroccan fashion in the past, but I have not been able to locate any examples of the kind of metacommentary that I am discussing here coming from them.

3. I hesitate to include Baudrillard here because he has generated so much negative publicity that few remember his more interesting contributions to the study of sign systems in contemporary cultures. The hyperbolic commentaries he published on the Gulf War (Baudrillard 1995) and 9/11 (Baudrillard 2002) are not what interest me. Instead, I have tried in the preceding few paragraphs of the main text to outline what I see as the explanatory utility of his earlier notion of the evolution from internal to external sign codes of social standing. I also think that he is not that far from the approach of Susman (1973) and Sennett (1977), who describe the move during the nineteenth century in the West from concern with character to a focus on personality, accompanied by a parallel concern with the presentation of bodily appearance, as the most important form of expression of the self (see Featherstone [1982] for an elaboration).

4. The *makhzen* is the term that historically has denoted the centralized Moroccan authorities, generally in the cities, who ruled over the countryside.

4 | Forgive Me, Friend

Mohammed and Ibrahim

EMILIO SPADOLA

In Morocco I tend—like many American anthropologists—to seek rapport with a smile. Retailers in Fes refer to American tourists by the code word *miska*—chewing gum—meaning they are all teeth and lips. (British tourists, in contrast, are *ad-dam al-barid,* which means cold blood.) Yet a Moroccan acquaintance of mine characterized Americans as tragically sad friends. The United States is so enormous, he said, and everyone so mobile, that "you Americans are always ready to drop a friend." He's right, in my experience. The friendly first steps of rapport are, if not the opposite of friendship, a firm defense against it. Defense against the long-term obligations and demands of friendship may be why so many American ethnographers have focused on these themes in Moroccan social life. Perhaps this shadow of contractual obligation is why my dearest friend, Mohammed, assures me in his inimitable English: "Ibrahim, I have no interest in you."

Rapport is anthropology's most cherished concept, the sine qua non of fieldwork. Without rapport, one merely observes from afar; with it, one participates. "That mysterious necessity of anthropological field work" (C. Geertz 1973, 416), rapport evokes not so much friendship as utility—an intentional spontaneity, suspended between levity and labor, sheer calculation and mere tolerance. Nevertheless,

Clifford Geertz famously commented that he and Hildred Geertz established rapport in Bali only by mistake. The Geertzes were observing an illegal cockfight when armed police raided it. Instead of "pull[ing] out our papers"—that is, instead of acting properly—the Geertzes fled (ibid.). Before this they had been intent on establishing rapport, "wander[ing] around, uncertain, wistful, eager to please" (ibid., 412). Fleeing the police was, in contrast, spontaneous and unintended, and the hospitality it established was entirely "accidental." Yet, Geertz notes, "it led to a sudden and unusually complete acceptance into a society extremely difficult for outsiders to penetrate" (ibid., 416).[1]

In the later essay "From the Native's Point of View," Geertz debunked rapport as a "preternatural capacity to think, feel, and perceive like a native" and advocated instead a technical and "a bit less magical" emphasis on "experience-near" concepts of personhood (C. Geertz 1983, 56, 58). Yet the Geertzes' ineptness in Bali suggests the converse: rapport freely emerges when the ethnographer fumbles and abandons technique; the magic of rapport is its emergence from accident. And precisely because it is "not a very generalizable recipe"— not a formal element of fieldwork—the mistake may lead to deeper ethnographic intimacy: their "accidental host," writes Geertz, "became one of my best informants" (C. Geertz 1973, 416).

Experimental or reflexive ethnographies, especially those written on Morocco in the 1970s and 1980s, intentionally (at times, infamously) stretched the boundaries of rapport, drawing in part on Geertzian themes of accidental or unintended connections. Their motivations surely differed; reflexive authors emphasized fieldworker-informant relations as messy, muddled, and, at best, negotiated— chiefly to refute ethnographers' authoritatively transparent recording of society and culture. But like Geertz, writers such as Paul Rabinow (2007 [1977]), Vincent Crapanzano (1980), and Kevin Dwyer (1982) sought to humanize rapport—even, however tentatively, engaging informants as something like friends. They did so with evident difficulty, emphasizing the agonies rather than affections of Moroccan friendships—the "brinksmanship," "domination," and "submission"

(Rabinow 2007, 47–48), the "scheming, intriguing, and manipulation" so "cloying—to the Westerner" (Crapanzano 1980, 78). And they recorded their own mistakes, accidents, and general failures of authoritative fieldwork form. But like the Geertzes' magical accident, these failures of intention did not so much discredit their work as identify "real rapport"—friendship—as a formal condition of ethnographic inquiry.

In this essay I look at fieldwork and friendship in Morocco and, more specifically, at my dearest friend Mohammed and me and our mutual affection, which has developed over the past twelve years of my periodic fieldwork and social visits in Fes. I explore these themes of friendship and fieldwork, of mistakes and unintended connections, between Mohammed and me, and in Rabinow's and Crapanzano's exemplary works of reflexive ethnography. In doing so, I suggest that what links friendship with mistakes in Morocco is what may come after the lapse, in a friend's forgiveness.

MOHAMMED AND IBRAHIM

I met Mohammed in Fes Medina in 1998. I was living in a Moroccan household near the neighborhood of Ayn Azlitan, using doctoral funding to continue studying Arabic after a summer at Middlebury College's language school. I was also meeting with *faux guides* (unlicensed tour guides) to discuss the regulation of tourist guides, the rise of unemployment in the 1990s, the novel regime of official guide credentialing, and persistent arrests and police brutality against guides. A fellow doctoral student recommended I meet two merchants he knew. The first was dour, smoking cigarettes and sitting on a stool at the sunny front of a tiny shop amid the rush of medina foot traffic. There was some talk—no rapport—nothing more. I went looking for the other man, who, the student said, worked in an enormous carpet shop between Moulay Idriss's tomb and the Qarawiyyin mosque.

The door is hard to find, the passageway cool and narrow, the walls sweating. At a small wooden door a grim young man, with a scarred face and black hair and eyes, looks me over, then leads me to a back room off the dark main atrium (the yellow lights are turned on only at the arrival of customers so that rugs can be displayed). A group of older men are sitting on a semicircle of low benches facing a loom. They are dressed neatly, but in working clothes, their rough woolen djellabas hanging on hooks; they exude labor and piety. A murmur of Darija, the Moroccan form of Arabic, comes from a weaver with a fringe of gray hair under a knitted cap, who is passing a yarn spindle under and over the warp of an emerging woolen carpet.

The floor is laid with blue and white tiles, the lower walls covered with exquisite geometric mosaics. Carpets lie draped over banisters, and little birds chirp and sing in cages hung high and low on nails along the walls. The room is cool, and the air thick with smoke from the men's pipes, which contain *kif*—an economical mix of strong black tobacco and mild marijuana common in working-class northern Morocco. Mohammed stands slowly to greet me, handing to another man his pipe, its long wooden stem tipped with a tiny clay bowl. He is my height, about 5' 9", but ten years older than me. He is also thicker, with short, graying brown hair, a square face, and a close-trimmed beard. Mohammed moves calmly and deliberately to face me, no excess smiling, nothing casual about him. (Years later, watching David Simon's *The Wire* on television, I start at seeing Avon Barksdale—Mohammed's darker-skinned doppelgänger.) Other men nod to me, and soon I am sitting, observing. A cushion is passed my way along with a hot glass of mint tea, which I hold, rim and base, with thumb and forefinger. Discussion continues, and unlike my usual domestic introductions in Fes, no one talks to me or seems concerned with me. Every few minutes a pipe is lit and passed; the low voices blending with birdsongs and the sharp flick of a lighter. I understand little of the discussion of something apparently serious; the seated men are attentive to Mohammed's words.

At dusk, Mohammed leads me up three dark flights within this enormous carpet bazaar to a terrace overlooking the heart of Fes Medina, where we listen to the echoing call to *Salat al-Maghrib*, the sunset prayer. He speaks, using formal Arabic and modest English, about the state's interest in tourism, but he emphasizes its neglect of social services. He points down to several visible ruins among the intimate crush of buildings—this one burned down; that one collapsed, filling with garbage. For ten years these have been slated for rebuilding, Mohammed explains. The street entrances have been nailed shut and notices posted, but nothing else has happened. Mohammed walks me downstairs and out to the cobblestone street just feet from the Qarawiyyin mosque. I leave with a new name, Ibrahim.

After one meeting, Mohammed and I have rapport, or something like it. He speaks openly, it seems to me. But I am not at all comfortable. A week later, I return to the carpet bazaar. Mohammed is accusatory: "Where have you been? You have been gone fully a week." I am accustomed to the affable guilt of acquaintances—*"Finik? Fin hada l-ghayba?"* (Where have you been? Where'd you disappear to?)—but this is serious. Mohammed's manner is both didactic and familiar, reproachful in the manner of my older relatives. I picture my twin uncles (both firefighters), my grandfather—I even imagine my Italian great-grandfather—who know me and rightly expect better of me; as in their case, Mohammed's toughness and sheer masculinity are intimidating. What's more, he is not my relative, and I am not at home. This serious and pious man, an autodidact born in the Rif Mountains, frightens me.

INFORMANTS AND FRIENDS

The conventional term for a longtime fieldwork interlocutor, one to whom one grows close enough to establish rapport, is "informant." It is evocative of "informer"—inevitably so, given the aims of research (Crapanzano 1980, 144). Rabinow's critique of ethnographic knowledge criticizes informants' "self-conscious" and "unnatural" positions (2007 [1977], 39) as cultural mediators, who must stand outside their culture to objectify it for the researcher (ibid., 131–41). At times, Rabinow accepts this as the necessary condition of ethnographic exchange as an "art" (ibid., 38); at other times, he faults his informant's skillful mediation of culture as "resistance" to "further penetration" (ibid., 38, 27). He dismisses his informant and language teacher, Ibrahim, as

> a packager and transmitter of commodities and services, a middleman, a government translator of official messages. He was packaging Arabic for me as if it were a tourist brochure. He was willing to orient me to the fringes of the Moroccan community, to the Ville Nouvelle [the recent colonial city] of Moroccan culture, but there was a deep resistance on his part to any further penetration. (ibid., 27)

Rabinow's attempt at rapport with Ibrahim occasions a reference to friendship, but only as its opposite, as a Moroccan cultural practice of manipulation. Responding to his informant's scheme to get money from him, Rabinow writes that Ibrahim "was simply testing the limits of the situation. Within Moroccan culture this is a standardized and normal thing to do." "I had been conceiving of him as a friend," he writes, whereas Ibrahim "had basically conceptualized me as a resource" (ibid., 28–29). Of course, given his criticism of ethnographic power, Rabinow's disavowal of interest seems doubly unjust. Is not the two men's relationship mutually—blatantly—instrumental? What of Rabinow's explicit aim of acquiring language skills and field data on which to establish his research, and eventually his reputation as a scholar? The episode is nevertheless worthy of comment for its evocation of friendship as a disinterested relation and, more specifically, as the effect of accidental intimacy.

Rabinow engages with another young man, Ali, who, like Ibrahim, "tests" Rabinow, "pushing and probing" and launching "testing thrusts" to establish dominance over him (ibid., 38–39).[2] Yet over time, he writes, "I had established real rapport with [Ali], more as a friend than an informant" (ibid., 46). This is accomplished, however, not by following fieldwork norms but by transgressing them, through committing "a grave professional mistake" (ibid., 45). Rabinow, still struggling with Arabic and still learning the cultural ropes, accompanies Ali to a wedding, mainly as chauffeur. Driving home, his resentment toward Ali overflows and Ali, his feelings hurt, walks the remaining miles home.

Rabinow credits his transgression for the renewed intimacy. He apologizes to Ali, Ali forgives him, and "from that point on, we got along famously" (ibid., 49). Moreover, his mistake gives Rabinow a deeper entry into prostitution and Sufi culture. He credits his misstep for its "fortuitous congruence" with "Moroccan cultural style"— that is, with "brinksmanship" (ibid.). But, of course, its success also rests on Ali's forgiveness. Rabinow might have examined the messiness of fieldwork in terms of that. But Ali's gesture remains absent from Rabinow's narrative: "He began to come around. . . . [By] that afternoon it was clear that we had reestablished our relationship" (ibid.).

In a subsequent chapter titled "Friendship," Rabinow describes befriending Driss ben Mohammed—who "had consistently refused to work as an informant"—"casually," "almost accidentally" (ibid., 142). This very refusal, however, occasions Rabinow's most cherished insights into Moroccan culture. Because ben Mohammed is not an informant but a friend, and the two men share "a certain trust" and "mutual respect" (ibid.), Rabinow freely expresses his troubled feelings on Islam and Muslims' assertion of supremacy (ibid., 147). The axiom of fieldwork that Rabinow had previously dismissed—"The informant is always right" (ibid., 45)—turns out to be true, for ben Mohammed's "flustered" admission to such a feeling offers Rabinow pure, disinterested access to "*the* fundamental [Moroccan] cultural distinction, the Archimedean point from which all else turned"— "the division of the world into Muslim and non-Muslim" (ibid., 147). Reaching a point of "fundamental Otherness" (ibid., 162) with ben Mohammed, there is nothing left to exchange, and no reason to forgive. Kevin Dwyer rightly notes that while Rabinow considers ben Mohammed a friend, the man himself "disappears behind a number of cultural generalizations" (1982, 278). This seems to be Rabinow's point, however, since culture is friendship's aporia, its condition and limit. And friends, like cultures, remain fixed and separate: "I had a strong sense of being American. I knew it was time to leave Morocco" (Rabinow 2007 [1977], 148).

Like Rabinow's work, Crapanzano's writing calls our attention to the informant relationship as a research construct, a formulaic relationship that, bound to the fieldworker's research "intention," leaves the fieldworker "entrapped" (1980, 144). His view of friendship in the field likewise rests on the accidental transgression of these limits, and here too forgiveness plays an unexamined part. Like Rabinow (1975, 2007 [1977]), Lawrence Rosen (1984), and Dale Eickelman (1976), Crapanzano (1980, 78–80) ascribes to Moroccan friendship all the intention, compulsion, manipulation—in short, domination and submission—of fieldworker-informant rapport. If, for example, Crapanzano disagrees with Eickelman's view of Moroccan affection as a continuous battle for domination, he nonetheless complements that view by showing that intimacy, as in Abdellah Hammoudi's (1997) "master/disciple" framework, involves a desire for subordination as well (Crapanzano 1980, 80). There simply is no pure friendship among Moroccans.

Crapanzano's evident friendship with his informant, the sad and marginal Tuhami, works because Crapanzano conscientiously enters into this exchange.[3] More poignantly however, *Tuhami* (1980) ends with an evocation of the men's bond that rests on Crapanzano's failure to satisfy its demands, his failure of intention, and what seems to me his silent plea for Tuhami's forgiveness.

At the end of the book, Crapanzano has returned to New York. Tuhami has written to him, the letters conveying little content but a desire to correspond. Before Crapanzano travels back to Morocco, however, a letter from Tuhami's half-brother informs him of Tuhami's death and "asks for a work contract" (ibid. 173). The final lines of the book evoke Crapanzano's sadness and sense of failure:

> Arriving in Meknes, I went to the factory where Tuhami had worked and learned that Tuhami had been dead for about a year. His boss was away, and the worker who told me about his death had not known him. The worker thought that Tuhami had perhaps had a bad liver. He died on the way to the hospital. I tried to find his stepbrother [*sic*], but no one at the address he had sent me had ever heard of him. I did not know his sister's address.
>
> Oh, Tuhami, that is the way it is with men. (ibid.)

Crapanzano struggles with arriving too late. Tuhami has been dead for a year; the image of his death on the way to the hospital compounds a sense of his marginality. Crapanzano's presence seems intended simply to make up for his absence when Tuhami died, to touch Tuhami through his family or someone else close to him. Crapanzano cannot do this, however, and his last line—addressed to Tuhami—acknowledges his own awful human weakness, his arriving too late, his not knowing or giving enough. Crapanzano's words to Tuhami end the book, because of course it is impossible for Tuhami to respond. The effect is an unwritten plea that no Moroccan, nobody, but Tuhami can satisfy: "Forgive me."

MISTAKES

By the end of 1998, I am spending more time with Mohammed at his home, a spacious but by no means fancy Fassi house. I meet his wife, Nadia, and their four-year-old son, Oussama. Oussama jumps and pretends to make karate moves; he has just started lessons at a local club. Nadia wears a head scarf and is polite but reserved. Mohammed hands her a copy of *Al-Quds,* a Jerusalem-based newspaper I had brought with me to the bazaar, and I don't see her for the rest of the evening. When, in the last days of my stay, my older sister Meema visits, she meets Mohammed, Nadia, and Oussama, and she and Nadia speak French together in the kitchen.

My four-month stay in 1998 is just a stint of language study, but the experience touches me. Returning home, I dream that I am riding a train to my death. Other people step off the train, but I stay on, thinking, "so this will end in death." Through 1999, Mohammed and I exchange letters. His tone is soft and apologetic:

> Dear Brother Ibrahim, First, I thank you for your kind letter. This means you still remember me. I pass you the *salamat* [salaams] of my small family, Nadia and Oussama.
>
> Brother Ibrahim, I hope we meet again in Morocco, because, as you know, I love this country very much.

Please forgive my tardiness in writing. I am always working, and when I return home I am very tired. Chalk it up to life's difficulty. The important thing
is that you are on my mind. Thank God who makes our pens speak for our fingers, and makes the postal service erase the distance. Your friend, Mohammed.

In 2000–2001, I return for a year of pre-dissertation fieldwork focusing on mass media and national subjectivity in Morocco, living
in Rabat but visiting Fes for weeks at a time. In Fes, Mohammed is
no less concerned than before with my social skills, my bearing, my
whole being. I make mistakes, but I am indisputably learning. One
day, he examines and corrects my physical pronunciation of the Arabic
alphabet. I am dubious, but then I discover to my amazement that
the letters *Qaf* and *Kha* emerge from the same point in the throat.
He notes that my gait is uneven—I am wearing out one side of each
shoe—and tells me I should walk more carefully. I should dress more
neatly, more professionally—I needn't provide ammunition to crit-
ics. We are walking in the medina and I pause to give money to an
old woman crouched against a wall. "Ibrahim," he sighs, "with the
right hand. We give with the *right* hand."

I am Emilio to everyone else, but Ibrahim—a Muslim name—to
Mohammed, his workmates, and his family. Mohammed asks me
nothing about my religion. But he does hand me a photocopied hand-
book of *salat* (Muslim prayer) instruction from the United Kingdom.
As we look through it, he notes with irritation several mistakes, or at
least cultural differences regarding the Prophet's and Ibrahim's titles,
and writes the correct versions in the margin. I am finding Islam
compelling—or, more precisely, Mohammed's emphasis on correct
behavior, correct speech, heedfulness. This suits the engagement I
have had from the age of sixteen with Zen Buddhism, meditating,
and my aspirations to self-mastery. Mohammed's lessons feel akin to
this in a way quite distant from the Abrahamic mélange of Christian
and Jewish cultures of my childhood: the warmth of Christmases
at my grandparents' house, hilarious Seders with my mother's Jewish lesbian community, and with my father and stepmother's friends
in rural Maine. (At one such occasion, as we welcome Elijah to the
table the doorbell rings—it is a Girl Scout selling cookies.) Here I

find my Zen master; he happens to be Muslim. Of course, with Moroccan etiquette and language comes a habitual and more comfortable invocation of God, but Mohammed's lessons are more precise, more to do with skillful bearing.

He works on my lack of attentiveness to other people. As an American liberal, I believe in listening to my feelings, which is good—but demands continuous self-absorption, endless attention to each emotional shift. It makes socializing an exhausting ordeal. Mohammed recalls me to a basic and obvious tenet of ethnography, to carefully watch others: "Ibrahim, you talk too much. When someone asks you something, say, 'Oh, I don't know anything about that.'"

The point hits home several times in the next week. I am with my Fassi household in Ayn Azlitan, and the father's Casablanca business partner asks me about Moroccan soccer players in the United States. I pause. I know absolutely nothing about professional soccer. But my usual inclination—American *miska* that I am—is to find a connection, something. I begin thinking of foreign players in the National Basketball Association, but stop. "I don't know anything about that," I say. The man, losing interest, turns back to my host father. I just listen and smoke a Marlboro.

A day later, Mohammed, his workmates, and I are sitting in a back room of the carpet shop. Fes is depressed, tourists are scarce, and money is tight. A black-and-white television is showing Tom and Jerry cartoons, but the sound is off. Instead, the room is filled with the music of finches chirping and singing. Mohammed has finished cleaning their cages, carefully scraping dung and feathers off the floors, rinsing them, and refilling containers for food and water. A manic young man comes bounding in: "I'm going to the United States next month!"

"What are you going to do there?" I ask.

"I'm marrying an American!"

"What are you going to do for work?" I ask, now concerned.

"I don't know."

"Do you speak English?"

"No."

I begin hurriedly looking for a piece of paper and a pen. *He's in trouble,* I think, *I must teach him some verbs!* I ask Mohammed for a pen.

"What for?" he asks. I explain.

"Ibrahim, look at this man." I look at the man, who has moved along to another conversation, another bench—he cannot stop moving. "Will you teach him anything? Sit here, eat these almonds, and relax." Quite right. In a minute, the young man is gone.

Perhaps the lesson makes little sense for an anthropologist who wishes to, and must repeatedly, establish rapport. Or perhaps these lessons of social mastery are more meaningful than rapport. Nevertheless, I am living them, and I am too wrapped up or enrapt to make ethnographic use of them. Meanwhile, the focus of my research, shifting by the end of my pre-dissertation stint to Muslim practices of *jinn* possession and exorcism in Fes, rarely enters our conversation. Mohammed encourages research: "Find a single thread and begin pulling. Eventually everything will show." But he dismisses the project with a sentence: "*Jinns* are real; they are mentioned in the Qur'an. But the *jinns* and humankind are different species of being and do not overlap or enter one into the other's domains."

By the end of my stay, Mohammed's fierceness, his exacting manner, still unnerves me. He says we are brothers; I am closer to him, he says, than even his own brother by birth. But I am occasionally suspicious; a lapse of trust occurs around several blankets I buy from Mohammed as gifts. I recall a price mentioned some weeks ago, but now he asks for more. Taking Mohammed's advice to be direct in my speech—as he says, *bi saraha, raha,* "with sincerity, there is ease"—I question him. He shows me two sizes of blankets, the smaller of which is sold for the quoted price; I have chosen two of the larger. I thank him for hearing me out. He tells me in English, "Good accounts make good friends."

Mohammed is a businessman and good with customers, but I am more taken with his friendship and his friends, to whom he is continually generous, kind, and dedicated. We are leaving Allal, Mohammed's friend who is paralyzed from the waist down and who lives on the second floor of a decaying and subdivided medina house. Allal's chest and arms are enormous from pulling himself up the stairs to his room, which has a bed, a gas burner, and a television. The bathroom, a hole in a floor, is one flight up. Mohammed and some of his working-class Fassi friends meet there. The tone is pious, but more jovial than at the bazaar. Crowded shoulder to shoulder in Allal's room, the men sit and watch soccer, laugh over *kif*. Some play cards and drink black coffee, packets of Nescafé that Mohammed and I pick up for Allal at a small shop on his street corner.

Leaving with Mohammed at midnight, I navigate loose stairs in the pitch dark. Mohammed shines his keychain flashlight on the stairs behind him to light my way. He reminds me to turn fully sideways to slip through the broken front door. "Don't rip your jacket," he says from below. The streetlights of the medina are broken; the stone street is an extension of the stairs and is too narrow for us to walk side by side. The street opens at the corner shop, now closed. Mohammed points toward another door up the street and tells me a story:

> A few weeks ago I stopped over there to see a poor family. They invited me in to sit down for dinner, but apologized that they had no bread. They have no money—not even for bread. I said I would come back in a moment with bread and walked to this corner store. They were sold out. It was very late—no more bread for the day. I know another family over on that street. I knocked, and the son said, come in, come in. I said, "I cannot. But do you have bread?" Yes, the son said. "Give me, please, two loaves," I said. I took the bread to the poor family. If one person has, it can be shared with another who doesn't. Even half a loaf is better than no bread. Last Friday, a friend said to me, "Mohammed, you should not be begging from people."

Mohammed pauses under one good light in the street. "Ibrahim," he continues, "we do not do such things for applause. I thought they respected me. But, in fact, I respect myself."[4]

Mohammed has little money himself, but he helps many people: his ailing parents—his father has Parkinson's, his mother is nearly blind—his younger brother, and his sister's children. And still (Mohammed shows me the savings book) he puts away some money for his own children's future education. "I am a good struggler," he tells me. And he must be, for Fes, that once towering monument of Moroccan knowledge and power, has become a ghetto. When I come from Rabat to Fes, and especially to the medina, I see the difference in people's faces and bodies; in Fes, everybody looks worried, creased, hurried, bent. "We are in a hole, in Fes," Mohammed says, "and we cannot even see out of it."

In the street a young man kisses Mohammed's hand. "Who is that?" I ask. It is a young man whose father is poor, who was doing very poorly in school, and whom Mohammed helped find his way. "How?" Mohammed suggested he sign up for barber school, but it was too expensive. Mohammed spoke to the head of the school to propose a scholarship: "Cut his tuition in half. The boy will pay one quarter, and I will pay the remaining quarter on a monthly basis." The headmaster agreed; the boy enrolled, graduated, and now runs his own barbershop in the medina. "He calls me 'Uncle' out of respect," Mohammed tells me.

On top of his carpet sales, Mohammed trains birds. The songbirds at the bazaar and in his home are not a hobby; he owns a small bird shop elsewhere in Fes that sells bird cages, food, medicines, and doves and finches. Mohammed buys fledglings and trains each to be a master singer (ma'alim), which he then sells to other bird owners to train their fledglings. He runs the business, stopping in once a day, shopping at the weekly bird market, and cleaning cages. But all the profits go to Moukhtar, a soft and scruffy old man whom Mohammed has hired to manage the store: "Moukhtar is a terrible businessman. He cannot close a deal. It is a lot of work for me. But he needs money." Mohammed reminds me that Moukhtar has painfully crippled feet, and that I must bring him something from the United States the next time I travel home. I ask what, inserts for shoes? Mohammed sighs and says, "What he needs is an operation. *Aywa, la ilaha ila Allah* [oh, well, there is no god but God]."

CONVERSION

I am with Mohammed on the terrace of the carpet shop at dusk. I hear the amplified and echoing call to prayer and see the city's swallows, sculptures in motion, writing surahs (Qur'anic verses) with their wing tips. Mohammed's lush red prayer rug is laid out toward the *qiblah*, the direction of Mecca. His body is gracefully bending and straightening, and then he drops, perfect vertical, to his knees. I hear his words, with a sound of longing: "Subhana rabbi al-ʿala, Subhana rabbi . . ." (Glory to my Lord, the Most High).

In August 2001, as I am preparing to leave Morocco to finish my course work, I convert to Islam. It is done haphazardly, confusedly, with a young man in Rabat who has pestered me to convert for months. Certainly, my research has become devoted to Islam, as I work with religious men and young Islamist revivalists who perform *jinn* exorcisms. But I am making decisions faster than I grasp them; I am thinking really of Mohammed. I'm leaving for New York, and this is my going-away gift to him, something that expresses our solidarity. Visiting Fes before flying home, sitting in the bazaar, I tell Mohammed. He responds quietly, "*La ilaha ila Allah*. Now we are brothers in all ways." He turns to one of the men and shares the news of my conversion. The man stands, takes my face in his hands, and kisses my cheeks very softly. Mohammed brings me home; Nadia already knows. She is smiling warmly and gives me a white Meccan robe.

I feel uncomfortable, even astonished. What on earth am I thinking? This going-away gift has quickly escaped my intention—it is no longer mine to give, nor merely Mohammed's to receive. Marcel Mauss's (1990 [1950]) wisdom is driven home: the gift is always already in circulation; we merely pass it along. But happily I am heading home, where I can shelve the issue. When I tell my mother and sister, however, their apparent fear surprises me. I try to explain that I am not turning into a fanatical Muslim, only figuring out what Islam means to me. *Salat*, I say, is my meditation. Then comes 9/11. The cauldron of identity politics is boiling over, and I have no wish to partake of its contents. I drop my efforts to learn *salat*.

I live in Fes again in 2003, to conduct the real body of my fieldwork on Muslim politics and mass media. My conversion becomes pressing once again, with Mohammed as much as with anyone. Inside I feel I have made a mistake, gone too far, and I just want the whole thing to go away. But nobody in Fes has forgotten. My host parents ask if I am still praying, and I say no. My host mother chuckles; my host father tells me it's all in the heart. The youngest son in the family is less forgiving. He tells me he gets a particular feeling from Muslims—which he does not get from me. He tells me I am really a Jew, only pretending to be Muslim for research purposes. I ask him what that means. "Shall I slit your throat?" he asks. I say nothing but am unnerved, spooked. I am entirely uncertain of what I am, but I feel fraudulent in the social role of Muslim. Sharing the house is unpleasant. I don't think—I don't know what to think. Will he tell others? Apostasy can be punished by death. A neighbor mentions for no apparent reason that the young man troubles him: "His brother is a good man, but he is not. He has a black heart."

I tell Mohammed that I am struggling. But I struggle with the telling—this is well beyond the pale. My sense of trust is askew, and I am frightened for my friendship with Mohammed. Mohammed asks me how serious this crisis is. If it is *irja*, reversion, and thus apostasy, he says, this is very serious and I should tell no one. It is not *irja*, I say, not at all certain what I mean. He repeats a saying, *Insan ibnu bi ʾatih* (a man is the child of his environment). But I can't run home; my work is here. I have no choice but to forge ahead. Mohammed reminds me to regret nothing.

In the following days, I resolve to toughen up. To learn what Islam is to me, learn *salat*, and, perhaps in performative fashion, practice my way to clarity. Mohammed advises me to think of it like yoga. "Practice," he says, "and one day it will be like water." I am with Mohammed as often as possible, most often at his home, playing with Oussama, who looks exactly like Mohammed and calls me *ʿAmi Brahim* (Uncle Brahim), and his adorable toddler daughter, Oumaima, who resembles her mother. I am not certain what binds us together. Mohammed refers to us as brothers and is less concerned with teaching me, more concerned with talking about politics; speaking about life in Fes, whom to help, whom to visit. We speak of family; I have married and my wife, Alexandra, visits Fes several times. There is no question that she and I will dine several times with Mohammed and Nadia, or that we will visit Mohammed in the bazaar to drink tea and talk. Mohammed knows I am practicing *salat.* On Fridays, I meet him at the bazaar and we walk together to the Qarawiyyin mosque for the collective prayer. When Mohammed is busy with customers, I do the ritual ablutions in the bazaar kitchen and visit the Qarawiyyin with the throng of men in the Fassi street.

Nevertheless, Mohammed and I rarely speak of Islam. When I do initiate such conversations, Mohammed is brief but, as always, edifying. I describe having a wondrous feeling of humility before God, a euphoric submission. Mohammed says that is unnecessary: "Just do your work, and when you finish your work, put it out of your mind, and take care of your family." One evening at Mohammed's home, I write up a genealogy of my family religions. There is not much I can fill in. The Judaism of my mother's Polish-American parents, whom I never knew; the childhood Seders, turning into my mother's current faith in the twelve-step program. My father's atheism, his Swedish- and Italian-American parents' disdain for clergy, and his grandparents' downright hatred of them. I give it to Mohammed. The next day, he enters the salon where I am dressing, and hands it back to me: "I don't need this to know you, Ibrahim. You are who is standing in front of me now."

A month later, I walk to Mohammed's house, but his wife, speaking to me at the door, explains that his cousin Jamal has died of a brain aneurysm. Jamal is a young man with a wife and two children. Mohammed considers him more a son. I call Mohammed. He tells me the death might have been averted, but Jamal's family assumed a *jinn* was to blame and for several days had called various *fuqaha'* to find a cure. We plan to meet at Allal's sometime after *Salat al-ʿAsr* (the afternoon prayer). I wait with Allal for several hours, and then several hours more. I smoke *kif* and gaze around Allal's tiny room, at radios piled up against the walls, at his cigarette stand adorned with a poster of Sylvester Stallone, at a small image of Osama bin Laden taped to a framed photograph of a young Allal. Mohammed arrives, composed but weary, and explains that we will attend the funeral dinner, but he needs to walk first. In the night air, we hear the call to *Salat al-Maghrib* (the sunset prayer). The *kif* was very strong and I am surely too stoned to pray—certainly for the prayer to be valid—but I am not sober enough to think straight. We stop at the door of a mosque near Allal's. Mohammed asks if I wish to pray, and I enter with him and crouch at the central fountain to perform ablutions.

Something happens. I hear a murmur. I have done something wrong—scooped water with my left hand, perhaps. I look up at Mohammed, who has been dealing with death all day. He grips my shoulder, narrows his eyes, and speaks to me in English: "You have just dirtied the water. And now it is time to pray. So finish now." I feel pale and panicked. My mind is splitting apart. Mohammed pulls me by the arm to join the line of men who will pray. In the first *rakya* (circle of prayer), we bow deeply. I am feeling calmer now, easing into *salat*. But there is an odd noise. My watch, loose change, and several cigarettes have spilled out of my breast pocket onto the mosque floor. My mind melts into panic again. Confused, stoned, I am certain that the presence of cigarettes on the mosque floor is shameful. In *sujud* (prostration), I try surreptitiously to scrape my cigarettes and watch and change toward my knee. The other men in the row pause to rest on their heels, but I lurch upward. Mohammed puts a firm hand on my calf and presses me to the floor. Prayer ends, and we walk toward the fountain.

Mohammed faces me, astonished, disgusted: "Why do you not know the ablutions?" My face, eyes, and whole body feel taut, terrified.

"I know how to do ablutions. I am *very, very stoned*." Two men, police, approach Mohammed. "Who is this?" one of them asks.

"He is a new Muslim," Mohammed replies, "from Holland."

The men look at me at length and finally walk back to their corner. Mohammed, more relaxed now, continues in English: "You must go slowly—and stay cool. A Muslim is always cool." A few moments pass as I try to breathe and calm myself. He continues: "You have taken me out of my prayer, so I will now pray again. You may pray with me, if you like, and remember to go slowly."

From the mosque, we walk toward the funeral dinner on dark, dirty cobblestones under broken lamps in the poor city. At the door, I stop, ashamed: "I am so sorry. Now, after the trouble I've caused, I should just go home." Patient as always, Mohammed tells me: "Ibrahim, God forgives. God forgives. Just remember that people do not forgive. People are a problem, and you have to be careful. Come into the dinner. You will feel better. Don't talk a lot. Just sit and listen."

FORGIVENESS

Ramadan approaches, and despite the warmth I feel with Mohammed and the general success of my fieldwork, the dissonance of my social performance in Fes heightens. The mosque episode has shaken me terribly, and managing my identity on top of my fieldwork is debilitating. Visiting Rabat I am calmer; a friend in the finance ministry sympathizes with my self-criticism: "How do you think *I* feel? My name is ʿAbd Allah [servant of God]." Back in the pious milieu of Fes, however, I tip into something worse, something despairing. I know what depression is, and as Ramadan approaches I feel it: as the weeks pass, I fall through depression's lower levels, into a black pit, falling with no one to catch me. I leave for Rabat to seek out more neutral, simpler ground. Ramadan comes, and I decide to stay, renting a house in the Al-Oudaya neighborhood from a kind elderly woman who hosted me in 2000. I will make the most of Rabat, working at the Bibliothèque Nationale and in the records of Radiodiffusion-Télévision Marocaine. I am mostly incommunicado, but as the month of celebration nears its end, I call Mohammed. He understands my need to do research in Rabat, but he is astonished that I won't came back before Eid. His voice cracks: "You're not going to spend even *one day of Ramadan* with us?!"

Several weeks after Ramadan, Mohammed and I sit alone in the quiet and empty bazaar. I know that I have to be honest and clear (*bi saraha, raha*). This is no longer 1998 or 2001. This has nothing to do with my etiquette. Whatever training I have had is over, and we are just two different people who have somehow maintained a friendship. I choose to be honest, to let it all out. I explain that I am working hard to understand my conversion, especially what is happening inside. But I cannot, in good conscience, continue to claim to be

Muslim in front of him. I need it off the table between him and me. I am ready to lose this friend.

Mohammed is quiet at first, then tells me this is between me and God and does not concern him. He then reminds me that I have a good heart, and that God will give me only what is in my heart. His warmth is overwhelming, and I begin to cry out the accumulated pressure of the field. Mohammed straightens up, saying something about being a man, and tells me calmly that while I was in Rabat he worried about me, and whether I was all right. It is just Mohammed and me, alone in early darkness in a three-story bazaar, and something—honesty, urgency—has been loosed. As he talks, he speaks of himself: "I am working all the time to help everyone around me—parents, brothers and sisters, children, friends. I am helping everyone all the time." Mohammed and I are holding each other's shoulders, his words pour out, and now he is crying: "I am working all the time—I have no one to talk to—and I am smoking this *shit,* which is *killing* me." I see his broken teeth, his baldness, his grayness, his weakness: "*I was so mad, I was so scared, Ibrahim. I thought you would never come back.* If I didn't hear from you, I would come to Rabat myself and find you. *But I didn't know where you were—*" Mohammed and I are both crying now, perhaps from the wounds, both unintentional and inevitable, that have accumulated over the years of an intense but tenuous relationship.

We need this space, we need it together, and we slowly recover. My heart feels light, joyous, refreshed. Mohammed chuckles: "Well, we were *thrown.*" We walk out the narrow, cool entranceway to the bazaar, into the night, past the closed shops of the medina. We link arms. "We are still brothers," he says, looking at me. "I can lose many things, Ibrahim, but I can't lose you."

FRIENDSHIP, FORGIVENESS, RETURN

With each mistake and each forgiveness we are deeper friends, Mohammed and Ibrahim. Mohammed and Emilio. By this name, too, I have slowly, decisively returned to the practice of Islam, reclaiming the pillars and the tradition as my own, and as a path open to my two children, Bruno and Orlando. As I perform *salat*, Orlando, my one-year-old, toddles across my prayer rug and joyfully pounds on my back. My heart opens and glows; love radiates outward in expanding circles to my family, my neighbors, my nation, the world. *Salat* feels good; I am burnishing a glass lamp, letting my heart shine. I describe it as light, but Mohammed is right, it *is* like water.

The themes of my friendship with Mohammed echo the Geertzian theme of accidental intimacy: something real arising in the mistake, the unintended act. To feel rapport requires exchange, gift, and counter-gift—and exchange means a possible mistake. By their incalculable, accidental quality, mistakes are quintessential gifts. And they are recovered through the return, the act of forgiving. But just as mistakes are not the end of friendship, neither is friendship (*contra* Rabinow) the end of fieldwork, a magical path to cultural essence beyond which nothing more need be said. Friendship is like fieldwork, a series of accidents in search of return, of forgiveness. But no return is guaranteed. Mohammed reminds me to "stand at the wall of Paradise, to help each person over the wall" without hope of reward: "You help them into Paradise. But this does not mean someone will stop and help you over at the end."

On my desk, I have a photo of Mohammed sitting in Fes with my oldest friend, Adam (we met when we were both four). As often as possible, I refer students, family, and travelers to Mohammed. I sent him the dean of a New York medical school and an absurdly wealthy New Orleans developer. After hearing about this man's astonishing shopping spree in Fes, I called Mohammed. "I'm glad that I can send you a big spender," I said.

"Ibrahim," he replied, "you could send me a dog, and I would be happy." Mohammed would forgive such a gift. He is a good forgiver.

NOTES

I am grateful to David Crawford and Rachel Newcomb, who prompted me to write this essay and greatly improved it, and to Vincent Crapanzano for his careful reading and generous comments. Columbia University, the Social Science Research Council, and the Fulbright-Hays Doctoral Dissertation Research Abroad program provided research funding; the Colgate University Research Council has helped fund my subsequent research visits. I especially thank *Anthropological Quarterly,* where an earlier version of this chapter appeared, and Roy R. Grinker for editorial guidance.

1. The theme of cross-cultural communication emerging especially through accident, chance, or risk is developed by James Siegel (1986, 294–307), to whose work I am deeply indebted for my reading of Clifford Geertz. Siegel characterizes the Geertzes' fortuitous flight as a matter of "intending something, of being taken for having meant something else, the result being an unanticipated flow of 'communication'" (ibid., 296). John Borneman pursues a similar logic in his intimate fieldwork in Aleppo, and likewise draws insight (it seems to me) from Siegel: "Where communication fails is where understanding might begin" (Borneman 2007, 62).

2. Rabinow's references to "penetration" (1975, 27), "probing" (1975, 47), and "thrusts" (1975, 48) bear comment. They accompany his general characterization of Moroccan intimacy as tests of domination and submission, weakness, and humiliation. This sort of aggressivity has not been my experience in Morocco—at least, if I was being tested, I overlooked it. Reading Rabinow's reflections reminds us that fieldwork conflicts arise as much from ethnographers' social performances as from foreign cultural norms.

3. For Crapanzano's incisive statement regarding the irreducible presence of the ethnographer—and a unique reading of Geertz's "Notes on a Balinese Cockfight"—see Crapanzano (1992, 60–69).

4. "I thought they respected me . . ." is a quotation from Mohammed's and other Fassis' favorite wise fool, Sidi Abderrahman al-Majdoub (d. 1568).

5|

Suspicion, Secrecy, and Uncomfortable Negotiations over Knowledge Production in Southwestern Morocco

KATHERINE E. HOFFMAN

Power relations inherent in the encounter between anthropologist and informant engaged the advocates of reflexive anthropology working in Morocco (Crapanzano 1980; K. Dwyer 1982; Rabinow 2007 [1977]). Their analyses have reconfigured the practice and writing of ethnography over the last three decades. Questions of truth, disclosure, and suspicion shape not only anthropologists' relationships in the field, but also the data that can be collected and the forms in which it can be presented to outsiders. Irfan Ahmad remarks in regard to ethnographic informants' frequent suspicion of the state that perhaps we should "also talk—after Geertz's 'theatre state,' Dirks's 'ethnographic state,' Messick's 'calligraphic state'—about the 'state of suspicion' (in a double sense) that defines contemporary times and anthropologists['] interactions therewith" (2008). Political and historical factors internal to Moroccan communities, especially rural ones, also shape the ways informants accommodate or reject particular researchers and their projects.

This chapter examines some instances of secrecy, suspicion, and obfuscation I experienced while conducting field research in Mo-

99

rocco, particularly among Ishelhin Berbers in the southwest of the country between 1995 and 1999. Three main themes emerge. First, in the last years of King Hassan II's reign, there was widespread governmental hostility toward researchers and activists, whether Moroccan or foreign, who were interested in Berber language, Berber culture, economic inequality, or the marginalization of rural and Berber populations. Despite Hassan II's opening toward Amazigh affairs, encapsulated in a 1994 speech, Moroccan nationalism was still oriented toward an Arab identity, and authorities were suspicious of researchers' motives for speaking Berber and working in Berber-speaking communities. Second, the Swasa (residents of the Sous Valley, in southwestern Morocco) had deeply entrenched practices of secrecy and evasion, even among themselves, through which they carefully controlled the circulation of information both in the countryside and to outside audiences. Third, Soussi practices of concealing and revealing information were informed by historically and politically situated ideas about what constituted knowledge, who had it, and who might mediate its transmission. All three of these fieldwork dynamics shaped my dissertation research and consequently the form of my first ethnographic monograph, *We Share Walls* (2008b), as well as various journal articles and scholarly presentations since 1995.

I should note at the outset that although I received no outright refusal of research permission from the Moroccan Ministry of External Affairs, I also never received any permission. I did receive a residency card in 1995 and managed to renew it for four years, and I renewed it again in 2008–2009 while conducting research for another book. Thus, at all times I was living legally in Morocco, yet I lacked an explicit research permit. In addition to dissertation research, during 1997 and 1998 I also served as a consultant for the Morocco Education for Girls (MEG) project funded by the U.S. Agency for International Development and the Moroccan Ministry of Education. That consultancy granted me full permission to observe instruction in primary school classrooms and interview teachers, students, their parents and siblings, and teacher trainers about gender equity in the classroom and conditions shaping family decisions regarding girls' education. Under the U.S. agency's auspices, then, I conducted classroom observation, an invaluable experience that provided insight into multilingual language management and the ways in which teachers' acknowledgment (or lack thereof) of students' native language abilities (in the Tamazight, Tashelhit, or Tarifit regional varieties of Berber) influenced student retention in school. Yet I never received a piece of paper from the authorities approving my doctoral research project in non-institutional settings. Without that official stamp of approval, many people in the Sous Valley and Anti-Atlas Mountains, where I conducted my research, were suspicious of my motives—making me, in turn, fearful of them. After all, they had the knowledge I wanted to understand, and they were under no obligation whatsoever to give me access to their lives.

ACCESS AND THE SHIFTING VALUE OF ANTHROPOLOGICAL KNOWLEDGE

Many Moroccan officials at multiple levels, not just in Rabat, resisted my requests for information about specific facets of Amazigh demography and cultural practices in the 1990s. Sometimes the reaction was dismissive; other times it was scornful. Some urban Arabs and various institutional officials dismissed as illegitimate what they believed to be a premise of my queries. For instance, an official of Taroudant Province insisted that my research into the numbers and locations of Arabic and Tashelhit speakers in the province was irrelevant because, he insisted, there was no such thing as Arabs and Berbers. The French had created this illegitimate distinction, he claimed, to divide and rule Moroccans. My attempts to clarify that I was not making claims about Arabs or Berbers but was rather seeking demographic information about spoken language did not appease him. Even outside of administrative offices, I frequently encountered resistance to my qualitative work by laypeople, mostly men but also some women, who questioned the legitimacy of studying seemingly banal, everyday life. Underlying their dismissal were particular epistemological claims: knowledge was religious, not secular; knowledge came from texts and formal instruction, not oral sources; and men had knowledge in greater quantity than did women, since women were unschooled and thus lived lives too closely circumscribed by their parts of the countryside.

This resistance to qualitative research presented complications for one aspect of my first extended research project on expressive culture, in which I collected and analyzed women's sung poetry, especially the genre called *tizrrarin* that was prevalent in weddings and other festive occasions but also in collective laboring and the kind of musical horseplay that accompanied young people's collective meals (*zerdas*) (Hoffman 2008 and 2002). In the 1990s, as I audio-recorded sung poetry and talked to people in the Anti-Atlas Mountains and Sous Valley about this verbal culture, both men and women tended to dismiss it as insignificant women's play. They did not prevent my recording it, and indeed they considered such recordings preferable to those of everyday speech, which they saw as more likely to be flawed or incriminating. Close musical analysis of these sung poems, in addition to the analysis of song texts I had completed for my dissertation, revealed substantial patterns of intergenerational difference in the production and competence of sung poetry. In a nutshell, older women's sung poetry exhibited greater complexity at multiple levels than did that of younger women, suggesting a decline in the mastery of poetic language that often accompanies processes of language attrition and shifts toward a national language (in this case, toward greater borrowings and use of Moroccan Arabic even among self-described monolingual Berber speakers). I published my findings in a 2002 article in the journal *Ethnomusicology* and presented them in French at the Timitar Off conference organized in conjunction with the 2006 Festival of World and Amazigh Musics, held in Agadir.

What happened next was a reminder that scholars cannot control what will become of their research, or how others will interpret their findings in the years after the data collection. After my presentation, a young audience member from the administrative center of Igherm, near my field site in the mountains of the Ida ou Zeddout region, introduced himself and asked why I had not consulted his rural cultural association about these songs, claiming that the association was compiling a collection of *tizrrarin* for publication. But his organization had not existed ten years earlier when I was collecting the songs; moreover, as we discussed, my goal was not to produce a compendium of decontextualized poetry and evaluate it for its artistic or cultural merit, but to analyze the social production of this verbal expressive culture. Given that in the late 1990s, I often encountered critiques even in the mountains that women's poetry was too particularistic and secular, the interest of this educated lay folklorist surprised me. Few Moroccans, other than my closest interlocutors, encouraged my work on *tizrrarin* at the time, and most of my acquaintances were bemused, albeit sometimes quietly pleased, by my appreciation of it. Yet less than a decade later, at the Timitar Off conference, I found myself the subject of critique not because I had worked on Berber expressive culture but because I had not worked on it enough. As further evidence of the significant political shift in attitudes toward Berber issues during the decade since my first fieldwork, at one of the coffee breaks punctuating the panels at the conference, the Moroccan television station 2M filmed an interview with me conducted entirely in Tashelhit. The interviewer enthusiastically explained to viewers that I was living proof that one did not have to be Berber to speak Berber, implicitly refuting the widespread argument among urban Arabic-speaking Moroccans to the contrary.

FABRICATED SUSPICION AND JEOPARDIZED RESEARCH

More serious than periodic rebuffs or scoldings, however, were concerted efforts to jeopardize my research altogether. The most glaring example from this period will suffice as an illustration. Despite the dearth of official encouragement toward research on Berbers, in the 1990s there were a significant number of publications on Berber poetry, culture, history, and folklore, as it is often called. In any market town or city with a Berber presence in the 1990s, there were certain newspaper vendors locally known for carrying the small pamphlets and inexpensive books read by young men in particular who were interested in the growing Amazigh movement. With the close association between poetry and music in Amazigh society, it was common in the Sous and Anti-Atlas then, and still today, for male poets to both publish texts and sing in collective duels and performances at festive occasions. At some point around 1997, one of the region's foremost folklorists and singing poetry duelers, who was also an elected official, allegedly spread the rumor that I was a spy. I heard this from several different sources, yet I had never met the man. The plausibility of this rumor to rural people greatly hindered my work, since people stopped wanting to talk to me. At one particularly low point in what I came to refer to as the Year of the Cold Shoulder, Ida ou Zeddout villagers asked "When are you leaving?" each time I visited the village. Peter Metcalf best characterized the anthropologist's response to such a situation. In writing about how people in the village in Borneo where he conducted research blew hot and cold with him, he comments that "it was exhausting to be permanently anxious about popularity ratings, like some second rate politician" (2002, 45).

Many villagers stopped talking to me altogether during this period, and without knowledge of the rumor for several months, I presumed I had inadvertently offended sensibilities somehow. It was only later that I learned that an official from the Ministry of the Interior had come to the village to interrogate residents about my behavior, questions, and close acquaintances. Villagers preferred to keep the government as far away as possible and out of their business, a pattern that I also witnessed during that period with an agricultural census and identity card registration (Hoffman 2000). When I finally met the hostile lay folklorist in 2006, in the city and away from the mountains, he immediately asked why I had not consulted him during my field research. He had the answers to the questions I was asking, he informed me; why hadn't I just asked him? Clearly he too held the epistemological orientation toward investigation that saw it as a process of inquiry of the informed by the uninformed in search of discrete and knowable answers; my own orientation, however, was that investigation itself yielded both new questions and epistemological critiques. In his framework, participant observation has no place other than allowing one person to witness what is already known by someone else, and consciously so. Moreover, in hearing this claim, suddenly I saw his sabotage of my fieldwork as the result not of political conviction but as a defense of intellectual turf. What he considered suspect was my failure to regard him, rather than Berber women themselves, as the source of knowledge about women's poetry. I attempted to explain the logic of my methodology, reminding him of the gender-segregated domestic and public spaces in the villages that require one always to choose between camps. Berber women would not have let me into their private spheres where I could see verbal expression practiced naturally, through speech and song, if I had relied on men rather than young women to make introductions. Moreover, I explained, I needed to spend my days with monolingual people so I could learn Tashelhit, for Moroccan men commonly switched into Moroccan Arabic in conversation with me. Regardless of the differences between his logic and mine, one person's petty jealousy in and of itself had unhinged the fieldworker's position, the ethnographic process, and the resulting text artifact. All of this was possible because an elusive man whom I had feared for years—because he seemed in a position of relative power to me—had made the grave error of considering the audiences for our texts as overlapping and me as his competition, even though he published entirely in Arabic and I publish in English and French. We have since established a collegial relationship through encounters at other conferences. But it is difficult to erase the damage done by that period in the early fieldwork that resulted from his presumption that only a foreigner with something unethical to hide would avoid a local folklorist with something valuable to reveal.

CONTESTED AUTHORITY

These and other field incidents brought into relief the kinds of knowledge that people considered valuable and who could reliably impart it. It has often been said that anthropologists tend to write about what their subject population considers important. Yet this claim elides differences and rivalries within a community. Metcalf (2002) writes eloquently about the obfuscation he experienced from one of his main informants on death songs in Borneo, and the way he used her rivals to collect some of the information she withheld from him.

Unfortunately, I had no such luck when initiating what was to be my first field project.

An earlier iteration of my research project, long before my work in the Anti-Atlas Mountains, involved fieldwork among young women of high school age in a boarding school in Taroudant. These young women, I hypothesized, served as economic, cultural, and linguistic intermediaries between people in the town and residents of their rural villages, and I intended to investigate the nature and texture of that mediation. Given the small proportion of rural girls who stayed in school past the sixth grade, these girls seemed to me to be exceptional and worthy of understanding. After an initial meeting with the school authorities, the headmistress of the boarding school found it acceptable that I administer a questionnaire to the girls, but only initially did she allow me to talk to the girls in the informal setting of their dorms. Despite what seemed to be her endorsement of the method of participant observation, after only three evening visits I learned whom she considered worthy of research, and they were not her charges. She had not considered, when granting me permission, that I would speak Tashelhit with the young women rather than Arabic; Tashelhit, she declared, is divisive, whereas Arabic promotes unity among the girls. I tried to explain that I was only speaking the language in which the girls chose to speak to me, but she was not convinced; Tashelhit was for the home, and it was suspect in institutional settings. Just talking to girls, she suggested, was peculiar behavior. She explained:

> You know, in Moroccan society girls are respected and reserved (*muḥtaramin*). You can do your research anywhere in society, with families, with boys, but to get together with girls and ask them their opinions—this is out of the question. You may do this in the United States, I imagine you do, just looking at your elections and the way everyone asks everyone's opinion, but in Morocco you don't ask a girl's opinion. There may be some fathers who don't approve, and as an institution we can't allow this. There might be some questions that you ask girls that they don't want to answer. For example, for us religion is something we don't discuss. We don't ask, "Are you Muslim?" or "Are you Christian?"

Quite surprised at the headmistress's suggestion that I would be so naïve and ill-informed as to ask a Moroccan girl which religion she followed, I responded, "Of course I don't ask about religion."[1] But she continued: "And there are certain things—for example, if you're asking about *la tradition* [tradition, in French], *al taqlid* [tradition, in Arabic], that's also something that is personal and people don't want to answer you. They want to keep their secrets to themselves."

Moreover, she insisted, selecting young women as my study subjects was a flaw in my methodology. "How can you generalize about the whole Moroccan population from schoolgirls?" she asked rhetorically. The possibility that I was not attempting such inclusive claims was incongruent with this administrator's epistemological orientation and heightened her suspicions of my motives. She also claimed that "no one does the kind of study you want to do. Everyone, Moroccan or foreigner, works with a questionnaire. No one goes into an institution and asks students directly what they think about this or that."

I tried to explain: "For a scientific study of language practices and ideologies, questionnaires don't provide all the necessary information. So the questionnaire I prepared asks questions, but what I really care about is how language is used and understood by people." She retorted, "So why girls? Why the boarding school? These girls don't represent society. They live in a very isolated world, they are confined to the school, and they won't tell you anything about society." I agreed to stop the informal conversations in the dorm and simply to administer what seemed a rather innocuous multi-page questionnaire.

Although the headmistress's idea about who was worth studying is ridiculous by both anthropological and feminist standards, her comment about tradition being private was echoed in some of the students' responses on the questionnaire I was eventually allowed to administer to girl boarders who volunteered to take it. The questionnaire, carefully translated into Arabic with the assistance of a local translator, asked basic demographic information about each girl's family composition and origin; the education of her parents and siblings and their professions; her language use in various contexts; her preferences in dress, music, foods, and hobbies; and similar questions that at the time seemed innocuous to me. It was clear from the types of music, clothes, food, and other cultural markers with which the girls aligned themselves on the questionnaire that they conceptually set themselves apart from their rural communities of origin. Many of them described their rural market centers as "towns" and themselves as urbanites, and on the questionnaire they crossed out—sometimes dramatically—references to Berber musicians and rural foods, for instance, as though to further distance themselves from those indexes of rurality. When I reviewed their answers that evening, I immediately recognized that for many girls the questionnaire was an opportunity to present an image of the self that more closely modeled their future aspirations than their present experience or their past. The completed questionnaires were unusable for the purpose for which I had intended them, but they were instructive for understanding both urbanization and Arabization through the schools.

What John Lennon sang in "Beautiful Boy (Darling Boy)"—"Life is what happens to you / While you're busy making other plans"—is surely just as true if you substitute "research" for "life." Fortunately I had brought index cards with the questionnaire that evening and had asked for student volunteers to leave me their addresses and village names so that I could visit some of them over the impending summer break. These home visits around the Sous Valley provided a deeply instructive introduction to the region's multiple land tenure systems as many of the students' parents were agriculturalists. Some of them worked land that had been sold inexpensively by the government in the 1960s and 1970s to encourage farming and were associated with cooperatives that allowed them to reduce expenses and pool their products, such as milk, for sale. Others were wage laborers in commercial agriculture, picking citrus fruit in the fields or boxing it in factories for export.

While the project with the students in the boarding school came to an abrupt end, the home visits led to what became my dissertation and first book project on the relationship between language, land, and gender in southwestern Morocco. One of the student volunteers who invited me to her village was Mina, of the Ida ou Zeddout region of the eastern Anti-Atlas Mountains. The first time I set foot in those mountains, after getting out of a shared taxi along the paved road and walking two hours with the local *fqih* (religious scholar) who had taken the taxi with me from Taroudant, I had what turned out to be a correct hunch: I had found a fascinating field site that would take years to understand fully, a place where people did not refute their Tashelhit language and Berber culture to seem more Arab, and where mothers socialized their children into Tashelhit language and social values. Perhaps most important, given the suspicion, secrecy, and uncomfortable negotiations over knowledge production I was already encountering, I met in Mina not only a fantastic field informant but also a steady and true friend who would help me navigate the land mines of doubts about my intentions in choosing to live so far from my home.

COMMUNITY-INTERNAL SUSPICION: KNOWLEDGE AT WHAT PRICE?

There is suspicion in anthropological fieldwork not only between the researched and the researcher, and between the researcher and those mediating access to the researched. Often, there is also suspicion among the researched, and these suspicions shape what a researcher can and cannot do. The question then becomes, what is the price of accessing certain kinds of knowledge or certain people? Lila Abu-Lughod writes eloquently about this in her first ethnography, *Veiled Sentiments* (1986). Living with an Egyptian Bedouin family, and benefiting from the advantages of being almost adopted into it, required her to socialize with certain families instead of others. Many researchers face this constraint in fieldwork. In what follows I discuss one particularly challenging turning point in my extended fieldwork when my host mother forbade me to visit an entire village or a lay historian there, whom she claimed was the victim of divine retribution.

In 1997, while riding atop a small Peugeot pickup truck used for transportation between villages, I met a one-armed man whom everyone called Bu Afus (meaning "arm man"). Bu Afus began talking about "colonial" history (the term the local people use for the French Protectorate of Morocco), perhaps spurred on by the continual comparisons people made between me and the French Captain Ropars, who had been the administrator of the Igherm Native Affairs post in the 1950s before Moroccan independence—a similarity grounded solely in our being the only two foreigners people had known there who spoke Tashelhit. I eagerly engaged in conversation with him about the French presence in the region, and as he climbed down from the truck, he invited me to his village to continue the conversation. This may sound unremarkable, but there may have been only four times in my four years of fieldwork in the 1990s when any Moroccan man spoke seriously with me about rural history. The history books overlook the kind of information he was offering, and I was eager to access it. Men's dismissal of me at that time as an interlocutor in serious matters like history was surely due to my spending time with women and, when in the mountains, wearing the regional dress as my hostesses requested. The visual cues I gave off indexed me as unsuitable for historical discussions, and this meant that my dissertation lacked the historical depth I longed for; this is surely part of what stimulated a subsequent book project on rural social and legal history in the region under the French Protectorate. Returning to Morocco eight years later to research this historical project, as a tenured professor and published author, I met with an entirely different reception from men. It has proven possible for me to access these rural histories both in oral form and in court registers from the mid-twentieth century, and this has been an important part of my field research since 2008. In the 1990s, however, I was starved for historical information, as there seemed to be so little published on the eastern Anti-Atlas Mountains.

For five months after Bu Afus's invitation, I thought periodically about how to get to him, given that a young man from his village had stabbed a young man in my host village in a dispute—an event that, understandably, had led to tension and an end of socializing between youths in the two villages. Following my inclination to test out ideas and see how people would react, but going against the Anti-Atlas Berber tendency not to announce one's movements until the very last minute (preferably when heading out the door), I started to tell villagers that I planned to visit Bu Afus and that I would need one of the village boys to accompany me on the hour-long walk between the villages. People listened politely to this declaration and did not respond either favorably or unfavorably until one late afternoon when I returned from socializing with the young women before dinner preparations were to begin. My host mother, Hajja, was at a neighbor's house when I stopped in. A dozen other village women—more than usual—were gathered in the courtyard, but I did not ask why.

With her peers and mine as witnesses, Hajja asked when I planned to leave for Bu Afus's village. I said that I didn't know and that I still had to find a boy to accompany me. Everyone was silent. The sun was setting. Hajja turned to me and spoke louder. She advised me sternly:

> Don't cut off your right foot to feed your stomach. You are just thinking of your stomach, your desires [shahma]), but if you think about them you'll cut off your hand. I am your hand, do you understand? You are like my girl [drrit]. [That village] is full of bad people.

I asked whether this was because of the knife incident, or whether Bu Afus was the bad one. She replied:

> It's everyone there, they're all bad people. If you go there from here, allah yahannik [literally, "May God be merciful"; colloquially, "Farewell]. Pull your head together. Go to Taroudant first, or they'll come looking for us. If anything happens to you [there], they'll say we are responsible. Here you're safe. Haven't I taken you to different places and you've always been fine? Tigert, Tizi, Tasga, Igherm, Issdrim [nearby villages]—you've been fine. Here you're safe; Lalla Aisha [the local saint] makes sure of that. But if you venture to [that village], so long. Do you know how Bu Afus lost his arm?

I said I had never asked. "In a bus," she said. "So it was an accident," I said. "Not an accident!" she replied, and went on:

> He buried his daughter while she was still alive. She looked up at him [gesturing with her arms in the air and her mouth gasping] and he threw dirt on her. Soon afterward, he took the bus to Casablanca and it cut off his arm. Tell me that's not God's revenge. His father, he beat him. His mother, she was no good. He has no asl [roots]. And so then look, even his own son, his wife left him, and he's divorcing her. He's no good. Just wait until you get into his house and see what he does to you.

Hajja continued her threat, periodically turning to our hostess and, referring to me, saying, "She doesn't understand. How can I make her understand?"

While Hajja pleaded, I gripped her thighs in surprise and fear, and our hostess assured her that I understood. I was indeed scared and repeated to her, "I understand, I'm listening, look if I don't understand, look at my eyes, can't you tell I'm frightened?" She took my hands in hers and turned to address our hostess, saying, "Look at her hands, they're cold, they're white. Okay, she's scared; she understands."

She then tightened her hold on my hands and pushed them to my chest, imploring: "Pull your head together [*smun ixfnm, gbl ixfnm*]. I've never told you not to go somewhere. When you left here and went to Tata, I never told you not to go. Anywhere you go is fine except for there. Think before you do something. Pull your head together."

I assured her that I wouldn't go to Bu Afus's village and that I would keep my distance from him. She repeated, "Give [that village] and Bu Afus room [*fkasn tisaa*]. Stay away."

She kissed my hands and then dropped them, rising to leave. Our hostess told me to go into the sitting room, and the women in the courtyard echoed her. All the while they had been murmuring to themselves and each other, "*saḥt*" (it's true, this is how it is). An unmarried woman in her early twenties said to me, "Look, if you want to talk to him, wait until you see him at the market. Sit with him if he wants to tell you about dates [her rendering of my comment that he knows history, *tarix*]. Sit in a café with him, but don't take as much as a cup of coffee from him. Don't drink tea with him. Don't eat from the same plate as him. Don't go to his house. Do you know what *smm* is?" I assured her I knew about poison. She continued: "If you don't care about your own health, think about the people [*ayt*] of the village. They'll be in trouble if he does anything to you. The *makhzen* [central government] now knows who they are; they've written down everyone's names."

I never saw Bu Afus again, and I still have never set foot in his village.

ETHNOGRAPHIC PRODUCTIONS AND
EPISTEMOLOGICAL ANXIETIES

In addition to monitoring my movements, the people I researched showed considerable anxiety about the final products of my work—the knowledge that would appear in texts, audio recordings, and still images—and how these renderings would be disseminated and used, and by whom. The issue of what would happen to the stories they told me and the events they shared with me was also a source of both secrecy and suspicion. Among those areas in which they were secretive were assertions about local custom and the circulation of visual images in the form of photos.

Stories about local custom of the "we do this, we do that" variety, they feared, could lead to their voices being broadcast on the radio without their permission. Radio Agadir was interested in such topics. For this reason, many people were careful about talking when my audio recorder was running. When I asked questions in a style different from their own interactive styles, women told me that I was "like Laarush," a female Radio Agadir interviewer. Besides, as the boarding school headmistress had said, asking about young women's traditions means "stealing their secrets." The very knowledge of custom was carefully guarded; it had multiple forms of value that could be used for assessing reputation, respectability, piety, and other characteristics not only of a person but also of his or her village.

Photographs, people feared, could be seen by unrelated males and thus compromise a patriarch's control over his daughters and wife, those whom he is supposed to protect not only from danger and material need but also from men's lascivious gazes and their evaluations of the patriarch's material wealth gleaned from women's appearance. Thus, I asked permission before taking photographs, and usually only older women and girls—rather than newly married, sexually active women—agreed to let me take their pictures. It was possible to photograph only women I knew already (and thus presumably would not endanger or embarrass). More recently, the ubiquitous fear has become postings on the Internet whether on Facebook or elsewhere—a development with implications for women's collective song and dance performances in public settings that I will explore further in a future publication.

CONCLUSION

The factors contributing to secrecy and suspicion in the fieldwork encounters I have described here, both internal and external to the rural Anti-Atlas communities in which I conducted research, culminated in a perfect storm at the end of the twentieth century. This storm encouraged the kind of secrecy and suspicion at which King Hassan II excelled, and for which he was reputed and feared. In the mid- to late 1990s, prior to the government's acknowledgment of human rights abuses (Slyomovics 2005), Tazmamart, the now infamous prison for political prisoners, was a dangerous topic of conversation. Amazigh activists were a thorn in the government's side, and there were no women in the Moroccan legislature. There was widespread suspicion of outsiders who were not tourists, humanitarian workers, Peace Corp volunteers, or spouses of Moroccans. Many people feared neocolonialism and could not quite see an alternative to an Arabo-Islamic national identity. Officials were profoundly uncomfortable with the increasing international attention to the voices of women, youth, and indigenous or minority populations. They saw my research project as threatening on all of these fronts. I encountered none of this suspicion in field and archival research in 2008–2009 in the same region. Within rural communities, people engaged in information management, since knowledge—about people, events, and places—was a valuable commodity, carefully moderated via verbal styles such as "he said, she said" reported speech that encouraged accurate quotation and a chain of transmission, accountability, and authority. Before there were cellphones, paved roads, and electricity, there was widespread uncertainty over people's comings, goings, and doings. People carefully managed and tracked others' material goods—even a handful of almonds hidden in the chest pouch of a woman's wrap (*tamalhaft*) aroused suspicion—since the norm was that everything should be shared. There was a profound uneasiness over newly emerging differences between people and their access to material goods, information, knowledge, and the perceived power associated with all three of these.

As the descriptions of fieldwork in Morocco in this chapter have illustrated, the ethnographic project and product hinges not only on the relationship between researcher and co-researchers (as we might consider our informants), and on dynamics of authority and truth that shape interactions between the scholar and the studied. Just as important are the intra-societal relationships and the historical contexts that have shaped these, as well as the orientations and access to knowledge that characterize the various participants in any research encounter. Knowledge is always partial, as the works in reflexive anthropology of the late 1970s and 1980s, grounded in Morocco, insisted to ethnographers. Or, as one of Metcalf's informants in Borneo told him, and as he titled his book, "They lie, we lie." Yet in a given fieldwork project, we might ask, who are the *they* who are lying? What are *we* lying about, too? Rather than letting the answers to these questions paralyze us, Metcalf urges, we might just as well get on with anthropology. To do this in Morocco, as in any place on which the ethnographic gaze falls, we must keep in mind the ways in which truth is mediated in particular historical moments and political climates, and the ways in which the political economy of knowledge emerges from its production, its circulation, and the assessment of its value. What deserves study, who should do that study, and what should happen to the products of that study are matters of concern not only to academic professionals but also to those who make the meaning in their everyday lives that anthropologists deem worthy of our collective attention.

NOTE

1. Ahmad writes of being suspected early in his dissertation research of being an "agent of the West," set on collecting harmful information about an Islamist group in India by conducting research in the school they sponsored (2005, 281).

6|

The Activist and the Anthropologist

PAUL A. SILVERSTEIN

In his afterword to Paul Rabinow's *Reflections on Fieldwork in Morocco* (2007 [1977], 166–67), Pierre Bourdieu cites Jean Piaget's famous dictum, "it is not so much that children don't know how to talk: they try out many languages until they find one their parents can understand," and concludes, "Ethnology will have taken a giant step forward when all ethnologists understand that something similar is taking place between informants and themselves." This is a striking yet curious statement. Curious because it portrays anthropology as an improvable, developmental discipline, in spite of Bourdieu's critique several pages earlier of the "positivist conception of scientific work" and his applauding Rabinow for having broken with the "refurbished positivism" of his teacher, Clifford Geertz (ibid., 163). Curious also because Bourdieu would not reflect on his own field experience in North Africa or his dialogical relationship with his own informants until twenty years later, at the end of his life (Bourdieu 2003a, 2004, 2008; see also Goodman and Silverstein 2009). Yet ultimately what makes the statement so striking and prescient is that it runs against the grain of anthropology's relativist recognition of radical otherness and posits instead the ultimate commensurability of anthropologist and informant. While one certainly may be tempted to read Bourdieu as likening informants to children, the reverse may actually hold, as it is the anthropologist who, like a child, must learn his informant's idiom and who tries out various interpretive schemes until he finds one his informant can understand. In any case, Bourdieu, through Piaget, has placed self and other in the same psychic family—if not mutually self-constituting, then at least convergent in their quest for understanding and communication.

But if anthropology is ultimately a dialogical encounter, what happens when anthropologist and informant already largely share the same idiom? What happens when self and other converge not only in the *in situ* moment of mutual recognition, but also in the presuppositions and life projects that underpin their dialogue? It is not merely a matter of today's anthropologists being better trained than their predecessors in field languages and having deeper experiences in the region before embarking on their official fieldwork. Nor is this convergence simply the result of the various phenomena loosely labeled globalization, through which the English language and American culture have become part of everyday life in many of the places that anthropologists traditionally study. Moroccans have always had indigenous categories for white folk—as *nasrani* or *aroumi*—although arguably these have now become so highly differentiated that merchants around Marrakech's Djemaa el-Fnaa can distinguish on sight the national identity of various shoppers. Americans are no longer curiosities in even the remote corners of Morocco, particularly for a younger generation brought up on heavy metal, pirated DVDs, and downloaded episodes of *Prison Break*. Most American anthropologists have had the uncanny experience of learning about new trends in U.S. pop culture abroad, where curiosity often abounds and the uptake is surprisingly rapid, if locally idiosyncratic. Anthropologists have long remarked on the elasticity of culture to incorporate and indigenize Western technology, media, and conceptual schemes (see Sahlins 1993), as well as on the intimate and mimetic processes that characterize cultural encounters (Herzfeld 1997; Taussig 1993).

What requires further specification are the ways in which the "doubling of self-consciousness" that Rabinow (2007 [1977], 119) describes anthropologists demanding of their informants—the "symbolic violence" whereby our interlocutors are forced to objectify their culture and reflect on what they normally take for granted—is already embedded in various forms of local cultural expertise mastered by North African ʿulama (Islamic scholars) and Berber *imusnawen* (sages) who have been historically called on to speak in the name of discursive tradition. And what is perhaps new are the ways in which such self-reflection and cultural objectification have come to be particularly practiced as a discipline by emerging groups of cultural entrepreneurs (activists, tourist professionals, journalists, and development intermediaries) one could describe only as indigenous anthropologists (or perhaps as "para-ethnographers," in the words of Douglas Holmes and George Marcus [2005, 240–42; 2012, 127–31]). Even without the presence of a foreign anthropologist, such groups engage in the very "participant objectification" that Bourdieu (2003b) later identified as the hallmark of ethnographic methodology, albeit for their own purposes and under their own (sometimes heavily surveilled and discursively regulated) conditions of knowledge production.[1] Such an increasing convergence of anthropologist and informant, of self and other, constitutes the methodological, epistemological, and political context of contemporary Moroccan ethnography.

AMBIGUITIES OF RESEMBLANCE

A class of local cultural experts (whether in the guise of ritual specialists, master speakers or scribes, politico-legal arbitrators, or intercultural mediators) may very well be a cultural universal and is certainly the condition of possibility for most anthropological fieldwork. In the case of my own field experience, the Amazigh or Berber activists with whom I have been working over the past ten years have engaged in a number of pursuits generally associated with anthropological inquiry. They have drawn on Arabic and French colonial philological, historical, and ethnological sources in order to identify an "authentic" Berber culture. They have recorded genealogies of Berber families to chart tribal segmentation and a history of movement across the North African landscape. They have collected material artifacts, recorded rituals, and transcribed oral narratives in order to preserve the cultural patrimony they fear is endangered by the forces of globalization and decades of state-enforced Arabization. While ostensibly (salvage) anthropological in orientation, such efforts increasingly draw on a transnational politics of indigenous rights that explicitly refuses the "museumification" or "folklorization" of culture that activists consider to be the legacy of anthropological praxis. Rather, they are committed to a vision of cultural development ultimately premised on a bounded vision of culture that entails territorial autonomy, socioeconomic self-management, and political self-determination—in the most expansionist imaginations, a *Tamazgha,* or Berber homeland, stretching from the Canary Islands to the Siwa oasis in western Egypt.

Such a militant politics poses non-trivial dilemmas for contemporary anthropological sensibilities and theories that have challenged bounded notions of culture and embraced a world of mobility and cosmopolitanism. Anthropologists must increasingly come to terms with having their research presence, data, and findings appropriated for activist political concerns that are anything but their own; with the practical opportunities and limitations such appropriation entails; and with the potential conflicts that can arise when the ideological commitments of anthropologists and activists prove to be divergent or even incompatible. Such tensions and negotiations call into question—indeed, reverse—the inherited disciplinary assumptions about the symmetry of interests and asymmetry of means between anthropologist and informant. They highlight the ways in which all ethnography is necessarily a dialogical production and challenge the conceit—what Kevin Dwyer calls the "false image of strength" (1982, 256)—of the anthropologist as the super-agentive, contemplative "total persona" that Rabinow and Bourdieu curiously maintain.

Beginning in the 1960s but accelerating after the early 1980s, Berber-speaking students and migrants based in Rabat, Agadir, and abroad formed cultural associations dedicated to standardizing the Berber language (Tamazight) into a modern, written idiom of information, literature, scholarship, and pedagogy. This involved both an archaeo-logical process of compiling a baseline cultural repertoire and a sci-entific method of classifying, codifying, and mapping the materials collected. To a great extent these activist-scholars were self-taught. University programs in anthropology or sociology were either non-existent or severely underfunded, casualties of state developmental-ist efforts to train students in technological fields, as well as broader national attempts to bolster Morocco's Arabo-Islamic cultural cre-dentials through prioritizing education in Arabic literature and re-ligious studies. The social sciences curriculum that did exist—such as Paul Pascon's rural sociology program—largely adopted a politi-cal economy approach that relegated culture to a secondary status of causation. While some activists did acquire university training in ethnology, linguistics, and history in France, the majority cobbled together their methods and theories in bricolage fashion, drawing on whatever tools and sources were ready to hand.

What activist-scholars lacked in means, they made up in energy and entrepreneurialism. They pursued their research and writing projects on weekends or after their jobs as schoolteachers or civil servants. They made use of holiday trips to their rural homelands to collect materials and interview older residents considered fonts of oral history and literature. One such activist, now based in the rural southeastern town of Goulmima, where I have been conducting re-search, returned to the region as a schoolteacher after many years in Fez and France in order to pursue such interests on a more regular basis and to give back more seamlessly to his community. For the last twenty years, he has worked with a blind poet of his parents' generation, recording the poet's *oeuvre* and transcribing it as best he can with the technology available. He is joined in this effort by two other local activists, each of whom is working with a different blind poet in somewhat competitive fashion, using their recordings to in-spire their own poetic endeavors and self-publishing their archival and artistic works as funds become available.

Moreover, these activist-scholars are voracious consumers of an-thropological and historical scholarship on all things Berber. Resources being limited, Berber associations always have a library containing photocopies of whatever materials activists have collected or visitors have donated over the years. These include recent works but also colonial-era scholarship, particularly on the local region, which activists tend to regard as authoritative, or at least replete with cultural and historical information they can mine for their own purposes. In some cases, the theoretical approaches deployed by these European scholars—such as the segmentary lineage theory underwriting the work of Ernest Gellner (1969) and even the structuralist approach to the Berber house used by Bourdieu (see Bourdieu 1970; Silverstein 2004b)—have become axiomatic in activists' cultural self-understanding. Activists' projection of authenticity thus becomes mediated by the anthropological record itself.

In this sense, my informants recognized me in the field not simply as an American traveler, but also as a fellow student of Berber culture, although one whose motivations were perhaps suspect. On numerous occasions activists interrogated me about my research, evaluating it certainly on the basis of its cultural or political relevance to their own projects, but also according to whether it met the standards of logical positivism they had consciously learned from J. G. A. Pocock. One such interrogator, Moha, looked at me in perplexity after my initial summary of my research, and rephrased his question about it to determine how exactly my approach fit into what he saw as the four competing anthropological models of Moroccan society developed by Edward Westermarck (1926), Ernest Gellner (1969), John Waterbury (1970), and Clifford Geertz (1979). Moha proceeded to give a quick (and quite accurate) summary of these different approaches for the other participants in the conversation, and he also mapped these models onto different political tendencies within the Amazigh movement. Amazingly, he afterward admitted he had never actually read the works in question, given his relatively poor command of English and his lack of resources to order books from overseas; he knew of the authors primarily through online summaries. The point here is not to minimize the various differences that divided me from my interlocutors. Their penchant for logical positivism derived more from their political upbringing within the *Qaᶜidiyyin* ("Basist") Marxist student movements and its associated closed, anti-hermeneutic epistemology than from any social science training.[2] They approached these issues as engaged militants, not as contemplative scholars. It was precisely this combination of convergence of knowledge and divergence of perspective that made such encounters particularly uncanny—at least for me. For them, I was yet another potential resource to be consulted and mined, not inherently different from the well-worn photocopies of colonial-era texts that lined their association libraries' shelves.

POSSESSION AND ETHICS

This simultaneous convergence in content and method and divergence in perspective had a number of unexpected effects on the conditions of my field research and ultimately the quality of the necessarily collective ethnographic production that emerged. In the first place, it placed certain limits on how I chose informants, or rather how informants chose me. In every case of field research, that choice—as Rabinow (2007 [1977], 75, 92) discusses in some detail—is always politicized, given historical divides based on lineage, ideology, or personality. Activist struggles add yet another, non-negligible layer of potential contention to be negotiated. Already suspected of "playing politics" (*siyasa*) for personal gain and endangering local life by attracting unwanted state attention, Amazigh activists are also accused of undermining the delicate mosaic of the ethnically and racially diverse southeastern oases with a divisive discourse of cultural authenticity. As if through magical contagion, my research with and alongside local activists marked me as dangerous in the eyes of many people, and whole groups refused any social interaction with me whatsoever.

Furthermore, my interactions were constrained by the internal divides between and among activists. As Rabinow (2007 [1977]) and Lawrence Rosen (1979) have variously described, Moroccan men and women are very strategic in building webs of engagement and networks of interaction, often in competitive and agonistic ways. Activism becomes another site for such building of self through the resources of interpersonal connections, and it is no surprise that a multiplicity of rival associations tend to flourish even in small-scale communities. Amazigh associations are differentiated less by ideological divergences than by generational identity or a history of past disagreements, and it is not unusual to find close relatives on different sides of an associational divide. This obviously creates a number of distinct pitfalls for anthropological research in these areas.

In my own field experience, I was first invited to the Ghéris Valley by Hrou, an activist and a past officer in Tilelli, the local cultural association, whom I had met while presenting my research at Tamaynut, an allied cultural association in Rabat. Hrou had left the region by the time of my subsequent field visit, but I ended up becoming close to his activist brother, Brahim, who quickly became my key informant and apparently close friend. Otherwise put, I quickly became his anthropologist. He had organized a number of activists from various local groups in a land rights protest about the sale of five hectares of collective tribal territory to an outside private investor, and while I had come to the area to study historical memories of resistance, not land rights per se, I quickly became enmeshed and enthralled in the case. After all, I told myself in good Geertzian (or perhaps Malinowskian) fashion, the job of the anthropologist is to study what is important to the natives, not what is important to the anthropologist.

It took me a while, however, to realize the costs of this association with Brahim—who, more than anyone in the area, was disdained for playing politics for personal gain, and about whom sordid rumors circulated widely. Over the course of five months of close interaction with Brahim, I rarely saw Hrou or those activists close to him. Other local intellectuals with whom I had worked before did occasionally extend invitations to me but specified that I should come alone, "not with your friend." Through the spatial trajectories of everyday wandering and his subtle comments on the qualities of others, Brahim masterfully steered me away from people who would offer a decid-

edly different perspective from his or who would challenge his effective monopoly on my presence (and the small material gains that
came with it). Indeed, it was only after a definitive rupture in my relationship with Brahim that certain other activists even agreed to talk
with me, and in doing so they provided me with a decidedly different (if equally slanted and equally partially true) account of the local politics I had been studying, including the land rights case itself.
Most significantly, I was able to re-establish a close connection with
Hrou and his comrades, thus eventually closing the circle of my research trajectory. Retrospectively, the rupture (which I will discuss
in more detail later) proved to be probably the most productive, if
psychologically extremely painful, event I experienced in the field.

Divides within the local activist community likewise created pitfalls for how I could disseminate the materials I collected in the process of my research. After nine months of fieldwork in Morocco, I
spent a summer in the archives in France, gathering all available
documents related to the Ghéris Valley from the period of the French
Protectorate. After Moroccan independence, the military administration repatriated the vast majority of its records of rule to France,
including the numerous *fiches de tribu* (tribal indexes) and *consignes
de poste* (transfer documents) written by indigenous affairs officers in
an attempt to create an authoritative history and ethnography of the
areas under their control.[3] While the archives are technically open to
the public, access is certainly smoothed by having a university affiliation, and in any case visas to France are difficult to obtain for many
Moroccans. I thus felt an ethical duty to share these materials with
the people about whom they had been written, to re-repatriate the
documents back to Morocco. With a full flash drive in hand, I shared
this plan with a French-trained Moroccan anthropologist in Rabat,
who himself had been active in Amazigh associations and knew the
area which I researched. He warned me that such a plan, however
magnanimous it may appear, risked severely backfiring, noting that
even though my informants seemed like anthropologists to me, they
were not trained to read archival documents and could misinterpet
French ideological portrayals as cultural truths. More significantly,

he reminded me that the documents often made reference to the collaboration of particular individuals and groups, and that these had the potential to become weapons in local political struggles, no matter how much I redacted the documents.

Still resolute in my ethical assuredness, confident in my ability to successfully navigate such political pitfalls, and suspicious that his warnings emerged in part from his own efforts to socially and intellectually distinguish himself from non-credentialed para-ethnographers, I proceeded with a modified version of my plan and left a select choice of redacted documents in the hands of a senior officer in the Tilleli cultural association in whom I had deep trust and who was himself writing a history of the region. I asked him to make the documents nominally accessible to the public, but to share them actively only with people he felt were relatively outside of village-level politics. One of those people turned out to be Ichou, his close comrade and the son of the former French-appointed *shaykh,* who had previously opened his family archives to me. When I returned to Goulmima a few months later, Ichou excitedly asked me if I had any more documents to share. As I seemed surprised by his curiosity, he explained, "You see, Paul, with those documents, people listen to me." A shared research interest in Berber culture and the history of the valley clearly did not translate into a shared sense of the utility of the research. Possession of both the anthropologist and the anthropologist's findings were seamlessly assimilated into a larger political game between and among activists—a game in which I was clearly a novice player.

INTERESTS

Convergent research interests and divergent political ones also raised the stakes in the "testing" Rabinow (2007 [1977], 28–29) describes his Moroccan informants engaging in to maximize the "resources" provided by the anthropologist.[4] In general, the "transitoriness" (ibid., 110) of the anthropologist's social situation heightens such testing, insofar as it forces a telescoping of the temporal lag between hospitality offered and reciprocity expected. My informants expended varying degrees of economic and social capital to facilitate my stay, and while "owning" me had some minor symbolic benefit to them, the redacted documents and occasional financial contributions to their households that I provided could only begin to repay my incurred debt.

The rupture with Brahim predictably occurred over these divergent expectations. The fact that I rented a house from him for an amount well above market price, brought him and his family gifts (albeit mostly symbolic) from my travels, and offered to pay for most of our meals and excursions together (offers he usually refused) led me to believe that we had achieved some equilibrium in mutual expected reciprocity. Only several months later did I link a repeated pattern of missing cash to my visits to his house. Through some pseudo-scientific testing and rough calculations, I discovered that Brahim had lifted several thousand dirhams ($300–400, or close to a month's wages for him as a primary school instructor) from me over the course of our relationship, which meant that the meals and excursions he generously offered were actually being financed through my own resources. The realization certainly had the clichéd effect of rupturing the social world I had taken for granted, forcing me to rethink my own understanding of local concepts of friendship, trust, and interestedness.[5] But just as important, it led me to think more deeply about the role of the ruse in Berber (and, more generally, Moroccan) constructions of selfhood, particularly in cultural contexts where stories of the jackal and the hedgehog are emblematic morality tales of local resilience.[6] It helped me to rethink my own categories of collaboration and resistance, which had pained me in my internal debates over sharing the archival documents. As complicated as my eventual, tactful distancing from Brahim proved to be, the experience was, as we like to tell our undergraduate students, a "learning moment."

But of course there was nothing at all peculiar about Brahim's material interest in my presence, or in his presumption of my own naïveté as an obviously guileless *aroumi*, ignorant of classic ruses in the local marketplace of knowledge acquisition. My ethnographer colleagues could no doubt relate similar stories. But my transitoriness appealed to activists in other, less obviously pecuniary ways. On the one hand, my foreign status seemed politically useful to activists in confirming the importance of their political causes, and I have fielded frequent requests for interviews by activists working for newspapers, websites, and radio shows. On the other hand, my transitory status (and no doubt my American citizenship) made me nearly legally untouchable, and thus tactically useful in activist politics that often attracted police scrutiny. During the land rights case mentioned above, local activists used me as a decoy to distract the security forces who periodically trailed them. In one instance, Brahim and his allies needed to meet to plan a protest march, so—as I later learned—they sent me and a fellow activist off to dine at a friend's place, correctly betting that the police were more likely to follow me, as a visible foreigner. When the police later brought charges against the activists for organizing an illegal demonstration, they used me as an alibi, insisting that they were essentially just entertaining me and that I obviously had no personal stake in the land case.

Just as important, my transitoriness as an anthropologist was iconic of activists' idealized vision of themselves, as people who study and speak for local tradition but are not bound by it. If many Moroccans idealize mobility and the adventure of clandestine migration to Europe (*harrag*), activists, as political players, particularly seek to maximize trans-local connections and experiences. A disproportionate number of Amazigh activists in Morocco are schoolteachers, journalists, and lawyers, members of liberal professions that require travel for education, and generally relocation to an urban center, if not to a foreign country. Moreover, even those activists who return home to ply their trades for the benefit of their local community seek to maintain dense, trans-local connections, either through periodic voyages or Internet-mediated communication.[7] A case in point is Mehdi, a Rabat-based activist who has positioned himself as a veritable fixer for foreign journalists or researchers interested in Berber culture, as well as for activists who occasionally find themselves in legal binds. Through years of face-work, and through his former position as director of a research center, he has managed to accumulate a portfolio of contacts that reach up to the palace, down to remote villages, and abroad across multiple continents. His standard mode of self-presentation relies on performances of transitoriness; he appears to be constantly in motion, whether moving from appointment to appointment or traveling across the country from one event to another. He carries three mobile phones that always seem to be ringing, and he purchases ten different daily newspapers in three languages so as to stay abreast of national and international developments. Most symbolically, he carries with him a large stack of business cards collected from contacts that he invariably presents as being very important people or renowned foreign scholars (some of whom, it later turns out, are only young graduate students). It has occurred more than once that I have later met someone at an academic conference whose name I first heard from Mehdi. Almost as if to suture such an evanescent outlook, Mehdi recently married a woman from Eastern Europe, broadcasting photos from the church wedding across activist circles.[8] For Mehdi, such trans-local connections not only form a social insurance policy, hedging against his periodic material and legal needs, but also confirm him as an activist in the strict sense of the term: an "active" spokesman for an authentic and endangered culture, but ultimately unrestrained by ties of kin, locality, or even religion.

CONCLUSION

Anthropologists and activists are mutually "good to think," to invoke Claude Lévi-Strauss (1963, 89). Their dialogical working through their respective ethnographic and para-ethnographic projects provides moments for reflection on the place of culture in a world that so often appears to be transitory and unsettled itself. While I do not have deep insight into the ways my research presence particularly altered the thoughts and practices of my Amazigh activist interlocutors, at least one recently recalled a past conversation and reflected on how my earlier questions helped him gain clarity on a particular (albeit minor) issue. But, by and large, I am quite certain that such effects were few compared to the unexpected and challenging insights I gained from our interactions—insights that occasionally reoriented my research project or at least my way of thinking for better or worse. Anthropologists do not control their destinies in the field any more than they do at home; fieldwork experiences are unpredictable, challenging, and—quite frankly—usually beyond the anthropologist's control. Conceits of the anthropologist as superagent or total persona or "objective subject," as Dwyer (1982, 265) perceptively noted, fail to register this dependence or the fact that anthropologists are ultimately the children—not the parents—in Piaget's idiom, struggling to find a language our informants understand. But what is perhaps most challenging of all is the fact that anthropologists no longer have a monopoly on their own idiom: their methods and models have been adopted by others on whom they depend for the de facto collaborative production of knowledge, but who often have radically divergent ideological interests. In this respect, Bourdieu's implication that anthropologists are like Piaget's children seems quaint. Resemblance may ultimately prove more academically and psychically challenging than difference.

NOTES

My initial ethnographic field research in southeastern Morocco was funded by generous grants from the Fulbright-Hayes Faculty Research Abroad Program, the U.S. Institute of Peace, and the Michael E. Levine Foundation. Follow-up research was generously funded by the Carnegie Corporation of New York. My deep thanks to David Crawford, Kevin Dwyer, Brian Edwards, and Rachel Newcomb for feedback on earlier drafts. Pseudonyms are used for activists throughout.

1. See Shyrock (1997) and Winegar (2006, 25–32) for a discussion of similar cases of the shared anthropological and local categories of culture among Jordanian Bedouin historiographers and Egyptian artists.

2. For a discussion of the conflict between Marxist and Berberist student movements, see Silverstein (2010).

3. On the indigenous affairs officers, their politics, and their textual technologies, see Bidwell (1973), Burke (1972, 2007), and Hoffman (2008a).

4. See Rosen (1979, 47) for a market-centric understanding of all Moroccan social relations (based on kinship or anything else) as "resources" that are ac-

cumulated and mobilized for personal gain. I do not have the space to rehearse my hesitation about the generalizability of such a dyadic model. For this essay, however, I do want to approach the anthropologist–informant dyad as a semi-commodified relationship.

5. See C. Geertz (1979, 204–205) for a schematic discussion of the semantic relationship between friendship (*sedaqa*) and truthfulness (*tasdiq*) as an open space of ongoing negotiation.

6. The collection and analysis of Berber folktales dominated colonial ethnology, and it also became a site for the early articulation of Berber activism (see, for example, Amrouche 1988 [1938]; Mammeri 1980). For representative colonial examples and post-colonial analysis, see Laoust (1930), Leguil (1985), and Yacine-Titouh (2001).

7. Rosen describes the long-distance maintenance of networks of obligation as central to what he sees as the "personal nature of political ties in Morocco" (1979, 53). Like Clifford Geertz (1979, 219), Rosen underlines the centrality of mobility to Moroccan personal status.

8. These photos provoked a minor uproar in the Moroccan media, underlining Islamist representations of Berbers as suspect Muslims and resurrecting a periodic moral panic over Christian evangelization and conversion in Berber milieus. On these questions, see Ben-Layashi (2007), Boum (2007a), and Silverstein (2011).

A Distant Episode

Religion and Belief in Moroccan Ethnography

RACHEL NEWCOMB

It was a bright June day in Fes, with perfect blue skies, just before the heat of summer would lie on the Ville Nouvelle[1] like an unquiet conscience. Today my Moroccan mother-in-law, Jamila, had been promising to take me to the tomb of Sidi Bou Ghalib in the medina. For weeks I had been interviewing medical doctors, herbalists, midwives, and women about reproduction, but this would be my first visit to the tomb of a saint known for his *baraka* (the spiritual power a dead person once possessed) and his abilities to heal those who could not have children. My romantic preconceptions about saints' tombs, known locally as *marabouts* or *sayyids,* had begun in my first days in Morocco as an undergraduate, when I can remember being enchanted with the white-domed tombs rushing past the window of my train compartment: round, alien, and mysterious against flat landscapes of winter wheat. Over the years I variously imagined them to be places of magic, of sources of religious power and influence for women, or of local resistance to the homogenizing influences of global Islam. Other people must not have been immune to their beauty either: the *Editions Lif* postcards that used to be ubiquitous in Moroccan *tabac* shops frequently sold pictures of the tombs, and I had my own collection of postcards, which I tacked up on various refrigerators during my graduate school days to remind myself of what lay "out there" still waiting to be researched. Yet although I had timidly tiptoed around a tomb near a village outside of Tata, where a Peace Corps friend was based, I had never focused directly on these tombs in my research. I had done related work: after college, I spent a year on a Thomas J. Watson Fellowship trailing various Sufi groups through Turkey, Egypt, Cyprus, Senegal, and Morocco, and I certainly saw plenty of saints' tombs during this time, but none of them ever lived up to what I speculated must be happening in the fictional tomb of my imagination.

A 1977 article on the topic by the Moroccan sociologist Fatima Mernissi inspired me to seek out Moroccan saints' tombs for my current research, particularly those designated as sites for women's reproductive difficulties. This was to be my first real visit to a tomb. Jamila had assured me we could stay as long as I wanted, though she, like most of the Moroccans I knew, was not particularly enthusiastic about *sayyids*. The middle-class Fassis who were the subject of my first book stuck to mainstream religious observances: prayer, fasting during Ramadan, and the occasional (particularly for women) visit to a mosque. They had little use for the secondary aspects of Moroccan Islam, such as the amulets written by *fqihs*,[2] or the reputed powers of holy men. They were also not willing to indulge me in conversations about *jinns* or other supernatural beings.

"We don't talk about them because this draws their attention," one of my in-laws once explained. "It's better to mind your own business so that the *jinns* don't bother you." Over the years I made it a habit to bring up these topics in conversation, but my friends were almost always dismissive.

On the road to the medina, we discovered that our taxi driver was married to one of Jamila's former neighbors. Instantly he and Jamila began chatting like family. Jamila introduced me: her son's American wife.

"She speaks Arabic. And this is their daughter," she said, gesturing at my daughter, Sofia, who had just turned one and was trying to fiddle with the car door.

"You speak Arabic? Are you Muslim?" he asked.

"Not yet," I said. This was my usual response. It was a fairly typical conversation. My mother-in-law was always proud I could communicate with people. But inevitably came the impasse. If she speaks Arabic, why is she not Muslim? When will she be Muslim?

"*Inshallah* [God willing], you will find the path," he told me.

"*Inshallah*," I responded.

We were nearing one of the main gates to the medina, Bab Ftouh, and he asked us for the exact address in the medina where we wanted to be dropped off. Jamila told him.

"The tomb of Sidi Bou Ghalib?" he asked, his voice taking on a slight edge. "You know that it's *shirk* [to pray there], don't you?"

By *shirk*, the driver meant worshiping others who are not God. Yet most Moroccans who go to places like Sidi Bou Ghalib's tomb would not claim to be praying directly to the saint himself. Even the word "saint" is a bad translation for holy figures like Sidi Bou Ghalib, since the term "saint" suggests that God has intermediaries. In Islam, humans and God are supposed to connect directly. Some Moroccans go to *sayyids* because of the *baraka* of the person buried there. You want children, for example, and the good luck and *baraka* of a particular saint is said to have helped some women with this. But for many, there is a fine line between asking Sidi Bou Whoever for some of that good luck and actually praying to a figure who is not God.

"Oh, we know it's *shirk*," Jamila assured him. "We're just going to visit."

The tomb was in the middle of the dusty square where the taxi dropped us off. We went through a door in a faded yellow wall and passed through a courtyard with cracked, uneven old tiles. We found ourselves in a covered area with a high, carved ceiling, carpets on the floor, and the tomb in the middle, a raised box covered with a green velvet drape. On the other side of the tomb was a mosque, and we could hear muffled voices chanting. A stout woman with Coke-bottle glasses, the tomb's *muqqadima* (caretaker), welcomed us inside.

Murmuring prayers, Jamila circumambulated the tomb in a counterclockwise direction, finally settling cross-legged on a carpet. I joined her, and Sofia broke free of my grasp. She wasn't walking yet but was intrigued by the various objects in the room: a low window covered with an iron lattice grill on which she could just pull herself up; a woman with temptingly hennaed feet who sat in the corner, resting her head on a suitcase. Another woman who had arrived with us sat on the opposite side of the room; she was young, and her unevenly hemmed djellaba and cracked feet suggested that she was from the country. She remained silent the whole time we were there. The woman with the suitcase told us she was from the Rif, and a little blue tattoo with notched marks over her eyebrows danced when she spoke.[3]

"I hear this saint can bring children," my mother-in-law said, raising the subject of my research. The *muqqadima* reported that she had been married for four years, saw the saint in a dream, came to Sidi Bou Ghalib, and was finally able to have a baby.

"I tell anyone who comes here that if God wants, by praying here, you can have children," she said. She looked over at the silent woman, who was now lying with her back toward us, facing the wall.

Another woman entered the shrine and lay down near us, watching us warily. Conversation drifted among various profane topics. The world economic crisis, particularly the plight of unemployed Moroccan immigrants in Spain. Stories of the *muhajireen,* the immigrants, we all knew and the problems they faced in immigration. There was also talk of an *ngafa,* a famous bridal attendant, who had recently died. *Ngafat* brought trunks full of tiaras, jewelry, and traditional caftans to weddings, and they helped the bride change costume several times throughout the night. This particular *ngafa* had worked at my own wedding, sitting in a back room on a bed like a queen bee while her assistants dressed me.

"Stop talking so loud! This is a holy place. Have some respect." The voice came from the woman who had just entered. Everyone turned to look at her. Small, wiry, and wearing a djellaba of yellow polyester, Rachida had the wary eyes of a cat and a mouth full of ruined teeth. The women apologized, and Jamila tried to draw her into the conversation. Rachida softened a bit. She could have been in her twenties or forties; it was impossible to tell because from the stories she was telling, she had seen enough difficulties in her life to age her prematurely. She was nervous and animated, and in other situations, her jittery movements would have suggested to me that she was a drug addict. From a rumpled plastic bag she pulled a bus pass, telling us how she got to ride the bus for free because she was handicapped— partially blind. She launched into a long tale: she was one of only two children left in a family; everyone else was dead; and she had bought many things for her only sister, who then beat her up, stole her television, and kicked her out of the house.

It was a strange story that went on and on, peppered with further misfortunes. Rachida reminded me of some of the women I had seen in the Fes nongovernmental organization where I used to listen to legal advice sessions—women who came with long, rambling stories of abuse and bad luck, which would end up with requests for money or justice, rights or advice. Was this a therapeutic tale for a sympathetic audience, or was Rachida looking for assistance from the women present? Why had she admonished us at the beginning, when she was now talking louder than anybody? What was the saint's relation to all this? I was keeping quiet, letting Jamila offer the correct emotional responses. Perhaps if I came back, developed trust, and found out who the regulars were, I would understand more. At moments like these, despite having lived for several years off and on in Morocco, and despite understanding the content of what the woman was saying, I still felt lost in translation. What was the proper response here? Eventually Rachida ran out of steam, and the conversation turned away from her and back to other topics.

My daughter spent most of her time crawling around the Riffi lady with the henna designs on her feet, who was sprawled on a carpet, which seemed to be what you did there—come in, pay respects to the saint, lounge, and talk. I was trying to mentally process ten different things at once. What the women were saying, whether I would be called on to talk about myself, how Jamila then expected me to present myself, what I could turn this whole experience into, anthropologically speaking. What Sofia was doing. Baby touches window, baby closes the splintered shutter, baby grabs feet of old Riffi lady lying on carpets, baby puts hand in mouth. What my own issues with religion were, and where this all fit in. What I believed, or didn't believe. The times I'd felt close to something divine—was this one of them? Could I just shut out the disquiet and try to simply be in this exemplary moment?

Eventually Sofia grew tired and began fussing. The women encouraged me to nurse her, so I did, and she fell asleep. I laid her down on her changing mat on top of a soft bed of carpets. The place had a soporific effect, and listening to the gentle hum of women's voices was like meditation. Who was the saint? Nobody talked about him. All the *muqqadima* could say was that he had lived three hundred years earlier. Did it matter? I began to think I could really get into the peacefulness of being here all the time, listening to the birds, in the cool quiet tomb with the women talking. Could we say that one could feel God's presence here, in the shared solidarity of the women present, gathering strength from their conversations, in the birds singing and my daughter sleeping beside me, in the embroidered gold calligraphy on the green velvet draping the tomb? Are such thoughts *shirk*?

But then Jamila got up to pray, leaving the room for the mosque behind the walls. Suddenly I was without a protector. I had been letting her carry all the conversation, unsure of how I fit in here, and now I was waiting for the right moment to launch into my anthropologist's narrative—hey, I'm here to learn more about Sidi Bou Ghalib, let me tell you why in idioms that might make sense, and can I come back and hang out more, by myself?

"Ahh, Ramadan's going to be hard this year," the Riffi woman said. "The middle of the summer. Such long days."

"What day does it start?" someone else asked. They debated. Rachida looked at me.

"Do you fast in America?"

Everyone turned. I could feel myself blushing and didn't know what to say. Later, responses that were not quite lies came to me. I could have said, "No, because I'm nursing a baby." Why hadn't I said that? I could have said, "Sometimes." This was true. In the past I had fasted for a day or two of Ramadan, just to see what it felt like. But somehow what popped out was: "No, because I'm Christian."

Was I even that, despite the fact that I had never been baptized, just because it was the religion of my parents? This has always been an easier answer: to claim membership in one of the religions of the Book. And then to launch into my very true spiel about how I think Islam is also a beautiful religion, and how I'm particularly attracted to the ways of the Sufis. Some Sufis understand this. Most Moroccan Muslims don't.

Jamila was just returning as the *muqqadima*'s anger was building. I could almost see her glasses steaming up.

"She shouldn't be in here! She's a *nasrania*, a Christian!"

Jamila tried to defend me, saying that I was in the middle of finding my path, that her son and I were raising our daughter as a Muslim. But the *muqqadima* was furious.

"No Christians allowed!" she said. She started telling stories about how infidel interlopers had tried to invade the sanctity of the shrine before, just to get in and spy on them. She and Jamila were both talking at the same time, Jamila invoking passages from the Qur'an about openness to the faiths of the Book. Was Sidi Bou Ghalib a mosque? Who made the rule that no Christian was allowed, if this place wasn't even a mosque to begin with?

Sofia, awakened by the arguing, began to cry.

"I just wanted to feel the *baraka* of the saint," I argued, trying to bounce and soothe my daughter. "I'd like to be Muslim, but I'm not convinced."

"Well," said the *muqqadima*, "you need to go to the Qarawiyyin mosque and find someone there who will talk to you. I don't know how to convince you." Jamila told me to give her money. I hurriedly shoved some dirhams into her outstretched palms. We left. I was shaken.

Improbably, Rachida followed us out. She patted me on the back and said not to worry, that the *muqqadima* was just a crank trying to line her pockets with donations. We walked for a while with her, and she continued to chatter. She gave us her phone number, though I couldn't understand why. I knew Jamila would never call her. At some point we shook her off. Jamila scolded me for telling them I was Christian. I tried to explain that I had wanted to be straightforward.

It wasn't a mosque; I knew Moroccans didn't want non-Muslims in mosques—except for the gigantic Hassan II mosque in Casablanca, the second-largest in the world, which you could enter for a fee. The tomb was either *shirk* or a holy place, depending on where you sat. If it was *shirk,* why did it matter that I was there?

Suddenly Jamila ducked into another doorway and pulled me in with her. It happened so quickly that I was taken off guard. We were halfway through the opulently carpeted space when she announced: "Sofia is going to visit Moulay Idriss."

Moulay Idriss founded Fes in 808. Was he therefore also *shirk,* like Sidi Bou Ghalib, and should we really be visiting anyone's tomb at this point? I had never been in here. I had no head scarf. There were hundreds of people milling about, men and women both, though probably five times as many women as men. Plenty of them had no head scarves. Some looked like they were not Moroccans but tourists from other parts of the Muslim world. The tomb was in a corner, to one side of a gigantic, red-carpeted interior next to an elaborate courtyard facing the sky. Jamila went to a corner, prayed, and lifted Sofia up to the tomb to touch the cloth while I tried to remain unobtrusive, watching our possessions. Then she handed Sofia back to me and got involved in a discussion with some other women. At one point a woman walked over to me, plucked Sofia from my arms, and started kissing her. This happened a lot in Morocco, but I still wasn't used to it. This time when the stranger grabbed her, I felt like someone was ripping out my soul. I was desperate to leave—where were the tomb authorities here? I would say anything if they talked to me, even *la ilaha ila Allah* (there is no God but Allah), converting on the spot. If someone tried to take Sofia away from me, I swear I would do anything. But I didn't feel right being here. I snatched my baby back from the woman, who had stepped just a few feet too far away for comfort, and tugged at Jamila's sleeve and told her we needed to go.

It was obvious that I wasn't going to be able to do my research on the role of saints' tombs in women's fertility practices unless a seismic shift took place: my conversion to Islam. So what was holding me back? I have always been both attracted to and confused by Islam. The abstract beauty and mystery of the Qur'an. The poems of Sufis, whose vision of God as both infinite love and the incomprehensible being our souls long to unite with, is something I could accept. Muslims have ninety-nine names for God, many of which are also attributes of goodness in the world: compassion, strength, justice, and so on. So why is it not enough to say that God is in these attributes, that the attributes themselves are God?

In the year after college when I studied Sufis, many people seemed to be willing to engage me this far in my assertions, particularly in Turkey. There I saw other things I liked: groups of educated men and women who met to discuss God as an instrument of social justice, sing the mystic Rumi's poems, and play traditional Turkish instruments. The mystical whirling of the dervishes in the Halveti-Jerrahi *tekke,* or dervish lodge, in Istanbul, a performance that was not a show put on for tourists but a weekly ritual, the dervishes pivoting on slipper-clad feet, their robes spinning out from their bodies like birds' wings. There were moments when I got so close to belief that I could see, in the right atmosphere, a place for myself in Sufi Islam: in Cyprus, for example, fifteen years ago, when I met the *shaykh* of the Naqshbandis in a tiny Mediterranean village—a charismatic man with a long white beard and twinkling blue eyes, who knew details about who I was without my even telling him. Like the best Sufis, he presented religious lessons in aphorisms that were easy to remember, even years later: *Islam is the sea on which the boat of Sufism floats. The shaykh keeps his eyes on his followers, no matter where they are in the world. He has "remote control."* I did the silent *dhikr* with the women of the Naqshbandis, all of us meditating on those ninety-nine names of God, thumbing sandalwood prayer beads, and chanting in the inner spaces of our minds. For a time I even tried praying and could carry myself into its meditative aspects, the feel of my head touching the carpet, the direct appeal to God through the *sura al-Fatiha,* the opening chapter of the Qur'an. All those years ago, it made sense.

But all this was before I became an anthropologist. Since then, these moments have been few and far between. Beyond God's abstract qualities, conversion would require that I begin to follow the rules. Rising before dawn to pray, repeating the prayer five times, covering yourself from head to toe, even when you're alone with God and there is nobody else to see you. Defending the faith against attacks, even when you're not quite convinced yourself. How, as an American feminist, would I explain polygamy? How would I get beyond the fact that women can't participate in prayer or fasting when they are menstruating? Look it up on the web: you'll find numerous discourses either arguing that women are weak and need their strength while menstruating, or that women are unclean, but neither of these answers makes me want to convert. And why are there different requirements for different faiths more generally, if they are all accepted by Islam as "of the book?" If the other faiths are all accepted by God, in a manner of speaking, then why do Moroccans insist on my conversion?

Sometimes, in the right circumstances, talking to the right learned scholar of Islam, I get answers that satisfy me. Then I think perhaps I could do this. And then I would be admitted to the tomb of Sidi Bou Whoever and could pray alongside the women there, could return again and again until I knew the regulars and being there became second nature to me.

But then I reach the second impasse: what conversion would mean for me as an anthropologist. Practicing the religion of the people you are "studying" smacks of the age-old prohibition against "going native." Despite the rallying cry of the crisis-of-representation-era-anthropologists that the walls of objectivity have come tumbling down, there are still implicit taboos, boundaries not to be crossed. You would think that one of these forbidden areas might be sex, yet it seems to be acceptable to date, marry, and have children with people you meet "in the field." Sex with informants sounds unethical, containing tinges of exploitation, but even that line is blurred depending on how you define the relationship.[4] If your significant other, whom you meet in the field (and who occasionally tells you crucial information about the culture), becomes your spouse, perhaps it is acceptable.[5] But religion seems to be the last bastion of separation between self and other. Certainly, we have our documented stories of anthropologists temporarily losing their minds in peyote trances or after the persuasive manipulations of shamans.[6] These instances, as Paul Stoller (1989) reminds us in his own account of sorcery in West Africa, get relegated to barroom conversations, and if they enter anthropological scholarship, then a certain distancing happens: analysis transforms experience into a discussion of others' realities, which are real to them and subsequently can make things happen—to them. What remains is the very real taboo against going native in matters of religion. But is this simply a holdover from the days when anthropology was closely associated with colonialism, and colonizers and anthropologists saw themselves as bringing science or faith or civilization to the natives while studying the myths of those whose lands they occupied?

I have American friends who are religious scholars and have converted to the faiths they study, but nobody in their field raises an outcry. In fact, when I told a philosopher colleague about my experience at the saint's tomb, she asked me,

"Why not just convert?"

If only it were that simple.

Katherine Ewing, in a compelling essay titled "Dreams from a Saint: Anthropological Atheism and the Tendency to Believe" (1994), writes of her uncanny nocturnal encounters with a Sufi saint while she was conducting research in Pakistan, and of the dreams that tested her own sense of our disciplinary boundaries. Exploring psychoanalytic and Sufi interpretations of her dreams, she acknowledges that accepting those Sufi interpretations would entail a radical rupture with the anthropologist's deeply ingrained interpretive frameworks. She concludes that despite professing a stance of cultural relativism, or a desire to acknowledge the validity and reality of our informants' life worlds, the anthropological community as a whole has ruled out the possibility of belief. Anthropological atheism, though difficult to overcome, is a major obstacle to the understanding and acceptance of us by the people among whom we conduct research. Moroccanist ethnographies, despite being in the vanguard of experimental and reflexive ethnographies from the 1970s through the 1990s, do not contain metaphysical encounters that seriously question the foundations of the anthropologist's belief systems, or lack thereof (ibid. 573). Ewing mentions Clifford Geertz's famous statement that the ethnographer should attempt to seek middle ground between "village atheist" and "village preacher," but she adds that one anthropologist, on returning to Sefrou, found that at least one local regarded Geertz as more of an "atheist outsider" (ibid.).

The anthropological literature on religion in Morocco still remains distant from its object. Few works wrestle with the question of belief, with the possible exception of Abdellah Hammoudi's *A Season in Mecca* (2006), which trains its analytical gaze on how fellow Moroccan pilgrims on the hajj interact with the global community of Muslims (as well as the Saudi nation-state) and on Hammoudi's tensions with the faith and his own position as both an insider and an outsider. But other works in the canon document religion as spectacle, whether studying trance and possession, the efficacy of ritual, or the more formal structure of the brotherhoods. There are the staid, sober brotherhoods of the elite and the frenetically possessed gatherings of the masses. Even Edward Westermarck's voluminous *Ritual and Belief in Morocco* (1926) spends most of its time not interrogating what God means to people, but chronicling ritual acts and localized superstitions. As for women, aside from older articles by Fatima Mernissi (1977) and Daisy Dwyer (1978), we have very little writing on women's participation, particularly in Sufism. Nor are there works that describe any researcher's attempts to study rituals or belief as an insider might, by giving oneself over to them.

Does this refusal (or inability) to fully participate in the lives of the people we study in matters of religion limit our ability to attain knowledge? How is this taboo challenged by "native" anthropologists, who are already members of religious faiths that they may also be studying?[7] Might a more open approach to belief bring us back to one of the original hallmarks of anthropological endeavor, that of comparison? In the old days of anthropology, comparison seemed to be about either finding our common humanity or pointing out differences that made us culturally unique. But a true comparison of religious beliefs could do more than that. It could highlight the very taken-for-granted prejudices we still bring to the field about the superiority of our own cultural traditions—whether those traditions are of scientific objectivity rooted in outsider atheism, or of a Judeo-Christian framework that we are, for some reason, still unable to discard.

Would conversion truly make me an insider? I doubt it. But to me, acknowledging my inability to convert to the religion of my husband and daughter (and thus open myself up to new anthropological spaces that I could then study) is loaded with baggage that is both professional and personal: religion is culturally specific, and I am a product of my own culture. It is not a question of culture in broad brush strokes—that is, Moroccan versus American. Even in my own country I would have a difficult time adopting a belief system in which some other American has been raised since birth. First of all, there would be the issue of finding a community of fellow believers with whom I have something in common. In Morocco, local aspects of Islam come with other contexts: the people who profess belief in the powers of the saint would not be the same kind of people as my in-laws, who follow a more modernist, textual version of the religion. To convert would not suddenly open me up to an imagined community of Sufi love poetry enthusiasts and trance dancers, which is probably a part of the Orientalist fantasy that attracts me. Rather, conversion would entail being fair to the orthodoxy of the people I know best in Morocco, practicing the five pillars of Islam even while my mind roils with questions and doubts that remain unanswered. The local Muslims I know back in Florida are either fairly conservative or completely nonobservant. I have met many Western converts, particularly women, but most of them have also adopted gender ideologies at odds with those in which I have been raised. These communities would be my options for local *ummas*,[8] not the group of women gathered at the tomb of Sidi Bou Whoever in search of *baraka*. And I would still be an outsider.

In addition to the problem of finding community, another cultural issue lies in the very complex nature of religion and belief itself. Belief is so deeply internalized that it remains like breathing or mother love, things felt that are impossible to describe. To ask "Moroccan religion," if I can even make so broad a generalization, to bend itself to my will and desires as a seeker or as an ethnographer is an insult to whatever that religion may be. Even within one country the multiple ways of addressing God depend on where one stands—on one's social class, gender, generation, and level of education. Is God an abstract force, a prime mover, a justification for the domination of one group over another, or a father figure whom, in a patriarchal society, one should never dare to question? As I have found through the years in my stubborn efforts to ask Moroccans to translate belief into idioms that I could understand, translation remains impossible, just as it is difficult for anyone to objectify something that has been internalized so deeply throughout an entire lifetime. I have no idea how the women at Sidi Bou Ghalib would conceptualize a religion that they've internalized since birth.

Stepping into a religion as an adult is not the same thing as donning a caftan for a wedding, learning to cook couscous properly, or marrying and having children with a Moroccan. Or is it? Some Moroccans have assured me that faith will come through repetition, through the repeat performance of prayer and other ritual acts. Just *say* the *shahada,* the profession of faith; just *do* Ramadan; just *pray,* and the rest will follow. But I doubt that my doubts would simply melt away. Even if I converted, my experience of living the religion could never be Moroccan, because I am not Moroccan and can't erase the years in which my own cultural sense of religion has been so deeply imprinted onto me. So, although professionally and personally I might like uncertainty to melt away while I imbibe the *baraka* of the saint, the more I know about Morocco, the more I realize that this is never going to happen. I'm embarrassed that I continued to cling for so long to the vague Orientalist fantasy that my ultimate rendezvous with a saint would somehow be transformative. But in a way, perhaps it was. Sidi Bou Ghalib's *baraka* was not be enough to open up the mysteries of the universe, or even Moroccan religious expression, but it did cause me to reflect on how complex the issue of religion in Moroccan society still is. What I am certain of is that most Moroccans are not of one mind about Sidi Bou Ghalib's powers either. At least there is consolation in realizing that many of the Moroccans I know would feel just as uncomfortable lounging around the tomb of Sidi Bou Ghalib as I ultimately did. And this fact alone tells us that there is still much to be learned.

NOTES

1. Most Moroccan cities are divided into two sections: the medina, the Arab quarter that existed prior to French colonization (1912–56); and the Ville Nouvelle, the new city that the French built close to or at a slight remove from the medina.

2. In Moroccan Arabic, a *fqih* is often a self-designated religious scholar who writes Qur'anic verses for protective and magical uses.

3. Most Muslims consider tattooing to be *haram* (forbidden by Islam), based on a *hadith* (a saying of the Prophet). In Morocco, the practice, largely confined to rural areas and women of older generations, is dying out.

4. Invariably, when my students read the Rabinow classic that supposedly opened the floodgates for discussions of the conditions under which we practice our craft, *Reflections on Fieldwork in Morocco* (2007 [1977]), they ask what made it commendable for this giant of anthropology to have sex with a Berber prostitute and even to be celebrated for his openness?

5. The taboo of the ethnographer's sexuality has been explored compellingly in Kulick and Wilson (1995).

6. There are some wonderful works that deal with this question. See, for example, Stoller and Olkes (1989); Favret-Saada (1981); Apffel-Marglin (2008).

7. In a very compelling essay describing her own problems with this issue, Frédérique Apffel-Marglin observes that in addition to not questioning the religious beliefs of native Hindus, Muslims, and so on, anthropologists don't accuse "fellow citizens" who convert to Christianity or Judaism of "going native" in matters of religion; rather, this applies only to those who "adopt a practice they have not inherited by birth, and that is not of Western origin" (2008, 25).

8. The *umma* is one's local community of Muslims or, more generally, the entire community of Muslims worldwide.

8 | Shortcomings of a Reflexive Tool Kit; or, Memoir of an Undutiful Daughter

JAMILA BARGACH

THE SETTING

Bougainvilleas of multiple colors—burgundy, yellow, rose, and white—draped the walls of what seemed to be a timeless corner villa and separated it from the small streets paved with a puzzle, hard bricks that made a funny buzzing sound when cars drove on them. Past imposing metal doors, a tiny cemented walkway led up the stairs to the inside of this art-deco villa where there was practically no garden, except for the branches of the bougainvilleas shooting outside. This was the main headquarters of the nongovernmental organization (NGO) Solidarité Féminine, SolFem for short. The villa had been built around the 1940s in the colonial period, in the heart of what was then French-bourgeois Casablanca, a neighborhood called Palmiers in reference to its lush vegetation of flowers and all types of trees, chief among which were its sizable palms. But Palmiers has fallen on hard times. Today, this once-prestigious and sophisticated neighborhood has turned into a crumbling, gloomy environment of decrepit villas, practically all of which have been condemned to death—some a sacrificial gift to hungry bulldozers and truck loaders at the service of ever-greedy promoters, others the victims of time and neglect. Some villas continue to be occupied, but all life is under siege within their walls. The streets are only a place of transition now, a place of passing through, because of the fear of aggression and theft.

Palmiers is a sort of *terra non grata* between the chic and the throbbing heart of Casablanca and Derb Ghellaf, one of the most infamous neighborhoods in the city, with extremely high density (mostly young people), high crime rates, drug trafficking, and the dangers attached to a general state of permanent delinquency. Though policed, Derb Ghellaf youth cruise neighboring quarters of the city and are often spotted smoking joints, drinking alcohol, and kissing or trying to have sex under porches in Palmiers, or squatting inside long-forsaken gardens. SolFem was able to afford this location because it was in the heart of a run-down neighborhood full of vacant villas that no longer functioned as a community. But its location was also a strategic choice. Here SolFem's activities are not likely to disturb conservative, bourgeois ethics, and the organization may be more accessible to the type of clients it serves.

SolFem was created in the 1980s by the extremely charismatic Aicha Chenna with two related missions: to fight child abandonment and to help promote a dignified life for unwed mothers and their offspring. A few words are necessary here to illustrate the boldness of Chenna's initiative. Today having a child out of wedlock in Morocco (regardless of the circumstances) is still considered one of the most heinous crimes that a woman may commit. Sex outside the marriage is considered religiously and legally as *zina* (illegal fornication)—which, under clauses 495–97 of the Moroccan Penal Code, is punishable by up to three years in prison. Second, by having a child out of wedlock, the woman dishonors not only herself but her entire family—which is considered as much, if not more, at fault than the woman—and often her ties to the family are subsequently severed. Last of all, the child born under these conditions suffers from negative stereotypes and treatments as she or he carries the terrible stigma of bastardy. Although the living situations of these women may take multiple forms (depending on such factors as age, place of origin, social class and status, and place of residency), once they are faced with an unwanted pregnancy, their condition generally shifts into awful uncertainty, fear, and precariousness as they have to flee, hide, and fend for themselves. In addition to the dire material aspects of what becomes a complex life, each of them has to deal with the trauma of betrayal, guilt, and shame. They suffer nightmarish worries about the destiny of the child to come and the deeply unsettling nature of what they are supposed to feel toward and do with these babies. All of these feelings occur within a social context that often treats the women with utter disdain and judges them only as offenders who deserve their lot.

Against this somber backdrop, a ray of light and hope arose with the work of Aicha Chenna. A woman in her early sixties today—a sort of Mother Theresa, as some journalists have labeled her—Chenna is presented (and presents herself) as the archetypal mother: caring, altruistic, gentle, generous, and exuding love and warmth. As a social worker in the late 1970s, she often witnessed the painful separation between unwed mothers and their children born out of wedlock, but there was one case that prompted her, as she said, to "do something, whatever, but something." This pivotal moment happened when a nurse snatched a nursing baby from its mother's breast, and the milk shot out and hit Chenna in the face. Forty years later, she still feels the warmth of the milk that symbolically transformed her, and the memory continues to motivate her.

In the bureaucratic and heavily suspicious environment of Morocco in the 1980s, Chenna dared to open a small center in the basement of a villa in what used to be the northernmost and poorest suburb of Casablanca, Ain Seba^c. With private funds, she set up a small food-producing company and paid unwed mothers to work there, giving them a source of livelihood that allowed them to keep their children. Chenna, together with a group of supporters who subsequently became a governing board, emerged from the Ain Seba^c basement and acquired the villa in Palmiers, where they created a professional pastry-production unit, a day care center, and a legal and psychological counseling center for the women. They also worked to secure shared-rent housing for the women in Derb Ghellaf, the crime-ridden neighborhood nearby. SolFem slowly became a beacon for equity and women's rights, and by the mid-1990s—as Morocco started to experience relative political freedom and a strong civil society began to emerge—the NGO became firmly established. By the beginning of the twenty-first century, it had purchased the original Ain Seba*c* facility, opened a lunch cafeteria in the Palmiers villa, and started running a catering service within the Casablanca hospital system. After a widely publicized visit by Princess Lalla Selma, the new wife of the newly enthroned King Mohammed VI, SolFem became a household name and was further legitimized by a generous gift from the king. Now SolFem manages multiple businesses, the latest being a traditional *hammam* (steam bath) and a spa.

One morning in October 2002, at 9:00—very early for a day in Ramadan—I took a taxi to the main avenue adjacent to the narrow, deserted streets where SolFem was housed. There was a sluggishness in the air that is very characteristic of Ramadan. Once I entered the building, I encountered mixed smells of honey, frying oil, anise, and sesame seeds lingering from the standard Ramadan menus made and sold the day before. The main room that served as the lunch restaurant was deserted, with the chairs stacked on the tables and pushed haphazardly into different corners. The floor was slippery, heated voices came from the kitchen, and the screams of children filled the air. I felt a sort of estrangement as I saw myself walking in this place, not really knowing how to carry out the mission I was entrusted with. I felt—and this feeling would be confirmed in my work with the unwed mothers—that the place was filled with a heavy sense of sadness and anger, as well as guilt. I tried to squelch my uneasiness and proceed rationally, but I continued with the awkward feeling inherent to situations in which the cues are mixed. In the end it seemed that the colorful bougainvilleas at the perimeter were the most agreeable and comforting sight this place had to offer.

THE ASSIGNMENT

I had just been hired as a consultant to evaluate the counseling center for unwed mothers at SolFem by one of its German funding agencies. This is routine work in this type of environment: funders need to know that the money they give is indeed being spent where it should be, and that the work is meeting the norms and goals that the funders initially set up for the institution. This evaluation was simply considered a sort of administrative follow-up task. At this point, there was no tormented questioning or concerns about whether the model proposed was good or bad, or even whether a model should have been proposed in the first place; there was a total ignorance of that model's surreptitiously coercive nature. My assignment was taken for granted: money is given to support a project, and results need to be evaluated. Period.

The way the administrative structure of SolFem operated at the time reflected the organization's growing pains. There were two main sections. First was a Center for the Support of Mothers in Situations of Distress, whose role was to receive, listen, and counsel the mothers in situations of distress and then orient them toward external or internal resources. The second section was a Program for Rehabilitation via Education and Training, which carried out and supervised the training program alternating between cooking, pastry, massage, sewing, and so forth, depending on the aptitude of the mothers. The mission of the rehabilitation program was also to work on creating and reinforcing mother-child ties. (There was also a human resource department, as well as the governing board, but I will not discuss those components here.)

My job as a consultant had two main aims. First, I was to examine the performance of the counseling center and evaluate whether the goal established at the onset of the funding had been attained in its entirety or, if not, how much of the goal had been attained. Second, I was to assess the ways in which the work at the center promoted gender equality as a whole within Morocco. The means of inquiry were left up to me, but my procedure and evaluation needed to be scientific. There was, undoubtedly, a highly normative aspect to this work that I was not familiar with at the time, especially drawing conclusions based on the use of quantitative and qualitative tools such as statistics, indicators, and life narratives obtained by interviews with the clients. With the possible exception of the life narratives, the other tools remain essentially problematic for anthropologists with my sort of training because they reduce the complexities and nuances of life experiences to simple concepts and/or numbers that are supposed to be all-encompassing.

After a decade in the United States, I had returned to Morocco a couple of years earlier, and I still thought with nostalgia about the classes I had taken in the United States. I was fresh from Rice University's Department of Anthropology, which, though not the first to call attention to the complex relationships between anthropology and its subject, is the entity to have been officially identified in the mid-1980s with the "crisis of representation" much publicized through the books *Anthropology as Cultural Critique* (Marcus and Fischer 1986) and *Writing Culture* (Clifford and Marcus 1986). The crisis emerged as the discipline shifted away from positivist models. Questions about the nature and production of knowledge became a major focus in cultural and social anthropology. In the graduate seminars and classes I took at Rice, we were, among other things, particularly attuned to the nature of the anthropological gaze; questions of hard, "scientific" language; and the way anthropological arguments are constructed. We often focused on how relationships are established between ethnographic fieldwork, data, and theory.

I spent eight years of my life working, reading, and evolving within the crisis of representation, exploring the tormented politics of anthropology and the colonial enterprise, and I realized that anthropology was not always put to noble uses. We learned that it was just a fallacy to think that, as anthropologists, we could be objective judges, or that we held the higher moral ground. We learned to be wary of "evaluating" the "other." We were often reminded to be aware of the "self" that does the evaluating, to understand that the anthropologist is not simply an observer akin to a researcher in a hard science laboratory, but the product of a culture, and her or his gaze is culturally mediated. Now, at SolFem, I was suddenly wearing a new hat that didn't match anything I'd learned. Like an undutiful daughter, I was cutting myself off from (or was I betraying?) my intellectual lineage, judging a service rendered, and doing so "scientifically" (whatever that meant!). It was now my job to assess with indicators and indices a much larger movement of "gender development" meant to promote a reformed society.

All of these elements were anathema to me. This was the privileged domain of sociologists, yet deep down I was mortified. I kept asking myself why I had accepted this assignment, what had motivated my choice. This essay is an attempt to formulate a commentary on this bewildering experience and to reconstruct, in retrospect, the effects and affects of this deeply personal reflexive moment, but it is also intended to be a reflexive exercise as it relates to anthropology.

As I walked into SolFem on this particular morning, there were twenty-one young, unwed mothers whose only common denominator was that they were caught with an unwanted and unplanned pregnancy outside established legal and social norms. Most of the women who could afford an illegal abortion never made it to SolFem, and the statistics showed that it was the poorest uneducated teenagers and young women who became the clients of this NGO. Once admitted, most of them worked at the restaurant after dropping their babies off at the day-care center in the basement, where other mothers like themselves tended to the babies. All of these young women had had extremely traumatic experiences, had a myriad of unresolved issues, and had been rejected by their own kin for "cultural" reasons. For me this was not culture as a text, as Clifford Geertz's famous phrase has it, but young women mad with suffering and confusion, some believing wholeheartedly what their society told them they were and convinced that their culture had given them just what they deserved. A very few others were angry, even furious, rejecting the label their society gave them and looking to debunk the social hypocrisy. They argued, and rightly so, that it was unfair to punish them and not the men who were equally responsible.

In an environment such as SolFem, the relationship between the unwed mothers, idiomatically referred to as "clients," and the staff members followed a clear class divide. The clients were from poorer social strata, while the staff members were typically from the middle or upper-middle class. The language divide was equally clear, with

Moroccan Darija (and sometimes Berber) as the language of the clients and French the tongue of the staff members. I was, of course, identified with the administration by the clients, as I spoke French and worked directly with the social workers. Clients would identify me as the *ustada* (the professor), and most of their conversations had one of two leitmotifs: they were victimized or they asked for forgiveness. In either case, their choice of words and phrases clearly indicated the feelings of guilt that haunted them. They truly believed that they had sinned and thus they assumed that, like many others they had met before, I was judging them. Blame was a condition they had grown familiar with; they'd witnessed it in all different shapes and colors and in many different forms. Inherent to my talking with them was a pronounced inequality, but I made a conscious effort to avoid talking down to them or harboring prejudices. They often wanted to be absolved, as if I had the power to offer them redemption, but they also denigrated the NGO and railed against the staff. Although their critiques emanated from their hurt or from what they perceived to be unjust treatment, their comments had the potential of cutting off the flow of funds to the association. Ironically, these young women, whether they knew it or not, held a power that could be wielded as a form of sabotage.

THE ARGUMENT

I came to this new consulting job with an analytical background that mistrusted the language of objectivity and objectivism and favored relativism, situated knowledge, historical grounding, and partial facts. I believed in relativist approaches. I favored interpretive methods and was open to the evocation, the fragment, and the memory as much as to the myriad literary methods of analysis, from conceits to symbols. But I was also very much aware that these were incarnated lives and that there were varying schemes that motivated individuals in their different worlds.

This "reflexive tool kit"—however empowering, however often it had yielded ethical and politically responsible, significant, or aware ethnographies—required me to reposition myself in ways that were extremely painful and intellectually challenging. To complicate matters, I was certainly animated by my own ideologies. I was a feminist, and I believed staunchly that society should grant equal legal rights to men and women. I worked in many other venues to promote gender equality.

Now I had to judge, to evaluate a service, grade it either good or bad, and measure a "movement" of gender equality. These goals were in utter contradiction with what I've called the reflexive tool kit; they assumed there was a standard norm for determining whether or not something works. But the main questions from my training would be: *Where does the norm come from? Who sets up these norms?* My assignment also presupposed that a movement can be adequately measured via numbers and statistics, but those were ethical issues that concerned structuring values that were highly abstract and difficult to render in the language of a mathematical equation. The stakes were totally different from an academic approach to ethnographic writing. How, then, was I to do my assignment?

Despite my aporia, I had to proceed through what I perceived to be a minefield. On the one hand, I had to convince myself that the "scientific" tools had their role, even if they were not capable of yielding a single truth. On the other hand, I had to limit my interpretive relativism. How could I do this while allowing for the voice of an individual for whom trauma is at the heart of experience? Ethically it could not simply be dismissed or discounted. The reality of the women's pain and the ways in which it was attached to the deep social structures in place captured my attention. In reviewing the existing literature concerning birth outside marriage in Morocco, I found that the corporal intricacies of human experience were often diluted because of the legal and administrative obsession with finding a solution.

After the first month of this inquiry, I asked the funding agency why they had chosen an anthropologist for this specific project. Their answer was unassuming and straightforward: they wanted statistical data as well as the "lived" experience. An anthropologist could deliver on both counts, while a sociologist tended to favor the data.

The agency wanted a "balanced" representation, given the precarious and unstable situation of the young women. Moreover, and perhaps more revealingly, associations and funding agencies are quite aware of the vehement criticisms of them as agents of moral decadence by conservative and religious extremists, who argue that this type of work in fact encourages debauchery and illegitimacy. Balanced reports combining narratives (heart-wrenching ones, at that) and numbers helped offset these sorts of criticisms.

FIRST ENCOUNTERS

My first encounter with the counseling center involved two social workers.

"It is a matter of chance; the group of young unwed mothers come and go. One may in a year find a 'nice' (*driyef*) batch and the next a 'not-so-nice' (*mashi-driyef*) one," the social worker said after I asked her how easily the women related their traumatic experiences.

"What is 'nice'?" I asked, incredulous. What could this norm called "nice" be in such a context? From this moment on, our exchange was fraught with suspicion. I realized eventually that the social workers played an odd game with me: when one was forthcoming, the other was critical or almost hostile, and then vice versa, as if they were playing "good cop, bad cop."

My first encounter with Oumnia, an unwed mother:

> Everyone can encounter problems in their lives [in other words, *I am not the only one*], but you know we were really, really engaged [*there is a social legitimacy to my sexual encounter with my boyfriend*], but he gave me pills and I was asleep when he did what he did [*I am not really responsible, he betrayed me, I am a victim beyond my will and consciousness*], and now it is really his mother who is creating problems [*there is a future dénouement to my ordeal, my precariousness and status of offender is temporary, and my normal life will resume*]. Ustada? [Do you understand?]

With the exception of a couple of young women, most of the others had stories that resembled or combined elements of Oumnia's tale. These were moments fraught with suppositions as their very being in SolFem largely determined their tales. They were here because they had a problem and needed a solution, and the counseling center was supposed to fulfill such a function.

These first encounters were important moments in that they gave me the larger frame that would, more or less, define most of the ensuing exchanges. The social workers' approach to the work was reduced to its most functional aspect: A young woman came in, she was asked to lay out the bare facts, and then much thinking would go into considering the choices available given the inherent constraints. What were the most advantageous contingencies possible? The outcome was delivered in an incisive, matter-of-fact, businesslike manner that, on a purely human level, was galling for me, given the trauma these women had suffered.

Most of the proposed solutions and mediations (which, of course, would take a long time to reach) were about "regularizing"—that is, getting the young women married or, if that was impossible, making sure the child was granted an identity. In essence, by working so diligently toward this outcome, the social workers were validating the venue of marriage as the ideal solution while further incriminating their clients for having sex outside of marriage. For a feminist this was infuriating, not least because unconsciously valorizing marriage in such a way was a reproduction of a patriarchal model that these women would be forced to fight on other fronts.

Through the accounts of the women, I could, in part, judge the service of the counseling center and gauge the extent to which these young women in SolFem had been transformed into "different subjects"— that is, into individuals conscious of their situations and of the options they would have to choose from. I had to listen to their litany of complaints about how they were used and exploited. Most of them were angry and in pain. The pain concerned not only their situation, but also the confused feelings they had toward their babies. They were angry that SolFem's procedures were often very slow and that their own aspirations or specific requests had no room in these dry, formulaic processes. The majority of the women felt that what the social workers did was effective, but their cold efficiency doubled the women's sense of guilt, heightening their sensitivity to the position they now found themselves in as compared to their previous lives. They were still being judged. What had they learned from being in SolFem? "Yes, we learn how to do things, but that is all," one of them told me. In essence, while there was a technical or manual competence involved in the directions they were given, these young women still did not understand the very nature of their marginalization or possess any feeling of empowerment. They complained about working hard, but each one of them was caught in her own world of pain and oblivious to her neighbor's problems. There was no venue to address the pain as a collective trauma or as a collective problem, which in some aspects it certainly was. How could I pretend to measure "gender equality" in the microcosm that is SolFem, let alone Moroccan society as a whole? The task seemed daunting, to say the least.

Each year about four or five consultants like me visit the counseling center. The social workers at SolFem had become proficient in various ways of dealing with consultants, from sophisticated indifference to effective expediency. They had developed a working method, as they said. They claimed that they had mastered all legal and administrative matters, family traditions and relations, and so forth concerning the unwed mothers, as well as techniques to influence or bring about change within all of these vital social and affective domains. When the unwed mothers came to SolFem, they were largely imprisoned in all kinds of fears and were prey to false hopes. The social workers saw their role as revealing what they called the "real" options available to these young women, even if they had to be "tough"—"because that is the language they [the women] can understand." As a consultant, I was concerned with only a single issue: the social workers' performance. I did not truly understand the complex reality in which the unwed mothers existed. If I were to calculate the social workers' rate of success—success meaning cases where a tangible solution had been found and implemented—I would say they were doing well, when I compared the number of women coming into the center and the solutions provided for them. However, if I were to judge the quality of the service—that is, how the service was rendered, the position that the unwed mothers occupied at the center—then the social workers were failing. Based on their experience, the social workers claimed that "what the unwed mothers choose to tell you is something you can't control, but you can only give them answers to what they tell you." Given what I witnessed in SolFem, they were right. Still, there was a sense in which this cold-hearted efficiency and domineering sort of paternalism was so contrary to my personal sensitivities, my beliefs as a feminist, and what I considered the NGO's noble mission that I found myself morally incapable of *not* judging, a volte-face from my initial positioning. But as time passed and I got used to SolFem and the multiple layers of interactions there, I started to discern how things could indeed be measured and how nuanced the act of judging could be.

APEX AND DÉNOUEMENT

I conducted individual interviews with the young women and organized a focus group exploring their imagination of the future. My selection of this theme—the future—came after much thought on how I could best understand what they had learned at SolFem, how they envisioned themselves in the future, and to what extent they could be (or not be) channels for greater gender equality within the country at large. As part of the evaluation process, I sat in a corner of the office during the interviews and noted how the question-and-answer sessions were conducted. Then I compared the individual interviews with the agreement signed between SolFem and the German funding agency I was working for—and with my personal beliefs about what constitutes good manners and what professional standards might be. As noted above, I was aware that these young women could easily sabotage the work of the counseling center. I also knew that the funding agency and Moroccans might have different definitions of "efficiency" and "professionalism." I was also very acutely aware that my own standards were "urban bourgeois," as I was reminded once by the social workers, and could in no way be the measure I should use to judge their work. But with these constraints, no effective evaluation could be performed, and yet an evaluation had to be concluded. In the end, my choice was based on three "objective" criteria: the efficacy in orienting the client, the expediency of the services rendered, and the manner in which the orientation was delivered.

One morning in Ramadan, I took my position in the back of the office, behind the two social workers who were working that day. The atmosphere was already tense, and it was only 10:00. Women came in either to ask for legal advice or to apply to be admitted to SolFem. The counseling center received them, so when they entered the office they really didn't know who was who (I told the social workers to introduce me, but I got only a shrug in response). I pulled my American clipboard out, and, as I adjusted the paper, a young woman came in. She stank to high heaven, and her djellaba was in shreds. She was no more than seventeen, and she carried a bundle that contained a newborn child. She collapsed in the chair and said that she had given birth just three days earlier. She had run away from the hospital and come to SolFem for help. One of the social workers asked her many questions about the biological father, her family, where she had resided during her pregnancy, and what she intended to do with the child, jotting down the information. Then she asked the young woman to step outside. The two social workers consulted for a while, called other organizations, and eventually found a vacancy in a Christian shelter located in another part of town. They called the young woman back in and told her with no preliminaries to take bus number 33 on the main avenue outside the villa and be sure to get to the shelter within three hours, or she would miss this "golden opportunity." They added that she could come back to the center after a few days, so that they could help her get some identity papers for her baby boy.

It was true that they had dealt with the woman efficiently, and they now proceeded to the next case. But I thought that their directions were not all that precise, and I wondered how this young woman, not a native of Casablanca, could find her way in this metropolitan maze. I had to continue my observations of the social workers, though, and I told myself that if the young woman had been able to find SolFem in the first place, she'd manage. The next morning, as I stood by the office door waiting to make a copy of a paper, I overheard one of the social workers say that the young woman had never made it to the shelter and "in*al dinumha ila rj*at u khdinaha, khaliha tmut*" (literally, "May God damn her mother if we take her in were she to return; let her die"; idiomatically, "Fuck her if she thinks we can take her in the NGO; let her die").

This was stated with such intense hate, contempt, and biting cynicism that I automatically stepped into the office and stared at her, incredulous; my jaw must have dropped quite obviously. All of a sudden it became clear to me that what mattered more to this social worker was that the work was done; the human beings for whom services were to be provided were apparently of no consequence. The social worker said "let her die" because she felt that the young woman had not respected what the social worker had done or taken her advice. The work she was doing was about her words, efforts, and directions, not about the unwed mother or the baby. The social worker held the truth—"mastered the reality," as both social workers were fond of saying—while the client had no voice, no say, nothing but the void and the road map the social worker made for her.

How did that performance measure up? Questions ran amok in my head concerning this first incident: Is this center a farce? How can I evaluate gender equality if one of the center's agents, the social worker, is not able to realize what she is doing? Is there any space for an ethical engagement in this work environment? Are these individuals at all able to develop some sort of critical distance from themselves and what they do? Should I be careful about not generalizing and assume that this was just an individual expression of this one person? Was she just caught up in work she saw as helping, without realizing that she was actually punishing the clients, and punishing them hard? I had no answers to these questions, of course, but I was deeply shaken by this incident and could not refrain from judging this performance not only as professionally deficient but also as lacking humanity. Was it because the funding agency was aware of these shortcomings that it wanted an evalution?

The second incident: One of the individual interviews I conducted with Fouzia, a client of SolFem, was particularly difficult for me. The difficulty lay in two elements of the exchange: first, Fouzia constantly wanted me to corroborate her statements; and second, I realized that she was a liar with many psychological issues, and that this pregnancy was not her first. In this interview I learned, for instance, that she had stolen some of the NGO's material, she had manipulated the social workers into accepting her as a client though she knew that SolFem's regulations limited the NGO's services to the first pregnancy, and she had found herself trying to strangle her one-year-old daughter one night when the little one couldn't sleep. Her account was appalling to me, as it revealed her as far from a "victim"—unlike the other women I had seen at the NGO and the typical client that SolFem described. Fouzia was cunning and violent, a liar and a cheat, and she didn't think about her responsibility for giving birth and abandoning two babies earlier. Most disturbing for me was the fact that she truly thought that I would agree with her and approve of her choices. I was not a psychoanalyst, and it was not my job to deal with her neurosis. Thus I came out of this interview literally holding my head—feeling confused, depleted, and especially angry. My anger toward myself, this woman, the NGO, and the entire system taught me a lesson that, in a way, explained (though it didn't justify) the unprofessional behavior of the one worker who often claimed that the unwed mothers lied more often than they breathed.

What had started out as a complicated process acquired further layers of complexity, as none of the women being evaluated fit what was supposed to be their initial profile or stereotype. Where did I take it from here? Contrary to my feelings at the onset of this adventure, when I thought that evaluating and judging was inherently a problematic position because of my intellectual affiliations, I now thought that *not* evaluating would be problematic on moral grounds because it was very clear to me that there were serious problems within this NGO. The question was how to evaluate it? My final evaluation combined statistical elements and life narratives. I felt to be honest I had to dwell on what I considered the irresponsible and unethical behavior of one social worker, though my statements in the evaluation were nuanced, given that the staff members' working relationships with the unwed mothers were far from ordinary. Through the life narratives and my subsequent work with these particular women and other women in the same situation,[1] I've had a privileged look into their lives. Because of the ordeals they experienced, a good number of these young unwed mothers had become incredibly good at deceiving, lying, manipulating, and using a number of other evasive tactics. I didn't realize this immediately because SolFem presented these young women only as victims (which indeed they are), a marketable image that appeals to funders. Thus, SolFem's board did not appreciate my report, and I was told that it is easy to be critical while they had constructed something that worked, albeit with problems. Years after this episode, the social worker in question left SolFem and even dared to sue Aicha Chenna, an affair much discussed in the newspapers and presented, especially by biased journalists, as the ultimate proof that the world of women's associations is corrupt and serves only its own ends.

Answering the question about whether this particular NGO was advancing gender equality within Morocco proved to be a nightmare. All I felt comfortable saying at the time was that the young unwed mothers who stayed in the center or simply came for legal counsel either already knew, or the center were made them aware, that: (a) there are special places where they could turn for support; (b) with the right knowledge, a woman can get certain rights (this research took place before the revolutionary legal changes in the family law of 2004); and (c) whatever their ordeal or problem, they were not alone—there is something identified as a collective women's problem. In addition, some of these women did spread the word about this collective problem in their neighborhoods and among their families and friends. Gender inequality was beginning to be recognized, but to argue that there was a movement toward it would have been overstating the case.

Through the interviews and my observations, it became evident that shame and guilt defined the young mothers' relations to their immediate social world and that by probing these two notions, I could discern and even measure the extent to which the social workers had succeeded in creating a different social world for their clients. In spite of my initial misgivings about the role of hard science and objectivity, it became evident that no single method of analysis would suffice to render an accurate picture of the effect that the NGO had on the lives of these women. While I still feel that the depth of their anguish could never be reduced to numbers or scales, certain aspects of the change in their relationship to their social world before and after their participation in SolFem's program were indeed quantifiable. Despite my feelings of impotence and frustration along the way, in the end, I found my work as a consultant to be an extremely rewarding experience.

The report I finally gave the German agency required a bit of sanitizing. I had to tone down all the psychological turmoil I had gone through with the counseling center and some of the unwed mothers, as well as my realization that service NGOs in general had an opaque kernel of predatory capitalism that was, in the end, contrary to their altruistic and reformist mission. Thus my final report began by describing a context, the objective of the study, and the methodology—and then I proceeded to fill in the blanks. The money the agency paid me was for the results and not for this subtext, which is an interesting comment on how this knowledge was produced and what I chose to give to the agency.

I want to close this essay with a final word concerning my "identity." I was born into the impoverished remnants of what had been an old, established, middle-class urban family, and I was raised amid much reminiscing about the family's "great" past and riches. The grandiose ruins of my father's past acted as a sort of shield that protected me from the immediate reality of the place in which I lived until I went to Mohammed V University, in Rabat. I remember witnessing the fall of the Berlin Wall on the television sets at the DePaul University Student Center after I began my studies in the United States in the late 1980s. I had left behind a Morocco that was still living through a period of severe government oppression; my awareness of this was heightened through my connections and affinities with the remnants of some political groups at Mohammed V University. Freedom (internal freedom in a Sartrean sense) had become my chief goal—freedom from my father's haunted ruins, from the pressures of government oppression, and from the strict conformity to rules that "good" girls from my social background were supposed to respect.

On one hand, I believed that being both a "native" and an anthropologist gave me particular advantages as a researcher in Morocco, especially knowledge of the language, and perhaps an easier understanding of what Clifford Geertz called "deep play," the profound meanings embedded in the flow of social action. However, my experience at SolFem forced me to recognize that one can be a non-native even at home because what one holds dear can be constantly profaned, if not shattered. Freedom was, in fact, at the core of what SolFem proposed to provide for these women. The NGO wanted to teach them to embrace the freedom of being mothers regardless of the circumstances of the child's conception—and regardless of the heavy personal price the women had to pay for being unwed mothers. My personal trajectory and my earlier fieldwork on issues of child abandonment and adoption had left me unfamiliar with this world, its codes, and especially the sometimes violent way this freedom was shoved in front of the women. Was it really freedom, then—did it deserve this label? I am still not really sure about that. But I am sure that this kind of freedom can never be measured, and that as long as we have the ability turn the eye inside, as the poet Aimé Césaire says, there is much that can be built if there is the right measure of distance and critique toward oneself.

NOTE

1. I conducted further fieldwork with these young women and others in different NGOs from 2002 to 2005. I am working on a book dealing exclusively with them.

9 | Reflecting on Moroccan Encounters

*Meditations on Home, Genre, and
the Performance of Everyday Life*

DEBORAH KAPCHAN

To Yahya

Perhaps home is not a place but simply an irrevocable condition.

—James Baldwin, *Giovanni's Room*

There is a story, always ahead of you. Barely existing. Only gradually do you
attach yourself to it and feed it. You discover the carapace that will contain
and test your character. You find in this way the path of your life.

—Michael Ondaatje, *The Cat's Table*

I encountered Morocco when I was twenty-four years old. It was,
in a sense, an accidental or at least a serendipitous encounter—but
then again, it may have been fate. Before leaving New York in 1981,
I was in music school studying flute performance. I was working on
my second BA, begun after my graduation from the English Department at New York University (with a minor in French literature), and
although I was feeling too old to be a freshman for a second time, I
didn't know what else to do. My only directive was a tired but work-
able cliché: follow your heart. So I began a second undergraduate de-

gree. It was a symptom of my inability to choose: writing or music? Music or writing? Okay, both.

When I wasn't practicing or riding the noisy subway from the East Village in Manhattan to Brooklyn to attend classes, I was either waiting tables or going to the New York Public Library—particularly the branch across from the Museum of Modern Art. It was there that I discovered the Smithsonian recordings of African traditional music. I was a wind player, but it was the recordings of the Gambian *kora* that finally gave me the push I needed to quit my formal studies of music and go to the Peace Corps office in downtown Manhattan in order to sign up for a stint in West Africa.[1] I didn't know what I would do for the Peace Corps, but I knew I wanted to learn as much as I could about a music that, for me, was magical. And I didn't have any money. It was, truth be told, a way to get out of New York, a (free) ticket, and a whim. And while the irony of using a government organization to escape a government of which I was highly critical at the time was indeed lost on me in 1982, I now can forgive myself my naïveté. When the Peace Corps called, I sold my Bang and Olufsen turntable, my collection of jazz LPs, and my books. I sold my rent-controlled studio in the East Village and even gave away my cats. I thought I was never going to return to the United States.

But despite the fact that I listed Gambia, Mali, Senegal, Sierra Leone, and Ghana as desired destinations on my Peace Corps application, West Africa was not "written" for me. Morocco was.

It is interesting that in Arabic one's fate is described as having been "written," like a script that we unknowingly follow. Of course, Islam is a religion of the Book, and literacy is thus accorded an almost mystical place in it.[2] But if language is what separates humans from animals, for Muslims only the hand of God writes fate: *kulshi fi-iyd allah* (everything is in the hands of God), especially destiny. For those who believe in *al-maktub* (what's written), the script exists prior to our enactment of it; it is predetermined and preternatural; we only narrativize it later to ourselves and others so it will make sense as history, as a life. Yet it's not necessary to believe in providence to understand that there is, in fact, an unconscious projection that issues from our bodies, that somehow "goes before" the five senses[3] and pulls us along as if on a string—as if we were following when, in fact, we are creating.

I did not want to go to Morocco. But I went. And what I found there was both my future and my past. That is, I found "home" and what in French is called *appartenance,* belonging. I use the French term because it includes the word "part." The infinitive, *appartenir,* also contains the word *tenir* (to hold). To belong is to hold a part of, to be beholden to, to at once belong to and possess. In 1982 I departed for Morocco; I became a part of it, and it became a part of me. In Moroccan Arabic one says, *erjˤt fi-hal-i* (I came back to my path, or state of being), or *erjˤt ˤand-i* (I went back to what belongs to me—that is, home).

I also use the French word because it was my experience in France that ultimately prepared me to recognize my home in Morocco once I found it, as I had already encountered North Africa in my eighteenth year when I spent the summer with a family in the Massif Central in France. For two months I talked for hours a day with the grandfather of the family, who had spent several years in Tunisia when he was a young doctor. We sat in his *salon Arab,* with his burnoose hanging on a coat rack in the corner and our chairs smelling of camel leather. He spoke Arabic and still dreamed of returning to North Africa in his seventy-second year of life (our ages, seventy-one and seventeen, formed a palindrome). Yet I had forgotten all of that until the moment I landed in Casablanca seven years later, when I came home to Morocco for the first time in my life.

Fate pulls us into the future with a string fabricated from our past.

Why is it that some places are home-like and others remain forever foreign? What is the alchemy of place and affect that spurs the ethnographic imagination? And what does ethnography accomplish when this simpatico feeling is missing? In this essay, I relate my life experiences in Morocco since 1982 to two key texts in the discipline—Paul Rabinow's *Reflections on Fieldwork in Morocco* (2007 [1977]) and Pierre Bourdieu's text on the "Kabyle house" (1970)—in order to understand ethnography and the ethnographic imagination as a potential homecoming that indelibly imprints both the individual and the social body, making one a part of something very different than that to which one has belonged before. In this way, ethnography stands in a mirror relationship to another kind of writing about home—namely, the memoir. If ethnography explores the worlds of others to understand one's own (Rabinow 2007 [1977], following Paul Ricoeur), memoir explores one's own world for the larger significance of what it means to "be" in the world—that is, to shed light on the worlds of others. Both genres recount memories (of things observed, felt, heard, and otherwise experienced) that evoke and create an affective space of interaction between writer, reader, and written. In both, belonging plays an important part, either as a being part of or as a holding apart. And although both live political lives in the public domain and are thus potential genres of activism (Tsing 2005),[4] ethnography distinguishes itself as a mode of knowing (that is, an epistemological endeavor) as well as a way of being (the method or ontology of fieldwork) that in addition produces a genre of knowledge transmission (the narrative ethnography). Due to its focus on the other, ethnography is particularly fraught with ethical conundrums and contradictions. To be effective, the ethnographic imagination must be projected, much like the string of fate that we are unconscious of but that pulls us into encounters, into what we write and what is written (for us), and also into the very sensate performances of everyday life.[5] Home is thereafter forever changed.

REFLECTIONS ON *REFLECTIONS*

After two years in the Peace Corps, my life had changed considerably. I was fluent in Moroccan Arabic, and I was married to a Moroccan high school teacher. Because of my language skills, I landed a job as an ethnographer in a longitudinal study of literacy directed by a University of Pennsylvania professor, Daniel Wagner (the results of that study are published in Wagner 1993). It was my job to do the ethnographic interviews with parents of the children in the study. The job came with two field sites and two residences—one in the small village of El Ksiba in the Middle Atlas Mountains (population around 20,000, mostly Tamazight speakers), the other in Marrakech (population now more than a million,[6] primarily Arabic-speaking, though with a sizable population of Tamazight as well as Tashelhit speakers). A small Renault Quatrelle took me between the two places.

When I first read *Reflections on Fieldwork in Morocco* (henceforth *Reflections*), I was twenty-six and living in a small *riad*[7] in the medina of Marrakech. As a newlywed, I had already spent many hours learning to cook, embroider, knit sweaters from oily goats' wool, and bargain with vendors in both cosmopolitan and rural markets. Had I gone native? Well, if going native means forging affective attachments with one's environment and losing what we now realize is the illusion of objectivity, perhaps I had taken that step.[8] I had gotten married to a Moroccan, and I gave myself to the experience fully. At that time of my life, I went to the public baths and looked with longing at (what I saw as) the noble bearing of pregnant women donning their caftans and djellabas after hours spent scrubbing themselves and each other. Femininity was an unambiguous art in Morocco (or so it seemed to me then), and, after several years of being an androgynous New Yorker, I desired it. More important perhaps, my body was ready to have a child, and I had fallen in love with the man I wanted to father it. I was a *bint* to my parents-in-law, a *lusti* to my sisters- and brothers-in-law, an ʿ*amti* to their children. I spoke Moroccan Arabic fluently, much better than I do today.

I dug into *Reflections* with relish, as I was immediately drawn into its first-person narrative. Indeed, before coming to Morocco I had shared Rabinow's weariness with the West and the "undergraduate ennui" that had propelled him far from home (2007 [1977], 3). I also appreciated his honesty, particularly when he said things like "I had gone into anthropology in search of Otherness. Meeting it on an experiential level was a shock which caused me to begin fundamental reconceptualization about social and cultural categories" (ibid., 29). Although not yet part of the anthropology clan, or privy to its initiation secrets or "clan taboos" (ibid., 5), I too had had the very core of my world rocked by an experiential encounter with difference in Morocco. Yet despite my initial enthusiasm about *Reflections,* my sentiments quickly turned to repulsion. That is not too strong a word. I had a visceral and almost violent reaction to the book. It's true that I had read only a few anthropology books before—Kevin Dwyer's *Moroccan Dialogues* (1982), Vanessa Maher's *Women and Property in Morocco* (1974), Elizabeth Fernea's *A House in Marrakech* (1975). All these books were in the library of the *riad* that came with my new job. (Indeed, Aisha, the maid and main informant in Fernea's book, had been working for the University of Pennsylvania's Literacy Project for several years by then, and when I took the job, we got to know one another.[9]) I was completely riveted by the idea that one could make a living doing what I was doing out of love: that is, learning a language and culture and writing about it. Indeed, I was hooked.

But *Reflections* stopped me in my tracks. I was shocked by Rabinow's facility in applying monikers ("wino cab drivers") and making judgments (Richard was "weak," and lacked "courage" [14]). The text was written by a man who did not speak Arabic except cursorily. He made generalizations that were sweeping and, I thought, unfair. Most importantly, Rabinow decidedly did not feel at home in Morocco.

All books are products of their time. It would be unfair to criticize Rabinow's first book from the vantage point of current affect theory (Brennan 2004) or the anthropology of the senses.[10] Since its publication in 1977, the notion of the informant has been duly criticized (Fabian 1992, 2000 [1983]; Marcus and Fischer 1986); the knowledge-power equation unpacked, in part by Rabinow himself (Rabinow 2008; Rabinow, Marcus, Faubion, and Rees 2008); and the Orientalist tropes that underlie even the most self-conscious research deconstructed (Abu-Lughod 1991, 1993). Nonetheless, I now ponder my deeply averse reaction to *Reflections.* At twenty-six I may have read very little anthropology, but I had been thoroughly schooled in post-structuralism and deconstructionism—Derrida's *Grammatology,* Foucault's *Archaeology of Knowledge,* Barthes's *Mythologies* (and, indeed, all his other works), as well as the works of Freud and

Lacan. This was my education as an English major at New York University from 1978 to 1982 (I also studied some literature). I was not naïve. But I was furious when I read *Reflections*. Why?

ETHNOGRAPHY IN BAD FAITH

Rabinow makes important contributions to anthropology by critiquing its attachment to social science and by elevating fieldwork—and its interpretation—to a place of centrality. He goes so far as to say that fieldwork "defines the discipline" of anthropology (2007 [1977], 5).[11] As a student of Clifford Geertz, Rabinow embraced hermeneutics and considered anthropology an art of interpretation (not a social science). When I read *Reflections* in 1984, this assertion was nothing short of life affirming—that is, it affirmed *my* life, and I realized that I had a name for what I was: an ethnographer. Yet something was not right. Rabinow, it seemed to me, remained impermeable, deflecting Moroccan culture instead of internalizing it. Although he acknowledged the role of intuition in fieldwork and had insights that often paralleled my own, Rabinow's experiences were largely spawned by conflict and tinged with judgment. He pitied the French misfit, Richard, a leftover from colonial times and, in Rabinow's words, a "failure." Rabinow described the children in the region where he lived as "fearless little monsters" (ibid., 84). The "big men" in the villages "liked to ask questions and not answer them," and they were interested only in domination (93). Mekki, the shepherd, "lacked intelligence" and was the "village idiot" (94, 95). And although Rabinow addressed the danger of making facile generalizations about large political movements like colonialism,[12] he nonetheless made plenty of generalizations about the Moroccan psyche, such as: "Material motives are never in disrepute in Morocco. It is only when they are absent that suspicion is aroused" (110); "In good Moroccan rhetorical style I had countered a strong gambit with an equally strong counterattack" (87); "The *qaid*—a soft-spoken and even-tempered man—one of the reasons, I might add, that he was neither respected nor feared—explained clearly that everything was in order" (88–89); and "Religious power, as most other things in Morocco, tends to be personalized, and manifests itself through particularly forceful individuals" (50). Such offhand comments made assumptions about Moroccan culture that I found unfair. Rabinow was painting with a large, Western, and decidedly cynical brush. Are all even-tempered men treated with disrespect in Morocco? Are all motives material? Is religion only about power and the cult of the person? Reading *Reflections*, one would think the answers to all these questions were "yes."

More important, however, conflict was the leitmotif of *Reflections*. In one pivotal narrative in the book, for example, Rabinow drops his primary friend and informant, Ali, on the side of the road to walk the five miles back to Sefrou by himself in the early morning hours. (They had been to an all-night wedding, and Rabinow, who was the driver, had wanted to leave much earlier than Ali, and was exhausted.) Rabinow explains:

> At the wedding Ali was beginning to test me, much in the way that Moroccans test each other to ascertain strengths and weaknesses. He was pushing and probing. I tried to avoid responding in the counter-assertive style of another Moroccan, vainly offering instead the persona of the anthropologist, all-accepting. He continued to interpret my behavior in his own terms: he saw me as weak, giving in to each of his testing thrusts. So the cycle continued: he would probe more deeply, show his dominance and exhibit my submission and lack of character. Even on the way back to Sefrou he was testing me, and in what was a backhanded compliment, trying to humiliate me. (48)

That Rabinow makes Ali a stand-in for Moroccans in general in this excerpt seemed to me unfair enough. But in fact Rabinow seemed to be describing a kind of gender-determined competition that, while present in Morocco, is certainly not unique to that country. While Rabinow may have been dramatizing for narrative effect, he clearly does not use drama theory to his advantage. (If he had drawn on Stanislavski, for example, he might have emphasized the protean aspect of human subjectivity and tried to understand what it was like to be in Ali's skin instead of nearly jumping out of his own.)[13] Instead of discussing the nuance of social and affective exchange, however, Rabinow narrates this story as an agonistic conflict between two implacable personalities inhabiting two unyielding positions wherein power and honor are at stake.

Rabinow's worry, if not guilt, about this episode led him to reflect on the importance of hospitality in Moroccan culture.[14] He ascribes Ali's haughtiness to his pride about being a good host,[15] and Ali's (self-imposed) penance for not being a good host is that he walks five miles home in the dark. The theme of hospitality is clearly an important one in Morocco, yet Rabinow describes it as another form of behavior that creates dominance and subservience—that is, a system of power. And while *diyafa,* or hospitality—like all aspects of the gift (Mauss 1990 [1950])—certainly includes those dimensions, it is also a deeply embedded ethos in Morocco, a practice imbued with social affect. I have eaten many meals with Moroccans—from the most humble to the most lavish—when the hosts knew the probability of our meeting again was almost nil. All gifts may be interested,[16] but at least for Muslims, the recompense may be in the hereafter: *haqqaq fi jinna,* "your recompense is in heaven," as the popular saying has it. I couldn't help feeling that Rabinow was missing the affective point.

But perhaps in his world at that time, he wasn't. Still, why had such conflicts never happened to me?

Rabinow defined the ethnographic field experience as a kind of symbolic violence, an encounter in bad faith:[17]

> To those who claim that some form of this symbolic violence was not part of their own field experience, I reply simply that I do not believe them. It is inherent in the structure of the situation. This is not to say that every anthropologist is aware of it, for sensibilities differ. The form and intensity no doubt vary greatly, but they are all variations on a common theme. (*Reflections,* 130)

While I cannot deny that symbolic violence is a part of human interaction (and perhaps part and parcel of home as well), the equating of ethnography and violence deserves a response.

VARIATIONS ON A THEME OF ETHNOGRAPHIC VIOLENCE: THE ROLE OF DISPOSITION

Unlike Rabinow, in Morocco I did not learn about conflict but about the *avoidance* of conflict. I learned about something called *al-khatr.*[18] *Khatr* is a word that is very difficult to translate. In Moroccan Arabic it means "will" or "volition," but it has a different affective valence than either of those English words. In classical Arabic it also means "vibration," "oscillation," or "something weighty" (Wehr 1993), and while there is not a neat conflation between classical and Moroccan Arabic, it is instructive to consider the full semantic spectrum of the word. In Moroccan Arabic it can also mean "morale," as in the expression *ma ʿandu-sh al-khatr* ("he's not in a good mood"). Someone who is patient and compassionate has a large *khatr* (*ʿand-u al-khatr kabir*), and when you don't want to hurt someone's feelings, you say,"*mabghitsh n-khasr khatr-u*" (literally, "I don't want to ruin [or break] his *khatr*"). To say that "someone possesses *al-khatr*" (*shi wahed and-u al-khatr*) is to say that that person is patient, long-suffering, and unlikely to be perturbed. In that sense, the word is best translated as "equanimity."[19]

Khatr is, in fact, a disposition, a "state of mind or feeling"[20] often oriented toward an object or someone else (one may be well- or ill-disposed toward a person, for example). As a disposition, *khatr* is experienced as if it resided in the embodied self (seemingly bounded and distinct from other selves), yet—like anger, happiness, irritation, and other emotions—*khatr* is determined by a variety of factors such as class, gender, environment, history, and social context. What's more, *khatr* is liable to be influenced in the present by the actions and feeling states of others—that is, it is an inter-subjective state of indeterminacy.[21] *Khatr* inhabits the area of in-between, where selves affect other selves and connection is realized, created, or broken.[22]

Like all important lessons, I learned about *khatr* the hard way. Trained in discourse analysis, I meticulously taped and transcribed all the data for my first book. My research assistant, Mohammed, would work with me for several hours a day, and we would sit together, listening to the tapes I had recorded of women in the marketplace, he transcribing the words into Arabic while I simultaneously wrote the translations in English. This dual transcription-translation process meant that I had the texts in both languages, but I also had the benefit of Mohammed's expertise if there were phrases I didn't understand. I had a toddler at the time, and we were living with my in-laws in Beni Mellal. I had one week left before our return to the United States and still had a lot of untranscribed tapes. My research time was limited. I asked Mohammed to come every day—morning and afternoon—impressing on him the amount of work to be done in the short time that remained.

"*Wakha, ma kayn mushkil. N-shufu ghdda insha'allah,*" he said as he was leaving that day ("Okay, no problem. See you tomorrow, God willing.").

The next day Mohammed didn't show up. The following day either. On the third day, I went to his brother Rashid's shop.

"Where's Mohammed?" I asked. All Rashid would tell me was that he had had to leave town.

I left for the United States soon after. I wrote my dissertation with the data I had, which turned out to be more than sufficient. But the following summer I was back in Beni Mellal, and, of course, I went to see Mohammed. After the necessary greetings and asking after his family, I awkwardly broached the subject of his disappearance at such a key moment in my research. "*Ma bghtish n-khsur khatr-ak,*" he said ("I didn't want to spoil your *khatr*, I didn't want to upset you").

Of course, my disposition had been disturbed, mostly because he had given me his word that he would be there (*ɛata-ni al-kalma*, he gave me his word) and then hadn't shown up. Initially I felt betrayed. But he explained to me that he had had to go to Rabat to take an exam for a job for which he was competing. Embarrassed to be putting his own interests before mine, he had decided to simply avoid the conflict and disappear.

I encountered this tactic often enough in my experiences in Morocco that I began to understand it as a cultural given—which is to say, it is something that Moroccans learn when they are young children. (In French, these givens are called *points de repères*, reference points, anchors that allow one to navigate the social environment.) When one understands that the avoidance of direct conflict may also be a transcultural ethic of care, one ceases to be (as) disappointed when conflicts of interest prevent the realization of personal desires. Respecting the *khatr* of another is also acknowledging that emotions are not independent, that in fact they are mutually constructed. That is why affective (and physical) withdrawal is sometimes the best strategy. When emotions and volition are not shared (as was the case at the wedding for Rabinow), then *khatr* has been broken (*al-khatr t-khsser*).

My experiences were qualitatively different than Rabinow's. For one thing, I fell in love—first with the place, then with a man. I saw a long future for myself in Morocco, and it was in my interest not only to understand but also to accommodate my sociocultural environment, to change, to modify, to fit in. Love, some would say, is like water: it takes the shape of its container.[23] But surely love is not required to do ethnography. Or is it? To what extent does the ethnographer's *khatr*, or disposition, determine his or her experience and perception? Must the ethnographer be in some way predisposed to (or have a rapport with) a particular cultural landscape (see the chapter by Emilio Spadola in this volume)?[24]

AFFECTIVE METHODOLOGIES AND THE LAW OF GENRE

Rabinow's focus on the agonistic is in part a result of participant observation, of "seeing" and "objectifying" instead of feeling and listening.[25] It is also a result of his discursive moment in intellectual history, namely a 1970s Ricoeurian phenomenology more attuned to "the prison-house of language" (Jameson 1972) than to gesture, feeling, and the senses. In light of recent theory that discusses affect as something that is shared and transmitted in a myriad of subtle, sensate, and unconscious ways (Brennan 2004) and in light of both sense-based and "radical empiricist" approaches to anthropology that stress the inter-subjective and indeterminate nature of experience,[26] reading *Reflections* today reveals not so much the fault lines between cultures as the ramifications of situational human encounter.[27] My intent is not to criticize Rabinow for his situated (and youthful) point of view, and certainly not to freeze his work in time. Rather, I ponder whether narrative ethnography itself is not a coming-of-age genre, an anthropological bildungsroman that teaches us about self, home, and belonging.[28] If so, it is important to remember that young men are socialized to come of age differently than young women. Indeed, Rabinow notes that during his fieldwork experience he "found the demands of greater self-control and abnegation hard to accept . . . [especially as he was] used to engaging people energetically and found the prospect of a year constantly on . . . [his] guard, with very little to fall back on except the joys of asceticism, productive sublimation and the pleasures of self-control, a grim prospect" (*Reflections*, 47). Is this not a young (Western) man's lament?[29] *Yimkan ma kansh ʿand-u al-khatr ʿala hadak-shi*—perhaps he didn't have the heart (*khatr*) for what he was doing.

The bildungsroman is a modern genre of European fiction that details the coming of age of its protagonist (Hirsch 1979; Moretti 1987; R. Stewart and Manson 2009). Unlike memoir and narrative ethnography, it is not always written in the first person, but it does tell a kind of hero story in which a youth (most often a boy, sometimes an artist) faces and overcomes obstacles in the journey toward adulthood. Implicit in the form are assumptions about a modern self that emerges into adulthood as an autonomous being, but that does so by learning about the rules and mores of a particular society. An anthropological bildungsroman, by extension, is one in which the hero or heroine grows up a second time in a second cultural context, the tacit understanding being that learning a new language and a new culture puts one in a state of innocence, a childlike state— what Rabinow refers to as being a "non-person" (*Reflections*, 46). To grow up is also to find, discover, often reproduce, and sometimes reinvent home.[30]

It is easy to read most narrative ethnographies, including my own (Kapchan 1996, 2007b), in this generic framework, as stories with a moral and emotional message as well as an intellectual one (Abu-Lughod 1986). Yet while both memoir and ethnography are confessional genres, in memoir one is accountable to oneself, whereas in ethnography one is accountable to others—of course the community of scholars one is writing for, but also and most vitally, the person or people one is writing about. Both memoir and ethnography contain truth claims: unlike the bildungsroman, they are assumed to be auto-biographical and based in fact or reality, yet there are different moral implications to each. Is "moral unselfconsciousness" really a virtue in ethnography, as Robert Bellah asserts in his preface to the thirtieth anniversary edition of *Reflections* (Bellah 2007 [1977], xxxi)? How would Richard feel if he knew Rabinow had said he was a "failure"? How would the characterization of "village idiot" sit with Mekki?[31] And would writing a straight memoir avoid these ethical dilemmas?

READING THE BERBER HOUSE

The first time I went to the High Atlas Mountains was in 1982. I was attempting to climb Toubkal, the highest mountain in North Africa. I never did reach the summit of that mountain, but I did learn a lot along the way. I had been in Morocco for only two weeks of what was to be my first three-year period of residence. Like Rabinow when he began his fieldwork, I didn't speak a word of Arabic at the time, but this wouldn't have helped much anyway, as the residents of these mountains are primarily Berber-speaking (though most now speak Arabic as well).

We spent the first day simply getting to the beginning of the hiking trail. We took a bus from Marrekech to Asni and then another bus to the town of Imlil, at the foot of the mountains. At that time, there were one or two cafés in Imlil and a few *hawant,* small stores that sold commodities like bottled water, matches, soap, sugar, oil, dried beans, and detergent. I was with two other Americans, one who had lived in the High Atlas for a few years and who spoke Tamazight (the Berber spoken in the Atlas Mountains). While my other companion and I sat in a café drinking sweet mint tea, he went off to talk to some of the locals. When he came back, he told us that he had arranged for us to spend the night in a *dwar,* a small village about an hour's hike up the first incline.

We had to hurry, as night was falling. We took our packs and started off. When we got to the cluster of houses that made up the village, our companion once again used his language skills to find our host for the evening. We were escorted into a small adobe house, and served a *dwaz*, a vegetable stew, with some homemade bread.[32] The man of the house spent a short time conversing with my friend in Berber, then left us to sleep. We didn't see the women, though we did hear them laughing gently in the next room.

A few things about this earthen house stand out in my memory. In fact, I saw only one room of it—the living room, where Moroccans entertain. The mattresses on the floor were made of cotton cloth with a floral pattern, stuffed with alfalfa straw, and sewn together with cord. The straw poked through the mattresses in places and made sleeping less than comfortable. The dirt floor had a loosely woven rug on it. There was a low, rough-hewn table between the two banquettes, and the blankets that we were given to cover ourselves were made of scratchy wool.

The next day we ate breakfast—bread, fresh-churned butter, and coffee—on the roof of the house as we overlooked the valley. We then thanked our hosts (I'm not sure if my Berber-speaking companion compensated them or not) and began our climb. Throughout that day we saw only a few people, mostly women collecting wood or working in the fields.

When the road got too rocky and our legs too weary, we rented mules from some boys near a saint's tomb and proceeded to the refuge, a stone resthouse where we were given a modest dinner.

Then we laid our sleeping bags down in the loft and fell into a deep sleep.

The rest of the trip was rather uneventful. We didn't make it to the summit but returned to Marrakech, where we immediately went to the public baths in the old city and were scrubbed almost raw by a rather rotund bath attendant.

Years later, in graduate school, I read Pierre Bourdieu's essay on the Kabyle house, in *The Logic of Practice* (1990). A French sociologist, social theorist, and *ethnologue*, Bourdieu encountered North Africa more than a decade and a half before Rabinow wrote *Reflec-*

Figure 9.1. Conversing with Berber women in the High Atlas Mountains, 1982.

Figure 9.2. I (behind, on the white mule) and Anne Staunton, a Peace Corps friend.

tions. Unlike Rabinow, Bourdieu worked in Algeria, and in particular in Kabylia—the Berber-speaking north. He went on to write about the way the repeated aesthetic practices of everyday life structure sociality and reproduced social class and "doxa"—"the pre-verbal taking-for-granted of the world that flows from practical sense" (1980, 68). He talked about "dispositions" and how they are produced (through socialization and education), while also generating (through unconscious repetition) one's "habitus"[33]—that is, the environment (religion, ethnicity, class, and gender) that creates the subject and, by extension, the society in which she or he lives (1977; 1990, 80).[34] "The habitus," says Bourdieu, is "embodied history, internalized as second nature and so forgotten as history . . . [It is] the active presence of the whole past of which it is the product" (1990, 56).

In the 1960s, before creating the above theoretical constructs, Bourdieu found himself in an Algeria still reeling from a violent war of independence with France (which Algeria won in 1962). Amid the traumatic upheavals produced by decades of violence, it is not surprising that Bourdieu was drawn to investigate an icon of stability—the Kabyle house.While his emphasis on space and practice was prescient, the categories Bourdieu used were very stereotypical, and one wonders if such clean dichotomies have ever existed in lived experience. Bourdieu delineates them as follows: "high: low:: light: dark:: day: night:: male: female:: nif (male honour): h'urma (female honour):: fertilising: able to be fertilised" (1990, 275).

There were other categories as well: mosque or field versus home; dry versus damp. Of course women were associated with the inner realms of the home—the low, the damp, the dark.

Paul Silverstein (2009, 178) has pointed out that Bourdieu's main sources for this information were not those actually living in the Kabyle houses, but those displaced through colonialism and living in resettlement camps, thus making these categories both an expression of Bourdieu's projection of a once-extant social unity ruptured by capitalism and colonialism—what Michael Herzfeld calls "structural nostalgia" (1997)—as well as an expression of nostalgia by those displaced, for whom the Kabyle house was an experience of loss.[35] Not only are these categories forced exaggerations, but Berber women—in 1982 Morocco in any case (see fig. 9.1)—were very much in the fields and outside. One might infer that Bourdieu's consultants were primarily men.

To say that my first foray into the High Atlas Mountains determined my own destiny is an understatement. Not only did my companions and I visit the sanctuary of Moulay Brahim—a saint whom the Moroccan Gnawa honor with pilgrimage every year—but we met a woman who was scaling the mountains barefooted on her way to the sanctuary. She was possessed, she said, by three spirits—a Muslim, a Christian, and a Jew. She was going to the sanctuary to persuade the Jewish and Christian spirits to convert to Islam. As a child of mixed religious parentage, this encounter held special resonance for me. But it also planted the seeds of interest for my book on the possession ceremonies of the Gnawa (2007b) some twenty-five years later.

This trip was fateful in another way as well, as I was ultimately to marry a Berber and live in a Berber house of sorts with our *shiliha*, my "little Berber" daughter, Hannah Joy.

You may be starting to think that this is a discussion of the performance of my everyday life, but the dénouement of this story is still to come. It happened in 1994, when I went to the High Atlas Mountains again. This time I was with Rose-Lynn Fisher, a friend of mine who is an artist and photographer involved in documenting Jewish culture in Morocco. We rented a taxi in Marrakech, and its chauffeur began the drive. As we climbed higher and snaked—always too fast for me—around the cliffside roads, I was shocked to find that almost every available space was occupied with displays of carpets, pottery, gemstones, and art aimed at tourists. If we stopped the car, young boys appeared from behind the rocks trying to sell us Berber jewelry and crystals that had been painted purple and were being sold as amethysts. The most surprising event of this trip, however, occurred in a Berber house. As we were descending a mountain, the driver pulled over to the side of the road without warning.

"We're going to stop here," he said.

Figures 9.3 and 9.4. My Berber mother- and father-in-law.

Figure 9.5. Hannah, the *shiliha* (little Berber), at eighteen months.

"Why?" I asked.

"There's something I want you to see. You'll like it. Come, we'll stop for tea."

I knew this driver and had employed him on previous occasions, so we got out of the car and followed. He stepped across a small waterway and walked down a path to a house. "This is a real Berber house," he said.

A woman appeared in clothes resembling those you see my mother-in-law wearing in the photograph (fig. 9.3). As I spoke no Berber, she spoke to me in Arabic. "*Marhaba* [welcome]," she said. "Look around. Everything you see is how Berbers really live."

The rooms of this adobe house were rather bare, but the basics that Bourdieu talks about were there. There was the supply room, the room with the animals—a goat, a meandering hen. There was a room with a handmade loom in it, a small, unfinished kilim strung across the beam. There was a cooking area, where a steaming kettle sat atop a smoking brazier. Just outside, water terraces had been built, channeling a small stream right next to the house for washing clothes and dishes. There was also an outdoor oven. In short, all the items of folklore that you might put into a museum were there, including clay receptacles, small glasses for tea, and copper and brass trays. There was even a woolen burnoose hanging on a hook by the door. The woman had transformed her house into a "living museum in situ" (Kirshenblatt-Gimblett 1998, 54).

There are several reasons why this commercialization of everyday life has occurred, not the least of which is the massive migration of men out of this area, and the consequent reliance of the women and those who remain (children and the elderly) on tourism (Hoffman 2008b). As Berber men leave, the women are left behind to become the cultural caretakers and the repositories of tradition. Women in this scenario bear the brunt of what they themselves refer to as "suffering"— *tamarra* (ibid., 93). But the men need to have place of return, a home. Hoffman documents, for example, the narratives of men in France whose everyday imaginations revolve around the idea of return, even though it is economically unlikely that they ever will. In the worlds of the male migrant in Europe, home is truly not a place but an irrevocable condition.[36]

But the fetishization of the Berber identity is also at play. As the autochthonous population of North Africa, Berbers become exotic lures to tourists as they perform their Berberness at music festivals and other spectacles in urban centers (Boum 2007b). While the Berber rights movement has quickly made cause with other international aboriginal rights movements, the Moroccan government has been slow to recognize Berber cultural autonomy since the "Berber question," as it is called in Morocco, puts the sovereignty of the king and the integrity of Moroccan nation into question (see the chapter by Paul Silverstein in this volume).

As an example of the performance of everyday life, the Berber house is iconic. It has been the focus of scholarly attention for decades, and now it is a site of both nostalgia and heritage. The ethnographic imagination has taken hold not only in the minds of scholars and tourists, however, but in the minds of the Berbers themselves, whose deals with savvy taxi drivers bring tourists to homemade heritage and homes-made-heritage. Seeing culture through the eyes of the other, the Berber householder makes her way in the world by theorizing (that is, objectivizing) her very identity, infusing everyday practice with a self-conscious logic of commodification.

REFLECTIONS ON THE ETHNOGRAPHIC IMAGINATION

Bourdieu theorized home. Bringing attention to the way the space of the Kabyle house and the everyday practices enacted within it create social structure, his work nonetheless reveals the essentialist categories projected by the ethnographic imagination of his time (both his and his Berber interlocutors'), particularly in regard to gender.[37] Despite his own deep theoretical engagement with the "field," Bourdieu situates the ethnographer in a paradox: namely, the intellectual process condemns one to observe the logic of practice and never to inhabit it.[38] Indeed, Bourdieu provides a stinging critique of anthropologists who deceive themselves by trying to adopt other beliefs. The sheer vehemence of his arguments against going native (which constitute a veritable leitmotif in *The Logic of Practice* [1990]) is enough to alert us to the sensitivity of this issue for Bourdieu. He worked in Algeria for years and was no doubt torn by the difficulty of doing research during and immediately after a scarring war of independence (Goodman and Silverstein 2009). No doubt Bourdieu was also torn by his affective attachments to the place and his inability to intellectually endorse those attachments. He notes: "Undue participation of the subject in the object is never more evident than in the case of the primitivist participation of the bewitched or mystic anthropologist, which, like the populist immersion, still plays on the objective distance from the object to play the game as a game while waiting to leave it in order to tell it" (1990, 34). And again: "All the attempts by anthropologists to bewitch themselves with the witchcraft of mythologies of others have no other interest, however generous they may sometimes be, than that they realize, in their voluntarism, all the antinomies of the decision to believe, which make arbitrary faith a continuous creation of bad faith" (ibid., 68).

For Bourdieu, the bad faith of the ethnographer comes from the desire to enter another's belief system without sharing that other's history.[39] For Rabinow, bad faith is simply inherent in the practice itself (see the chapter by Rachel Newcomb in this volume).

RETURNING HOME

Rabinow deconstructs the scientific voice of Bourdieu and his generation, giving us a subjective account of fieldwork. Rabinow's very discomfort with the everyday nature of the ethnographic encounter, however, becomes the platform for analyzing and putting into question the anthropological episteme. The reader of *Reflections* is left with the feeling that Rabinow did not feel at home in Morocco. Indeed, Bourdieu seems more at home with his subject and—ironically, if unconsciously—more emotionally invested in North Africa.[40] Yet we find strong tones of Bourdieu in Rabinow's conclusion to *Reflections:*

> Otherness was not an ineffable essence, but rather the sum of different histori-
> cal experiences. Different webs of signification separated us, but these webs
> were at least partially intertwined. But a dialogue was only possible when we
> recognized our differences, when we remained critically loyal to the sym-
> bols which our traditions had given us. By so doing, we began a process of
> change. (162)

This was Rabinow's truth in 1977. But it was not mine at the age of twenty-six. Nor is it now. Of course, we are all products of our history. But when I first read *Reflections,* as a non-initiate into anthropology, ethnography was less about the hermeneutic dialogue between "webs of signification" and more about creating new affective indexes for home. I did not feel the need to be critically loyal to the symbols of my upbringing. On the contrary, I was making a concerted and critical effort to create new symbols, ones that were connected to a structure of feeling that was, at least initially, foreign to me. And I was moving through the world as a sentient and not just a thinking being. I was not interested in holding my ground in order to debate, but in learning to inhabit a new aesthetic position.

Was this because of my own habitus? Was I trying to escape one culture by immersing myself in another? Would I never be admitted to the anthropology clan because of the impurity of my motivations—that is, because I was driven by an unconscious logic of practice rather that a self-conscious drive for theory (after all, I had left New York in search of music)? Perhaps I would have said so not too long ago. Now, however, I realize that this, too, is anthropology and that one's own habitus, like those of others, constitutes "a set of rules with which improvisation plays" (de Certeau 1984, xxii).[41] However one goes about it, knowledge is produced.

Exiles, like artists, seek out new aesthetic systems and try to domesticate them—that is, to make them their own, part of their home.[42] After all, for a musician to have something "under her fingers" is to have it be part of her repertoire, to have it be second nature. One of the reasons ethnomusicologists have not been tormented by self-critiques of going native is that (at least since 1960) it is assumed that one goes to the field to become "bi-musical" (Hood 1960). And to become bi-musical is to acknowledge that new aesthetic orientations are not only desirable, they are attainable.[43] As Bourdieu notes, they are a "state of the body" (1980, 68). Aesthetic style is not in the blood. It is not even in history, though our histories may predispose us to certain aesthetic systems more than others. Aesthetic style, like *khatr,* is in the body, and with time and repetition it becomes a habit.

Rabinow, following Geertz, broke ground by making anthropology less a science than a humanistic and interpretive endeavor. More recently, scholars have defined ethnography itself as a genre of art, one driven by an ethnographic imagination to be sure, but one that makes use of embodied experience, translation, and the techniques of memoir in order to critically engage difference (Sharman 2007). As anthropological bildungsroman, narrative ethnography is nourished by an ethnographic imagination deeply interwoven with the performance of everyday life.[44] This ethnographic imagination is projected into "the field" of fieldwork, much like the unconscious string of fate, pulling us into encounters, into what we write and what is written (for us). Deeply embedded in the sensate world, ethnography's perennial if implicit subject is the human propensity to create and recreate home amid the shifting evanescence of aesthetic practice and affect.

Thirty years ago I set out for Gambia and landed in Morocco. Fortunately, the West African aesthetic that I had so longed for existed in North Africa as well (Kapchan 2007a). Indeed, before I left New York, my flute teacher gave me one of his recordings and inscribed it with the words, "Let Morocco get into you." I listened to that advice. And despite divorce and the death of loved ones, I still feel like I am coming home, even thirty years after my first landing as a Peace Corps volunteer in 1982. It is a feeling. It happens especially in Marrakech. I get off the train, breathe deeply, and feel, "I am home."

NOTES

1. It is easy to think back nostalgically to the idealism inspired by President John F. Kennedy, who is credited with creating the Peace Corps, and to be embarrassed when reading his suggestion that "young college graduates would find a full life in bringing technical advice and assistance to the underprivileged and backward Middle East . . . In that calling, these men would follow the constructive work done by the religious missionaries in these countries over the past 100 years" (Leamer 2001, 337–38).

2. See Messick (1993) for a fuller discussion of the logocentrism of Islam.

3. To speak of the five senses is really just a convention. Different cultures recognize other senses, and, indeed, we can easily speak of proprioception (sensing one's body in space) as being the sixth sense, and intuition being the seventh (Csordas 1993; Guerts 2002).

4. As genres, both memoir and ethnography have what Bakhtin and Medvedev (1985) refer to as inner and outer orientations—that is, they are meaningful within the rules and themes prescribed by their genre while also living political lives in the world.

5. Insofar as the ethnographic imagination has been Orientalist, we see its negative power. Its positive charge, however, is that it is profoundly humanist.

6. http://en.wikipedia.org/wiki/File:Morocco-demography.png (accessed January 20, 2012).

7. A *riad* is a traditional Moroccan house with an interior courtyard or garden.

8. What does "going native" mean if not losing an "objectivity" that has come to be seen as a master narrative of rationality?

9. See Fernea (1998) for a further discussion of Aisha and the ethnographic project.

10. The anthropology of the senses, as well as theories of embodiment, was the logical outgrowth of the phenomenological anthropology to which Rabinow ascribed (see Howes 2003, 2004; Stoller 1989; Jackson 1996).

11. The notion of fieldwork as the center of anthropology is no longer current. Since Rabinow wrote his book, anthropology has had several "turns," both historical and theoretical. While fieldwork has not disappeared, it has been transformed significantly (see, for example, Asad 1993; Clifford 1988; Crapanzano 2004).

12. Speaking of generalizations, Rabinow writes: "What at first seem to be the broadest and richest concepts, capable of organizing and clarifying the most material, turn out to be the most impoverished" (2007 [1977], 122).

13. See Sklar (1994) and Foster (2011) on "kinesthetic empathy."

14. Why hospitality is pertinent here is not completely clear, as Ali did not host the wedding—he only invited Rabinow to attend it.

15. Ali himself does not use the word *diyafa* (hospitality).

16. In my first book, I talked about this interestedness by referring to the phrase ʿatini, n-ʿati-k, "give to me and I'll give to you" (Kapchan 1996).

17. When he realized, for example, that in order to understand the particular workings of colonial power and its effects in the region, he had to have oral histories from several different people for whom these stories were still painful and embarrassing (and who thus did not want to speak about them), Rabinow engaged a marginal person—someone with nothing to lose—to tell him a version of the story. Not wanting this marginal person to represent the community, the others ultimately felt obliged to open up to Rabinow. It was a kind of coercion, a form of blackmail. "My response," admits Rabinow, "was essentially an act of violence; it was carried out on a symbolic level, but it was a violence nonetheless" (2007 [1997], 129). The information that Rabinow wheedled out of his informants in the village of Sidi Lahcen concerned the complicity of the region's *qaid*, or mayor, with the colonial powers, and the suffering that ensued because of that in the wake of independence. Rabinow had uncovered the village's "dirty secret." What power that revelation had for official or unofficial

versions of Moroccan history is hard to evaluate. What is sure is that providing a context for its narration required covert action on the part of Rabinow, and he was aware of it. It is laudable that Rabinow was able to write about this, but we are left with the cynical question of "why do ethnography at all?"

18. *Al* is the definite article "the," which is usually attached to a noun.

19. Such an attitude is often equated with fatalism, a state in which whatever happens is considered to be "written" (*al-maktub*). In such a state, one says *al-hamduʾallah ʿala kulishay* (thank God for everything [that comes your way]) or *al-hamduʾallah ʿala kulli hal* (thank God no matter what).

20. The second edition of The Oxford English Dictionary defines "disposition" as, among other things: "6. Natural tendency or bent of the mind, *esp.* in relation to moral or social qualities; mental constitution or temperament; turn of mind. 7.a. The state or quality of being disposed, inclined, or 'in the mind' (*to* something, or *to do* something); inclination (sometimes = desire, intention, purpose); state of mind or feeling in respect to a thing or person; the condition of being (favourably or unfavourably) disposed *towards.* (In *pl.* formerly sometimes = mental tendencies or qualities; hence nearly = sense 6.) b. A frame of mind or feeling; mood, humour . . . 10.a. Physical condition or state; state of bodily health. *Obs.* †b. Normal or natural condition (of mind or body). *Obs. rare.*"

21. On embodiment and indeterminacy, see Csordas (1993).

22. See Grosz (2008) and her analysis of Deleuzian vibration.

23. Wallace Stevens says something similar of human nature: "Human nature is like water. It takes the shape of its container," http://www.goodreads.com/author/quotes/42920.Wallace_Stevens (accessed January 20, 2012).

24. Rapport—from the French *rapporter,* to bring or carry back (to someone or something)—is an interesting concept in this regard. In English we say that a rapport is "established," "built," or "created"—that is, it is not historically determined so much as it is physically and emotionally cultivated.

25. I allude in the title of this section to Derrida (1980).

26. Howes (2003, 2004); Jackson (1996, 1998); Stoller (1989). See also Deleuzian-influenced ethnography like K. Stewart (2009).

27. Of course Clifford (1986) noted the "partial" nature of all anthropological knowledge not much later than the original publication date of *Reflections.* See also Rabinow's response to Clifford in *Writing Culture.*

28. Abu-Lughod notes that even with the best intentions, informants may feel scandalized after an ethnography is published (1990). What is the way out? She later suggests that storytelling is the most humanistic and least injurious way to transmit knowledge (Abu-Lughod 1993).

29. It is not my intention to essentialize gender identities, only to recognize that cultural discourses determine genders and determine them differently.

30. As Bourdieu notes, quoting Claudel, "'connaître, c'est naître avec,' to know is to be born with, and the long dialectical process, often described as 'vocation', through which the various fields provide themselves with the agents equipped with the habitus to make them work, is to the learning of a game very much as the acquisition of the mother tongue is to the learning of a foreign language" (Bourdieu 1990, 67).

31. Indeed, in his foreword, Bellah credits Rabinow with demonstrating that "knowing in the human studies is always emotional and moral as well as intellectual," while further asserting that Rabinow's "unselfconsciousness about the moral dimension" is the "most valuable contribution of the book" (2007 [1977], xxxi). Yet while Rabinow does give us his emotional reactions to a series of cultural obstacles, he does not in fact tell us how to "know" emotionally, and certainly not morally, as Bellah implies he should. Indeed, emotional "knowing" was not Rabinow's concern in 1977. And that, to a large extent, was the source of my negative reaction to the book. Indeed, in retrospect I realize that the very lack of self-consciousness that Bellah found so endearing was, to me, inflammatory.

32. The stew is called *dwaz*—from the Arabic *dawara*, to turn—because one "turns" one's bread in it.

33. Dispositions arise from one's habitus but also contribute to its making and structure.

34. For Bourdieu, dispositions arise from class-based practices, aesthetic systems that in turn determine stances and somatic orientations toward oneself and the world. And while dispositions are structured, they are also generative— that is, they create new possibilities as well as reproduce past structures. The canonic quotation from Bourdieu's *The Logic of Practice* says that what he calls the "habitus" is comprised of a "system of durable, transposable dispositions, structured structures predisposed to function as structuring structures, that is, as principles which generate and organize practices and representations that can be objectively adapted to their outcomes without presupposing a conscious aiming at ends or an express mastery of the operations necessary in order to attain them. Objectively 'regulated' and 'regular' without being in any way the product of obedience to rules, they can be collectively orchestrated without being the product of the organizing action of a conductor" (1990, 53). Furthermore, he states that "this system of dispositions—a present past that tends to perpetuate itself into the future by reactivation in similarly structured practices, an internal law through which the law of external necessities, irreducible

to immediate constraints, is constantly exerted—is the principle of the continuity and regularity which objectivism sees in social practices without being able to account for it; and also of the regulated transformations that cannot be explained either by . . . mechanistic sociologism or by . . . spontaneist subjectivism" (ibid., 54).

35. Silverstein explores this point by deconstructing the metaphors of "rooting" and "uprooting" employed in the tradition of social theory and scholarship on post-colonial populations.

36. See also Silverstein (2004a) and Goodman (2005).

37. In *The Logic of Practice*, Bourdieu critiques the "practical logic" of structuralism that compels the analyst to find a coherent system, stating that his essay on the Kabyle house was "perhaps the last work [he] wrote as a blissful structuralist," before he realized that he had to look at "incorporated dispositions, or more precisely the body schema, to find the ordering principle . . . capable of orienting practices in a way that is at once unconscious and systemic" (1990, 9–10).

38. This led Bourdieu (1990) to explore the paradox of objectivism and subjectivism and to delineate a theory of practice whereby the unconscious and embodied actions of social actors—from cuisine to kinship structures—both reproduce social structure and provide a way to transform it.

39. Bourdieu uses the term "arbitrary"—which is to say, not logically. The "antinomies"—or paradoxes—of belief are found here, in the conscious decision to embrace a belief system that has arisen from a different habitus, a forgotten but present history. While this may present a paradox, it is a common occurrence, particularly in conversion or in any kind of new discipline of the body (Mahmood 2005). Foucault calls such action a "technology of the self" (1988).

40. See particularly Bourdieu's mention of his propensity to understand a "mountain peasant" (1990, 14).

41. De Certeau notes that social agency often takes place in small acts of domesticity. He provides several metaphors for this. One is that of a reader who transforms the text of an author by bringing his or her own life and interpretations to it. Another is that of a poet, for whom the (social and determined) rules of meter and rhyme stimulate new discoveries. Yet another is that of a renter who does not own the place where she lives, but nonetheless inhabits it and makes changes to it with "acts and memories" (1984, xxi–xxii). The ethnographer is also reader, poet, and renter, affected by and affecting the quotidian and sensate world by moving through borrowed spaces and inhabiting new forms of home.

42. Think of Pablo Picasso or Paul Klee, Thelonius Monk, Randy Weston, or even James Joyce or Gertrude Stein. All these artists benefited from their encounters with different aesthetic and cultural systems.

43. The concept of bi-musicality is not, of course, unproblematic. In his article, Hood says it is necessary to have a "natural aptitude for music" (1960)—which begs the question of rapport, habitus, and disposition.

44. If ethnography is a coming-of-age genre, a story of initiation into both another culture and, by extension, another self (that is, the self revealed only in the encounter with difference), it is not insignificant that Rabinow ends *Reflections* by gesturing toward a new cultural acquisition: Vietnam.

10 | The Power of Babies

DAVID CRAWFORD

Children are of obvious importance to farmers in the High Atlas Mountains of Morocco, as the main source of farm labor and as a preeminent cultural value. Villagers expect to have children, pity those who do not, ask about having them, pray to have them, and consider any equivocation about the desirability of parenthood to be a weird misunderstanding or a form of mental illness. For most of my time in Morocco, I was a researcher without children, so I existed in kind of bizarre, liminal state. I had the material resources and apparent capabilities of a man, but I lacked—willfully, it seemed—an essential component of full masculinity. From a villager's perspective, what sort of man fails to produce children? What sort of man fails to even try?

I understood this vaguely during my initial fieldwork, but its significance became forcefully apparent much later after I managed to marry and begin the journey toward fatherhood. When my wife was at home in the United States, six months pregnant with our first child, I was in Morocco looking forward to providing the culturally correct answer to the questions my rural friends always asked: Yes, I was married. Yes, we were going to have a baby. But I didn't get that far. Before even leaving Marrakech I was sapped by the marriage question.

Early summer, 2002. I was waiting with a few other passengers for the taxi to depart the stand outside Bab e-Rob, waiting for the final places to fill, chatting in the dust and the heat with the doors open and our feet sprawled out. A portly man had heard me buy my place using Tashelhit (Berber), so he began with a typical, all-purpose Arabic greeting (*salaam wa aleikum*) followed by a raft of Darija phrases and then moved to more obscure Tashelhit greetings that both say hello and test whether it makes sense to continue in Berber. Preliminaries concluded and bona fides established, he moved on to the issues that matter: (1) Where are you from? (2) Are you married?

I had never answered the second question affirmatively in Berber, and when I did a barrage of alien queries rained down on me, from the original interrogator and a friend of his who quickly joined in. I stalled. I sputtered. They were talking at once. I was trying to reply. My child was not yet born, I explained; I babbled about the sonogram, saying that the child "would be a boy." The single men clambered from the cab to smoke cigarettes together at a safe distance. The car was our own. It belonged to the dads.

Liberated from the unmarried "men," my fleshy questioner could barely contain his excitement. He narrowed his eyes. Do you give it to your wife often? How many times a night? How many days a week? He giggled and used hand gestures to ensure that I understood the verbs. How many children do you expect to have? The two fathers chortled with triumphant delight at my evident embarrassment. I was obviously new at this.

How lucky we all were to have children, they exclaimed, offering examples from their own active connubial lives to make me feel comfortable with the questions. They proceeded with fervent advice about everything, including the appropriate frequency of copulation (three times a night) and the sensible number of children to have (five to eight—they couldn't agree on that one). The simple act of saying I was going to have a child divided the taxi between the men and not-yet-men, and for the first time I was on the manly side of the fence. I was a little breathless. I had unknowingly changed my ontological status, transformed myself into a newly sensible, virile kind of being with features that rural men read as safe and familiar. This was not just about sex. This was about sex within marriage with the explicit aim of producing children—certainly not the sort of locker-room banter that I had been socialized to perform. And I did not even have a baby yet. The idea of children changed my social location and opened up avenues of inquiry that had been closed before. As it turned out, the reality of children would prove far more complicated than the idea, as I will discuss below.

PARTICULAR KIDS IN A PARTICULAR PLACE

In this chapter I want to examine the contradictory power of babies, in Morocco and elsewhere—their power to change relations among adults and the understandings that adults have of their relations. The vignettes I will draw from are taken from two periods when my children were visiting the village in the High Atlas where I have done most of my fieldwork, one visit in the summer of 2004 and a second in the summer of 2009. The village is small (approximately 200 people) and poor (little potable water and no electricity while I was there). Villagers support themselves as farmers, mostly, though wage labor is becoming more important. A few caveats and contexts are necessary before we begin.

First, this is not just any village. I have consistently been surprised at how variable Moroccan villages are, so it is difficult to draw on the one I know best to explain all of Morocco, all of Berber Morocco, or even all of the High Atlas region. We will have to take what I have to say as a very particular experience and let others weigh in on how it accords with the rest of the country.

I have been writing about this place for a decade now, so I will skip my rapturous evocation of the irrigation canals, ululating women, and high pastures. I have a whole book on that (Crawford 2008), and with the photographer Bart Deseyn, I am working on another with pictures. For our present purposes, what is important is that the village is very steeply built up the side of a mountain and is served by a rudimentary dirt road rather precariously clinging to the canyon wall. There are numerous places where a misstep would plunge a person hundreds of feet down, and there are no guardrails or warning signs. This particular village is also hygienically horrifying. Children commonly play in and with excrement of various origins. There are poisonous snakes, mosquitoes, lice, scorpions, flies in nasty churning clouds, vicious dogs, and bedbugs. The invisible microfauna, too, are prolific and virulent. There is no refrigeration. The nearest health clinic is at least a couple of hours away, when it is open and if it has medicine. I live most of the year in Connecticut. By Connecticut standards, this village is a very stupid place to take children.

Finally, my children are not just any children. I know that all parents say this. We all see our little ones as precious and unique. But objectively children, like villages, are variable, and it makes sense to understand something of their peculiarities if we are to understand the interactions between these kids, this village, and the process of doing anthropological fieldwork. They will surely hate me when they grow old enough to read this, but I think this rough introduction is necessary to understand what follows.

My son, Calum, is irascible by nature—though, in fairness, not all the time. He was nearly two years old during the 2004 visit and six years old in 2009. He sometimes growls at people he doesn't like, especially in Morocco, or hisses like an angry cat. Calum once exploded at a *faux guide*—one of those ubiquitous young men who try to harass you into buying things—"What's your problem? Why are you bothering us?" so forcefully that the guy actually stopped bothering us. Calum clearly has no problem expressing himself, which is pleasant when he's satisfied, but he can be impatient. He likes to dance and show off, but he can also be intensely shy. He's very inquisitive and asks questions about everything all of the time, and he likes to frame these in obscure vocabulary when he knows it. (He mused to me once that there must be different kinds of mosquitoes since, as he said, "some are nocturnal, some are diurnal, and some are crepuscular.") He's also a bit of a fascist. He likes rules, even if he does not like following them, and he is often dismayed in Morocco by the number of people who do not seem to be conforming to the rules he has dutifully internalized. We will discuss this more in a moment.

In contrast, my daughter, Lula, is quite sweet. She was less than a year old and still being breast-fed during her two trips in 2004, and she was five years old when she returned in the summer of 2009. Her ambient mood is cheerful rather than disgruntled, though when she does want something badly she outdoes her brother a hundredfold in monomaniacal intensity. She has autism and is not very adept at verbal communication, but compared to most kids on the autism spectrum, she is adaptable to new routines and surroundings. She has always attempted to make her surroundings fit the routines she knows and understands, especially when she was younger.

So these are the babies and this is the village. We turn now to the interaction between them and how this has transformed the practice of fieldwork for me, as well as the role of my children in transforming some of the ideas I think through and with as an anthropologist. I hope to show that, materially and ideally, babies are powerful.

IDEAL BABIES AND THEIR MATERIAL DOPPELGÄNGERS

The 2002 taxi ride that began this chapter landed me eventually in Tagharghist, the village where I work. My friends there were as excited about my transformed personal situation as my fellow passengers in the taxi, but far more polite. Nobody asked rude questions about my wife. Villagers were obviously thrilled I was married, and excited that a child was on the way. In many cases I'd say "relieved" was the real reaction. Women focused on questions about my spouse—when she would come, why she wasn't with me at the time—and this entrée seemed to allow them to have longer and more general conversations with me than in the past. It gave them a framework for asking what was going on in my world without directly asking me questions about myself. During my initial fieldwork this had been a difficulty. There had been skirmishes between senior men and a variety of women (from pre-teens to grandmothers) regarding the question of my marriageability, with women asserting their right to bargain with me as a potential spouse and men trying to stop them. So now, in 2002, the long fight was over. *That* issue was resolved, and anybody could talk to "Daoud" without being accused of conducting "marriage" negotiations. I put "marriage" in quotations here only because a permanent monogamous relationship is not what all of the women were trying to negotiate. Some divorced mothers in particular were very practical about the material advantages marriage might have for my research and for their households.

My return in 2004 began just as well. It was the first time we actually brought our children to the village, and they were seen as beautiful and we were viewed as blessed. Lula's autism had not yet been revealed. She was active and alert, and the village girls fought to carry her around on their backs. Calum was busy, silly, and engaged. Methodologically, we found our fieldwork enhanced. My wife fit comfortably into the desired social category of "wife and mother." Everything seemed to be going swimmingly.

Still, it was clear that things were not entirely as I might have hoped. Just as I was not then and could never be a typical village guy, I was not a typical father either. Abdurrahman, my main host in the village, had installed an iron railing across his rooftop porch—deliberately, he said, to keep my children from falling off. He had also built a sort of gate that prevented the kids in my part of the house from falling down the dark, steep, irregular stairs in the other part. Meanwhile, his own kids and grandkids scampered up and down the precarious stairways like spry little goats, with nobody taking much notice.

I was rather insulted. While trying to resist the anthropologically delicious feeling of Being at One with the People, I had nonetheless succumbed to it. All my post-marriage visits without my kids along—that is, with only virtual kids—had made it seem like I had crossed some threshold and was now more fully integrated into, and more culturally synchronized with, the village. But these gates and bars were solid iron reminders that I was not one of the villagers. My children were not like their children. Mine needed to be protected, coddled. Mine needed the enhanced treatment that I obviously required (and secretly denied needing) as a foreigner, a city person, a *nasrani* (Christian).

It did not take long for Calum to demonstrate that they were right, too, as he nearly ran off a roof when he escaped from our part of the house, then reached between the bars and pushed heavy earthen pots off the edge of the house to crash ten meters below in the road. In the first instance he nearly killed himself, and in the second he almost killed people passing by. Abdurrahman and I took the truck down to souk and bought chicken wire to put over the bars, a second line of defense. My two-year-old went from being fairly typical in my mind to being a creature of supernaturally destructive powers. Why was my child so much more dangerous, and endangered, than the village children?

Understandably, this began to make my wife nervous. And then one of the village children dropped Lula, our baby, out of her cloth sling and onto her head, and all attempts at transcendental cross-cultural synthesis ground to a halt. A poisonous snake bit a neighbor, and she died as a result. My wife got dysentery and had to be evacuated with Lula in the "ambulance" (a jeep with a dirty mattress in back). The experiment was over.

Still, we didn't give up. There seems to be some mechanism in the brains of parents that renders the bad parts of the job fuzzy and hard to remember. The drudgery of the infant years is erased, for instance, and over time children again come to appear cute and desirable. This mechanism worked on us. The details of 2004 eventually faded from our minds, and we came to believe that, in 2009, we could return to the High Atlas with our then more robust children and things would turn out great.

Calum and I arrived first, in late May, and it was almost immediately apparent that my bright, engaged six-year-old was not going to be the charming anthropological accessory that I had dreamed about. Calum was intensely shy at the start, given that he couldn't understand much, and I was made aware of how important his verbal skills were to his self-confidence. Without them he was paralyzed and frustrated, and he took his frustration out on anybody who tried to engage him.

In the village it took me a while to get him to go outside so that I could work. I was trying to be casual, to behave like any father in the village. Children play outside. So I gave Calum careful instructions on how to be safe, what parts of the road to stay away from (the edge, essentially) and told him to play where I could see or hear him. Naturally, his first independent act was to go where I could not see him and climb up on a boulder dangerously perched above the abyss. This sent the women of the village, many of whom were working on their roofs cooking and doing laundry, into a kind of collective paroxysm. They could see Calum was in danger, but their screaming at him had no effect at all, so sensible older children were sent to intervene. Other children were made to pry me from my attempt to work on a village household survey. Calum and I were brought together for another talk about safety. Several village grandmothers gave me the talk. I translated it for Calum as best I could. We were both humbled, father and son.

Even that was not going to satisfy the village women, however. They put three girls in charge of Calum, three girls who followed him everywhere and physically restrained him whenever, in their view, any danger might be present. Since danger was ever present for this unpredictable blond boy, and the most dangerous thing that could happen to the girls was that anything happen to Calum, they erred on the side of caution. Calum was dutifully prevented from doing almost anything at all. He certainly was not allowed to run along the road, throw rocks, or wrestle like the other boys. Most of this was OK with Calum—throwing rocks and wrestling were against the rules back home, and the village boys played far too roughly for him—but being pushed and pulled around by girls was simply more than he could stand. He asked me to teach him the Berber words for "enough," "go away," "stop," and "leave me alone." His attempts at communication only made the girls giggle, and the angrier he got, the funnier they found him. The giggling eventually left Calum livid and crying.

And there was the kissing. Moroccans kiss children. It started when we landed, continued in Marrakech, and became insufferable in the village. Everybody, it seemed, felt he or she had the right to kiss Calum, and Calum seemed to have no right to resist. He would shriek, "Daddy, they're not even *related* to me," invoking his own kinship system to highlight the impropriety of it all. He had been sternly lectured in school, after all, that strangers are not allowed to touch you, and that they are certainly not allowed to kiss you. Now, here in Morocco, a whole nation of strangers disregarded the unassailable prescriptions of American kindergarten teachers and went about kissing willy-nilly—with their victims having no recourse at all! What made it worse was that I would not defend him. "They kiss me right in front of you!" he would say accusingly, aghast that I would not stand up and honorably defend him from this sick and horrible intrusion. I taught him that he needed to grin and bear it, to tolerate diversity, in the saccharine words of every university's multicultural relations center, but the closest he got to gracefully accepting the situation was a low growl and a pout. We did not stay very long in the village this time, and I did not get much done.

But we did not give up. With time my boy calmed down and started to adjust. We had things to do in Marrakech, and we got ourselves into a rhythm and began to make it fun. I would take him with me all over the medina, for instance, and his job would be to find our way home. We had our own café, where the waiters knew our preferred breakfast selections, and our *halaq,* where Calum got his hair cut and I got shaved. If Calum had yet to tolerate intrusions on his body, he had at least reduced the violence of his reactions. He was overjoyed when, after a month, his mother and sister joined us.

I was thrilled too, though this also was the beginning of what I took to be the difficult part of the trip. I would now be taking my autistic daughter, my marginally adapted son, and my non-Berber-speaking wife, Hillary, to a part of rural Morocco that everybody but me seemed to think was unsafe. Colleagues, friends, and relatives told me the plan was crazy, and while I laughed off their paranoia, I was quietly worried. Hillary and I had discussed our concerns for months beforehand. Our focus was Lula. There was no way to know if she would eat the food or use what bathroom facilities there were in the village; there was no way to know if she would embrace the differences or freak out. We were not sure we could keep her safe. In the village I had struggled to warn people, to explain what autism was. I said that they should expect my girl to be a little different, for her to be "slow" in some ways, but still "smart" in others. There is really no shorthand way to describe the idiosyncrasies of a child with autism, and my attempts to do so in Tashelhit made me sound like an idiot. There was nothing to do but try.

OUR LAST FIELDWORK

We arrived in Tagharghist on foot late one afternoon. It was hot, and we were thirsty. We'd walked the final seven kilometers after our rental car had resolutely refused to make it up one of the steeper grades. It was June, and the majority of able-bodied villagers were hard at work threshing barley. Our arrival was known, however, and Abdurrahman popped in to give us warm Cokes and offer tea, but then he had to get back to threshing. Most people were too busy to leave their work, and anyway we wanted to collapse in the shade. This was perfect for the younger children left alone in the house. With the adults busy at the *inraren,* or threshing areas, the youngsters could examine us.

It did not take long for a small clutch of children to creep into our part of the house, led by Calum's former managers. Pressing up the stairs, quivering in the shadows of the doorway, they suppressed what giggles they could and hoped to be asked in. Eventually they were beckoned in and lined one wall of our courtyard nervously, looking at us quizzically, not sure of the next move. There were seven of them, ranging in age from two to about nine. They knew Calum and me, but most had never seen Hillary and Lula, and the young girls desperately wanted to inspect the exotica.

Calum, for his part, was acting as tour guide, talking to his sister and mom, explaining to them what he knew of the village from his previous visit, which mostly amounted to how one should be careful or these girls would herd you around like a chastened sheep. He pointed out Jamila, the bossiest of the girls, and would have nothing to do with any of them. At first Lula did not seem to notice the kids. She was busy drinking her Coke and sweating from the long walk up the road.

All at once Lula looked at the kids and said sternly, "Miss Lisa's class, line up. Time to go outside." The children looked stunned. "Miss Lisa" was Lula's beloved teacher, and after the announcement Lula popped up and ran over to the village children, then stood at the end of the "line" she perceived them to be making. Calum charged after her to ensure that she would not do anything wrong, that she wouldn't push or otherwise hurt one of the younger children. He is used to shadowing her, and since he had been shepherded by the older village girls, he was particularly eager to enforce the safety rules he had been made to follow.

But Lula was not up to mischief. She seemed genuinely excited at the prospect of playing with the children. She loves school, and in the days prior to our trip she had been asking for some of her friends from special education classes. Now that she had some children to work with, she was going to make herself a school. When the "line" didn't move, didn't behave as it should, she had to figure out what to do.

She said brightly, "Time to sing!" and brought little wooden stools over for the children to sit on, then ushered them into the seats. She began instructing her "class" in the circle-time songs that she had learned at school, beginning with a simple tune that involved singing each child's name in turn. Hillary asked all the children their names, and helped Lula insert Khadija, Malika, Rashida, and so forth into the song. The children quickly caught on and belted out their names and the English words to the song.

After singing for some time, Lula shifted gears and introduced "ring-around-the-rosy." She was unfazed by, or unconscious of, the language barrier, and the fact that the children were not familiar with dancing in the round simply meant that they needed instruction. This Lula provided. She laughed as she grabbed their hands and demonstrated how a proper ring-around-the-rosy works. She gazed deeply into their eyes as they sang, and the children grew increasingly animated and involved in the activity. Self-consciousness melted away and everyone followed Lula's lead in the song and dance.

Everyone except Calum. Calum was doing everything he could to disrupt this scene. He is a terrific brother to his disabled sister under typical conditions, but this was atypical. He was used to accommodating Lula, translating her. Now she was communicating with the inscrutable mountain children, and he could not crack the code. Hillary kept Calum somewhat at bay, but Calum was certain that Lula would get hurt or hurt somebody, and he was wildly jealous of her success at socializing. Lula ignored him and blithely continued to pretend that she was a teacher and the village children were her students. The children seemed perfectly thrilled with this arrangement.

Lula then moved on to patty-cake, and finished with "Goodbye Friends," inserting all the children's names in the song as if a typical school session had ended and they should all go home. It was astonishing. From a parental perspective, this was the first time we had ever seen our girl fully in charge of a situation. It was the first time she had willingly been the center of attention, and was one of the first times she was able to reach out and communicate effectively with a group of typical children. Where Calum, the supposedly typical kid, was handicapped by his inability to speak, Lula's autism had made her notably adept at nonverbal communication. Where Calum was shy and confused at the difference in culture, Lula apparently had transcended it. As she does in her own cultural world, Lula applied the script that seemed most appropriate, and it turned out to be a smashing success. It was one of the happiest moments of our parenting lives.

Later, when the village was settling down from their workday, we took the kids for a walk, and Lula again demonstrated her confidence in greeting people. She watched the older children finish pouring barley into sacks and scooping up chaff; she looked curiously at the sweating mules still tied to their posts. She excitedly held hands with any child who approached her, as Calum sulked and growled with hostile embarrassment. Lula did not notice the local lack (of toys or English-language skills, for instance) and the village children didn't seem to notice hers (on autism as a "discourse of lack," see Crawford and Haldane 2010).

Our joy was short-lived, however. The adults were back, dinner was being made, and I continued to try to "explain" my daughter. Her ability to play in an apparently appropriate way made explanations for her behavior seem unnecessary to my fellow fathers, and it was clear that they were beginning to wonder what my problem was. They crossly insisted that my children were fine, that I should stay in the village for the rest of the summer, and that I should not talk of my children in a way that suggested they were problematic in any way. Probably, the other fathers seemed to suggest, I should not be talking about the children so much at all.

Then, standing in front of us, Lula began to pee. She peed and peed, as she'd been holding it since we arrived, and she posed beatifically in her expanding puddle of urine, hands on her hips and a smile on her face. Hillary had tried to take her downstairs to the one real toilet in the village, but it was the hole-in-the-ground kind, and Lula was having none of that. It had taken us many years to teach her to use a three-dimensional toilet, and two dimensions were one less than she was willing to tolerate.

There we were. Abdurrahman was deeply embarrassed. I was embarrassed. Hillary sprang up to take Lula out of the room, and Abdurrahman got a towel and began to sponge up the pee. I tried to take over. He wouldn't let me. None of us knew what to say. Abdurrahman kindly suggested that it was no big deal. I tried to say that I *had* tried to explain. But I had no recourse, no discourse of autism to explain my daughter (and no way to explain my son's antisocial behavior, either). My village counterparts had no effective way to convince me that I did not have to explain. Fatherhood for them was evidently not fatherhood for me.

Before we left the village, maybe for the last time, I sat at the saint's shrine talking with Mohammed Id Baj. He was an old friend, and I had not yet seen him on this trip. It was early evening, and he was resting on a rock, tracing lines in the dust with his walking stick.

"You have two children, right?" he asked.

"Yes," I said, motioning across the gorge, "right there. A boy and a girl." Lula was singing with the village girls, and Calum was visible at the bars of the patio.

"So important," he said. "Children are *the* important thing."

"Yes," I agreed, not knowing what else to say, and we sat there still and silent, listening to the burbling of children at play. I asked about his kids, the ones who had married and those who had migrated. After a short time Mohammed's oldest son, Omar, staggered up the road with a huge log across his shoulders, looking like a penitent bearing a cross. Omar was trailed by his own son, also named Mohammed, who was imperiling the log carrying by winding between and around his father's legs. Sweating, exhausted, and smiling, Omar greeted me and propped up the log while he stopped to talk to his father.

Grandfather Mohammed insisted that grandson Mohammed come out from behind his father and kiss our hands, which he did. Then the grandfather tousled the boy's hair and heaved himself up to a standing position with a *"ya Rbi"* ("oh Lord"). He then hugged me warmly, and we said good-bye. I watched them move up the road: the strong young man bearing his heavy load, his father bent over his walking stick, and the rambunctious boy for whom all this walking was play. I knew that I should get back to work.

CONCLUSIONS

The first point I take from all of this is that despite decades of anthropological angst about our social position as ethnographers, we still routinely underestimate the significance of our family status. We anthropologists "don't like children," as Lawrence Hirschfeld put it bluntly (2002), or at least we do not appreciate their scholarly significance. We remind ourselves that we tend to be white and wealthy (at least in rural Moroccan terms), that we are overwhelmingly middle class in a Euro-American cultural sense, that we are mostly liberal politically, and we know that gender matters profoundly just about everywhere. Most of this is well understood, and we take it into account when we write ethnography. However, it matters a lot more than we think that many of us are single while we do our initial fieldwork. We work alone. We live alone. Our project is our own. We are bizarrely and often unself-consciously self-absorbed. While this volume provides some fascinating counter-examples (see the chapters by Rachel Newcomb, Deborah Kapchan, David McMurray, and Karen Rignall), the norm for U.S. graduate students doing fieldwork has been a state of romantic detachment and deliberate childlessness—a condition that allows one to be self-absorbed, which is to say absorbed with the anthropological project at hand.

In rural Morocco this is so weird as to be almost unbelievable. To be deliberately unmarried and childless is, I would argue, as salient a factor in making us seem alien to the natives as any other feature of our identities. Race, culture, class, and politics matter at home, so we notice how they matter in Morocco. Marriage and children are not much of an issue at home, especially for men, or they become important much later in life than they do in Morocco. I believe this is why we underestimate the local salience of our marital and parental status. There is good work on the theme of marriage, childhood, and parenting in Morocco, from the writings of Elizabeth Fernea (1975) and Susan Schaefer Davis (1983) to those of Deborah Kapchan (1996) and Rachel Newcomb (2009). And there are sporadic cases of family and children being cited in relation to fieldwork (McMurray 2001). Still, the present volume represents a significant breakthrough in terms of the number of authors who reveal their family status and its range of implications for their fieldwork.

Second, in rural Morocco marriage and family operate quite differently than they do in Connecticut. Even the idea of fatherhood had been magic in Morocco. It seemed a common category that helped Moroccan men understand me. Barriers dropped. I was accepted, even embraced, in new ways. I enjoyed new freedom and new sorts of conversations. I encountered Morocco differently. However, the cultural and class-based differences in the practice of fatherhood erected a whole new set of barriers and re-inscribed the distance between my world and that of the Moroccan mountains.

It is hard to say how this would have been different in Moroccan cities, but in my social class in my country, children are a project chosen by people, usually in their late twenties or thirties, often after careers and other serious issues have been settled. Children are separate from careers, generally a drag on them.[1] In the United States children are an option, usually, and not having them is certainly an option. Whatever visceral joy they bring, children are also something like expensive pets or accessories, symbols through which we perform middle-class, usually heterosexual, status. We middle-class Connecticut parents measure each other via our children, too—at school, soccer practice, PTA meetings, and birthday parties. We judge and are judged on the performance of our children, both how well we transmit important values to them and how promisingly they augur success as adults.

In rural Morocco this is not true. Having children is culturally critical, but beyond that fathers are not much judged. Children are around—everywhere, all the time; they are the proverbial water that fish hardly notice. And while one obviously moves from being a child to begetting them, the social world in general is infused by children and childhood. That's one thing that makes operating as a parent in Morocco easier than in the United States. There is no separate childless sphere, no interregnum when you languish long years between being a child and having them yourself. In fact, like Omar, you spend much of your life as a father simultaneously being a son—not in the abstract sense of "having" a live father, but actually living in your father's house, subsisting off his resources, and doing his bidding while you yourself are also a father. You father and are fathered at the same time. Many rural Moroccan men are at least grandfathers when they finally inherit land and begin to independently control their own domestic domain.

Also, in rural Morocco children are responsible for parents rather than the other way around. Care flows overwhelmingly from younger generations to the older. While I will work for something like two decades preparing my children for middle-class life (including saving a small fortune for them to attend college), my rural Moroccan friends can expect to be bathed in their children's devotion and care long before their wee ones are teenagers. The rural Moroccan father does not typically work to ensure the success of his son. The son works to ensure the comfort of his father. The existential transition from son to father is not necessarily smooth or unproblematic, but it does not involve a wholesale reorganization of the self. It does not constitute a change in career. Children are valuable economic resources for fathers in the mountains; they play a crucial role. They are not expenses but producers, laborers, thinkers, actors in the rural household economy.

Finally, while I have made arguments about the important economic operations of households before (Crawford 2007, 2008), I have more recently come to appreciate the role of the household in cultural transmission and transformation. Mostly this is because I have now experienced it. My children have literally made me a different person. They have undone what I was as a single man and refocused my entire life on them. This was not apparent to me until I attempted to combine the two lives—my single self who did anthropological fieldwork, and the dad who raises kids and teaches college. The two selves did not mesh well. The old me is somehow gone. My new household means that much else is new, too.

My evident transformation suggests that "culture" is not diffuse and final, a sort of ether that permeates us all during childhood, casts us in a specific cultural way of being, and then wafts away. Culture is an ongoing process, a lifelong process, a process that happens between rather than to people. The people nearest to us do some of the most important acculturating, and nobody is nearer to a parent than children. My children have re-acculturated me while I thought I was cultivating them in what we might call a process of dialogical ontogenesis. This is the real power of babies: they build adults. My children have reworked me in ways that I cannot resist any more effectively than I deflect their begging to hail the ice cream truck or their pleading to cuddle when they should be sleeping. My babies are powerful in ways that make me rethink my relationship to Morocco, to anthropology, and more.

NOTE

1. This situation prompted *Anthropology News* to inaugurate a series about work-life balance. Such a "balance" is a bald admission by anthropologists that "work" and "life" are different sorts of things, with children part of "life" rather than "work." Arguably, writing this chapter is my attempt to integrate children and career, production and reproduction.

11 |

Afterword: Anthropologists
among Moroccans

KEVIN DWYER

The essays in this volume address topics that, for a long time, were present only at the margins of academic anthropological discourse, if they appeared at all. Issues like the anthropologist's "identity"— the implications of the anthropologist's origins and how anthropologists construct themselves in the field; the attractions and perils of friendship; the impact of the anthropologist's family on fieldwork; suspicion of and hostility toward the anthropologist and competition between the anthropologist and others in the field; the tensions among the many aspects of an anthropologist's humanity, and between the roles of researcher and judge, between "scientific" observation and judgmental evaluation; the temptations of religious conversion; the fieldworker's deep, often extreme emotions in certain situations; the researcher's uncertain "control" over the fieldwork situation and the importance of unintended consequences, accidents, and mistakes—these are just some of the many topics these essays treat that were rarely explored in the anthropological literature up through the 1960s. These topics were seen as largely irrelevant to the knowledge-gathering aims of the discipline, and writing about them, reflecting on the anthropologist's own feelings and actions while in the field (what has come to be called anthropological "reflexivity"),

213

exposed authors then, and sometimes still does, to accusations of self-centeredness; of emphasizing their own presence, personality, and role at the expense of conveying knowledge about the other; of using language betraying too much emotion at the expense of cool, objective discourse. Today it is widely accepted that such accusations are fundamentally misguided and based on the illusion that knowledge of the other exists in a timeless and context-free domain, independent of the particular anthropologist who—situated culturally, geographically, and historically and with his or her personal and behavioral dispositions—tries to construct it. As the essays in this volume demonstrate convincingly, when anthropologists show and question themselves in their encounter with the other, our knowledge of the interaction gains in depth and complexity, as does our understanding of both the other and ourselves.

If the topics mentioned above were so rarely dealt with prior to the 1970s but pervade the essays on Morocco in this volume and appear frequently in anthropological writing today, we might wonder how this shift came about. To consider this we need to look back at U.S. anthropological writings on Morocco over the past four decades and characterize the general context within which they were produced.

SOME THIRTY ETHNOGRAPHIES, THREE PERIODS, THREE THEMES[1]

Ethnographies, Periods

There are perhaps some thirty ethnographies on Morocco written by U.S. anthropologists during the past four decades, testifying to a particularly rich period for U.S. research on Morocco and for U.S. anthropology as a discipline.[2] Not only did U.S. anthropological study of Morocco come to rival and outdo French research on France's former colony, but in the first decade or so of this period—roughly from the early 1970s through the early 1980s—U.S. anthropological practice and writing were being critically re-examined and a number of fertile new approaches were emerging, partly in response to world events and the U.S. role in them. These approaches were at times indebted to, at times reacting to, the predominantly empiricist Anglo-Saxon traditions of ethnographic study. It is not surprising that there was some overlap in these two areas, with the new developments in U.S. anthropology being in part reflected in innovative anthropological research on Morocco.

These anthropological studies of Morocco were written in a geopolitical context where, over a long period—at least from the 1940s up to the present—Morocco played an important strategic role in U.S. foreign policy. While this does not directly account for the attention the country received from U.S. anthropologists—there were other reasons, such as the significant attention already paid to Lebanon and Tunisia through the 1960s and the difficult political relations between the United States on the one hand and Algeria, Libya, and Egypt on the other—it does provide some of the structuring conditions within which this work was carried out. With Morocco occupying an important strategic position, funding for research in and on the country faced no insuperable obstacles and, as Brian Edwards makes clear in his stimulating 2005 study, starting in the 1970s the anthropological writing on Morocco was important in shaping U.S. perceptions not only of Morocco but of the broader Arab world and was important in discussions in Morocco, too.[3]

Starting in the 1970s, some ethnographic writings on Morocco owed an intellectual debt and much of their overall impact to Clifford Geertz, who was a major creative force in U.S. anthropology from the early 1960s through the next four decades. Geertz did important work on Morocco (after his earlier, groundbreaking works on Indonesia that were innovative in theory, subject matter, and writing style), and he advised and oversaw the doctoral research of a number of anthropologists working on Morocco from the mid-1960s on, among them Tom Dichter, Dale Eickelman, Paul Rabinow, and Lawrence Rosen. Yet the character of U.S. anthropological work on Morocco goes well beyond Geertz's influence. As Susan Trencher (2002) persuasively argues, the three innovative Moroccan ethnographies she concentrates on (Rabinow 2007 [1977], Crapanzano 1980, and K. Dwyer 1982)—she also discusses a study of the Amazon by Jean-

Paul Dumont (1979)—are best viewed as signs of broad changes in U.S. society as a whole, and only Rabinow, of the four authors Trencher discusses, worked directly under and was strongly influenced by Geertz. Besides, in many places where Geertz's work is referred to, it often serves as foil or target rather than as guide (this is true for Rabinow's work as well, with this volume's essays providing many examples for both authors).[4]

The ethnographies on Morocco written by U.S. anthropologists over the past four decades fall loosely into three consecutive periods.

1. Works from the 1970s to the mid-1980s.

This was a period of deep re-examination and fundamental questioning of both anthropology and of the U.S. role in the world. Anthropology's participation in political and military projects was one target of this questioning, and this was related to the worldwide rejection of colonial rule and its legacy and, in particular, to hostility toward U.S. aggression in Vietnam and its other foreign adventures in the Middle East and elsewhere. Works on Morocco published during this period (only some of which reflected these concerns) include Vincent Crapanzano's *The Hamadsha: A Study in Moroccan Ethnopsychiatry* (1973) and *Tuhami: Portrait of a Moroccan* (1980), Paul Rabinow's *Symbolic Domination: Cultural Form and Historical Change in Morocco* (1975) and *Reflections on Fieldwork in Morocco* (2007 [1977]), Dale Eickelman's *Moroccan Islam: Tradition and Society in a Pilgrimage Center* (1976), David Hart's *The Aith Waryaghar of the Moroccan Rif: An Ethnography and History* (1976), Daisy Dwyer's *Images and Self-Images: Male and Female in Morocco* (1978), Clifford Geertz, Hildred Geertz, and Lawrence Rosen's *Meaning and Order in Moroccan Society: Three Essays in Cultural Analysis* (1979, containing a lengthy essay by each of the authors), my *Moroccan Dialogues* (1982), and Lawrence Rosen's *Bargaining for Reality: The Construction of Social Relations in a Muslim Community* (1984).

2. Works from the mid-1980s to the mid-1990s.

During this period the challenges to traditional anthropology became an organic part of the discipline, signaled by George Marcus and Michael Fischer's synthesis of the unrest in *Anthropology as Cultural Critique* (1986), and took place in a context marked by the failure of orthodox development theory, new development initiatives from international multilateral organizations such as the International Monetary Fund and the World Bank, increasingly sharp societal strains within "Third World" countries, and gains in strength by local and grassroots groups in civil society. Ethnographies of this period include Eickelman's *Knowledge and Power in Morocco: The Education of a Twentieth-Century Notable* (1985), Elaine Combs-Schilling's *Sacred Performances: Islam, Sexuality, and Sacrifice* (1989), Henry Munson's *The House of Si Abd Allah: The Oral History of a Moroccan Family* (1991) and *Religion and Power in Morocco* (1993), and my *Arab Voices: The Human Rights Debate in the Middle East* (1991, focusing on Morocco, Tunisia, and Egypt).

3. Works from the mid-1990s to today.

Internationally, this period witnessed the 11 September 2001 attack on New York City's World Trade Center and, subsequently, the United States–initiated wars in Iraq and Afghanistan and the broader so-called "war on terror." In Morocco, King Hassan II's almost four decades of rule ended with his death in 1999, and his son succeeded to the throne as Mohammed VI. There was continuing dynamism in Moroccan civil society and the promulgation of a new family code (the *Mudawwana*) in 2004, which significantly strengthened women's rights. Morocco also suffered several "terrorist" attacks in the century's first decade, and many Moroccans continued the pattern of emigration, often clandestine and endangering their lives, while others returned from abroad.

Not least among the changes in Morocco has been the rapidly growing number of university-educated Moroccan men and women and, among them, many who know English well, who study social science at the university level, and who are able to examine how a relatively recent group of Western scholars—distinct from earlier groups of mainly French colonial scholars—were studying Morocco since the first decades of independence and interpreting the country for international audiences. These conditions underlie Edwards's remark, cited more fully in note 3, that the U.S. anthropological texts on Morocco "are part of what Moroccans themselves grapple with and respond to in contemporary cultural and intellectual production" (2005, 268–69).

Consequently, we are not surprised to find Moroccans examining this discourse about them—Hassan Rachik's *Le proche et le lointain* (2012) is a good example. In this work Rachik, a professor at the Faculté des Sciences Juridiques Economiques et Sociales, Hassan II University in Casablanca, examines not only the classic French ethnographies but also focuses on "*l'anthropologie interprétative*" in the final chapters, examining Clifford Geertz's writings on Morocco as well as Crapanzano's, Eickelman's, Hildred Geertz's, Rabinow's, Rosen's, and mine. In this context it is also unsurprising that some works by U.S. anthropologists have been translated into French (C. Geertz 1968, Rabinow 2007 [1977]), and some into Arabic (K. Dwyer 1982, Eickelman 1985).

Among the works of this period are Susan Ossman's *Picturing Casablanca: Portraits of Power in a Modern City* (1994), Stefania Pandolfo's *Impasse of the Angels: Scenes from a Moroccan Space of Memory* (1997), and books by most of the authors in this collection—Deborah Kapchan's *Gender on the Market: Moroccan Women and the Revoicing of Tradition* (1996) and *Traveling Spirit Masters: Moroccan Gnawa Trance and Music in the Global Marketplace* (2007b), David McMurray's *In and Out of Morocco: Smuggling and Migration in a Frontier Boomtown* (2001), Jamila Bargach's *Orphans of Islam: Family, Abandonment and Secret Adoption in Morocco* (2002), my *Beyond Casablanca: M. A. Tazi and the Adventure of Moroccan Cinema* (2004), David Crawford's *Moroccan Households in the World Economy: Labor and Inequality in a Berber Village* (2008), Katherine Hoffman's *We Share Walls: Language, Land, and Gender in Berber Morocco* (2008b), and Rachel Newcomb's *Women of Fes: Ambiguities of Urban Life in Morocco* (2009).

Three Themes

In these global and national contexts, many U.S. anthropologists were moved to address more explicitly the nature of their presence in the field and how their identity—origins, class, gender, civil status, and so on—influenced their research. They shifted their focus from classic anthropological topics (kinship and marriage, economic and political structures, land use practices, and so forth) to topics that involved the relationship between the local, regional, and global; the importance of mobility; questions of social justice; gender issues; and the role of the political. And they moved to explore a variety of forms and styles to better convey these new aspects. We see these matters becoming central concerns, although in very different ways, in the books produced during this period and in the contributions to this volume.

To trace how these ethnographies expressed these shifting concerns, I will focus on three themes that I believe are related in an organic way to changes over the past four decades that have taken place in Morocco, in anthropology, and in the relationship between the United States and the world: (1) presence, or how the anthropologist is "positioned" in the text, how his or her relationship to the community appears, and how the character of fieldwork shapes the experience and the book about it; (2) subject, or how the author defines the subject of the study and what the study's focus is; and (3) form, or the form, style, and structure of the written work.

Presence

One of the most significant innovations introduced by anthropological texts in the first period, from the 1970s to the mid-1980s, consists of placing the anthropologist in the text as a human subject. Crapanzano foreshadows this in his 1973 book when, in his opening vignette, he finds that the trance music has a "dulling effect" on him and "an irritating one" (xiii). In this early work the anthropologist's presence is not examined reflexively, but we see the anthropologist in the picture, in the moment; we read of his responses as a human subject; and we meet an early, somewhat jarring, example of what will become a major theme in subsequent works.

A short while later, in works by Rabinow (2007 [1977]), Crapanzano (1980), and Kevin Dwyer (1982), the anthropologist is deeply reflexive and plays a key role in the text, although each author does this with radically different emphases and to significantly different effect. In Rabinow's work, both self and other—"reconstructed," "condensed," and made to seem "progressively . . . neat and coherent" (2007 [1977], 6)—tend to lose solidity and disappear behind abstract formulations. In Crapanzano's, where the informant's words are provided in short excerpts, the psychoanalytic perspective tends to overshadow the anthropological, as Crapanzano admits (1980, 10), with the author's encounters with Tuhami resembling psychoanalytic sessions in being strictly separated from everyday life and in the two men's meeting only during these sessions (during which a field assistant was always the intermediary) and never outside them.[5] In *Moroccan Dialogues* we witness a series of "events" seen from the anthropologist's perspective and then read the extended dialogues (translated and lightly edited) about these events between the anthropologist and a mature, still-active Moroccan farmer, showing their different perspectives and the give-and-take, changes of direction, and abrupt ruptures that conversations often display; and allowing readers to appreciate—or so I hoped in writing the book—the strengths and weaknesses, the defenses and vulnerabilities, of the participants and to appreciate also how their relationship provides a commentary on the relationship between their societies.

Not all second- and third-period texts place the anthropologist squarely in the picture or in the moment, but doing so is characteristic of many of them. A good example is Pandolfo's work, in which she recounts on the introduction's first page an incident that "directly implicate[s]" her (1997, 1) as she is compared, in her role as anthropologist, to "a prominent actor in the French military and ethnological history of southern Morocco" (ibid., 2). This story becomes a possible allegory for the anthropologist's presence and operates as "an ironical warning, a challenge" (ibid., 3)—a "challenge" that, in appearing at the start of both her fieldwork and her book, is one the rest of her fieldwork and the body of her book are designed to answer.[6]

Other signs of the anthropologist's "positioning" during these decades are the explicit attention paid to (1) the question of identifying and naming individuals, (2) the nature of the exchange between anthropologist and community, and (3) the implications of the anthropologist's civil status. Naming and identifying the anthropologist as fieldworker and author is obviously a founding convention of the ethnographic genre, but whether and how to identify community members is problematic and has usually not been discussed explicitly—a contrast between self and other that exemplifies what I called in *Moroccan Dialogues* their "structured inequality" (K. Dwyer 1982, xix), in which the anthropologist, typically from a "metropolitan" country, earns credit for authorship that will materially advance his or her career while Moroccans, inhabitants of a "Third World," "peripheral" country, benefit little from the research beyond, perhaps, some satisfaction in personal relationships and modest material earnings; gain no significant improvement in life chances; and face, in many cases, risks and dangers from exposure. Although many authors over recent decades address this contrast, their answers are varied, often a consequence of the particular position occupied by community members. McMurray, for example, disguises identities since many of the people involved in his research were engaged in illegal activities (2001, xi); in other cases, authors defend using real identities because the figures appearing were public figures (K. Dwyer 1991); in still others, authors provide a mixture of real identity and disguise depending on the context of the research (K. Dwyer 1982, Bargach 2002, 19; Hoffman 2008b, 42).

In a number of recent ethnographies of Morocco, overt attention is paid to the exchange between anthropologist and community. One good example is Crawford's, where we read that "a collaborative project like this makes it difficult to know who is owed what" (2008, xiii)—a phrase that might provide a convenient excuse for shifting to another topic. Yet Crawford goes on to relate in detail, over almost a page and a half, how he compensated individual villagers and the village as a whole for the various kinds of assistance he received, while noting that, in exchange, "these mostly illiterate villagers have, in effect, given me a career" (ibid.). Related to the issue of exchange is the discomfort some anthropologists have shown with the traditional term "informant," no doubt because it implies instrumentalization, one-way communication, and hierarchical relationships. For example, Hoffman systematically uses the term "consultant" (2008b), and Crawford employs the terms "research partner," "interlocutor," and "friend" (2008).

We also see a more deliberate effort to indicate the anthropologist's civil status: Is the anthropologist married, and if so, how does or doesn't the spouse fit into the fieldwork project? Does the anthropologist have children, and if so, where are they during the fieldwork? What are the anthropologist's age, origins, and cultural and class background, and how might these influence the research? Many authors provide answers to these questions either explicitly or implicitly. Crawford's book, again, gives us some detail on how his change in status from bachelor to husband to father across his fieldwork experiences changed his relationships with villagers (2008, preface), in ways that many of us who have worked in Morocco will find familiar.

Among issues that remained undiscussed in the anthropological literature through the 1960s were the anthropologist's sexuality, and marriage between an anthropologist and a national of the country studied. Rabinow recounted, anecdotally, his experience with a prostitute in Morocco (2007 [1977]), and the sexuality "taboo" has now been definitively breached by, among others, Don Kulick and Margaret Wilson (1995). There are a number of instances of marriage in the Moroccan ethnographies I have been discussing, but the marriage tie remains largely in the background (Munson 1991, Kapchan 1996, Pandolfo 1997). Newcomb 2009 provides a picture of her wedding and a short discussion of the ways in which her marriage to a Moroccan influenced her fieldwork.

Subject

Books of the first period, from the 1970s to the mid-1980s, were largely concerned with local situations, social relations, religious beliefs, and neglected issues of power and injustice (for example, Crapanzano 1973 and 1980, Rabinow 1975 and 2007 [1977], Eickelman 1976, D. Dwyer 1978, K. Dwyer 1982, Rosen 1984). As we move into the second period, however, we see more frequent references to hierarchy and power, sometimes on the local and sometimes on the national level (Eickelman 1985, Combs-Schilling 1989, K. Dwyer 1991, Munson 1993). And in the third period we find this concern broadening to include questions related to international hierarchies of power and social justice, with greater attention being paid to mobility and to the impact of globalization (McMurray 2001, Bargach 2002, Slyomovics 2005, Crawford 2008, Hoffman 2008b[7]).[8]

Studies also are more frequently multi-sited, in line with the general trend in anthropology noted by Marcus (1995). This trend could already be seen in my *Arab Voices* (K. Dwyer 1991), and it continued in other works (Ossman 1994, K. Dwyer 2004, Kapchan 2007b). Also receiving more attention recently is expressive activity in the arts and in play (Ossman 1994, Pandolfo 1997, K. Dwyer 2004, Kapchan 2007b). Also, there is evidence of growing interest in middle-class settings, as in Kapchan 1996, Dwyer 2004 (which also shows Moroccan feature films using middle-class settings more frequently), and Newcomb 2005.

Works treating issues of gender in Morocco have been of continuing importance throughout these decades, reflecting the global emergence of feminist movements and activism that started in the 1960s, gained force in the 1970s, and began to be seen in Morocco toward the end of the 1980s, as well as the anthropological discussions around sexual orientation and cultural notions of masculine and feminine (in the first period, see D. Dwyer 1978, Davis 1983; in the second period, Combs-Schilling 1989, S. Davis and Davis 1989, Kapchan 1996; in the third, Hoffman 2008b, Newcomb 2009).

Form

Considerations of form were directly tied to the questioning of anthropology articulated during the 1970s and early 1980s. The first ethnographies of the early and mid-1970s (Crapanzano 1973, Rabinow 1975, Eickelman 1976, Hart 1976) raised very few of the formal questions that were to permeate subsequent work—Rabinow's second book refers to his first as "more traditionally anthropological" (2007 [1977], 7) a description that could also apply to the ethnographies just mentioned. We do find an early challenge to traditional form in Crapanzano's 1973 book, in which the reader, even before the book's "Introduction," is ushered into "A Hamadsha Performance" (as the four-page section is titled)—an episode I referred to earlier—that shows the anthropologist witnessing a religious brotherhood ritual trance and dance performance. But, on the whole, these early writings constitute a sort of generation zero, setting the stage for what was to come, but not yet formulating the concerns that were to dominate in many of the works of the late 1970s and early 1980s.[9]

In Rabinow's and Crapanzano's second books (2007 [1977] and 1980, respectively), and in my *Moroccan Dialogues* (K. Dwyer 1982), considerations of form were inseparable from the broader challenges these works posed to orthodox anthropology. As Rabinow says, his book is "a reconstruction of a set of encounters . . . a studied condensation of a swirl of people, places, and feelings" made to seem "neat and coherent . . . to salvage some meaning from that period for myself and for others" (2007 [1977], 6). His fieldwork experience, like a journey, moves forward—the progressive chapter titles are one sign of this—to end in an encounter with a "friend," with anthropologist and "friend" feeling "profoundly Other to each other" (ibid., 161). Crapanzano's opening sentence presents his book as "an experiment . . . whether successful or not I cannot say" (1980, ix), and later he describes it as "an experiment designed to shock the anthropologist and the reader of anthropology from the complacency . . . [of] writing and reading ethnography. . . . It is for this reason . . . that I have tried not to follow a conventional form in writing about my encounter with Tuhami" (ibid., xii). In my preface to *Moroccan Dialogues,* I discuss "feeling at odds with the main traditions within anthropology" (K. Dwyer 1982, xv) and explain that the particular experience, the research project, and the form of the book all emerged in the course of interactions in the field and in reflecting on them, rather than following from a plan developed prior to the fieldwork. My main aim in writing a text built around an "event + dialogue" motif (ibid., xvii) was not to produce "a faithful record . . . of the experience," a task I viewed as "impossible," but "to preserve in the text . . . what one believes to be crucial in that experience . . . here, the structured inequality and interdependence of Self and Other, the inevitable dialectical link between the individual's action and his or her own society's interests, and the vulnerability and integrity of the Self and the Other" (ibid., xix).

Placing formal concerns front and center has been a hallmark of many of the ethnographies that were written after these three. In some of the best, we see an increasingly explicit and self-aware effort to introduce, discuss, and display a variety of genres in order to convey the richness of cultural and emotional life in communities and among individuals, and also to give a more complex portrayal of how the anthropologist fits (or doesn't fit) into these communities. For example, there is discussion of photographs, television shows, and wedding videos (Ossman 1994), the presentation of song (Kapchan 2007b, Hoffman 2008b), the use of maps or drawings and poems (Pandolfo 1997), excerpts from fieldnotes (Crawford 2008), frequent appearances of life history and interview material, and varied uses of photographs, with some of these works combining several of these genres.

ESSAYS JUXTAPOSED

The ethnographic chapters in this volume present a great variety of fieldwork experiences that often extend concerns articulated over the past several decades, sometimes challenge them, and, on occasion, introduce new ones. In this section I group them in a rather subjective manner that reflects my own sense of the authors' partially overlapping concerns. First, I will discuss essays that focus on how anthropologists, in their encounters with Moroccans and Moroccan society, are pushed to construct themselves in new ways (van den Hout, Rignall, Crawford). Second, I will address essays about some of the problems that arise when trying to apply Western concepts to contexts quite different from those for which they were tailored (McMurray, Bargach). Third, I will focus on essays about how anthropologists find their way through complicated, multi-layered situations where they are faced with hostility and competition but also with friendship and support (Hoffman, Silverstein). And, finally, I will discuss essays that show anthropologists dealing with the tensions and dilemmas involved in identifying with, joining, and becoming an integral part of the lives of Moroccans and of Moroccan society (Spadola, Newcomb, Kapchan). As I explore the essays in this way, I recognize that I will not be able to do justice to their quality, subject matter, intricacy, and more-than-occasional flashes of humor, nor to the full range of each author's ethnographic imagination.

Charlotte van den Hout, Karen Rignall, David Crawford:
Confronting the Other, Constructing the Self[10]

These three essays, presenting three very different field situations, provide insight into some of the complexities involved in constructing oneself as an anthropologist, and we see that, even for the experienced anthropologist returning to the field, these complexities are never definitively resolved.

Van den Hout, coming to Morocco for the first time and beginning her first anthropological fieldwork in a psychiatric hospital in Salé, a city adjacent to the capital Rabat, starts out with an assumption she believes she shares with many, that the important languages in Morocco are Modern Standard Arabic (Fusha), Moroccan Arabic (Darija), and the several varieties of Amazigh (Berber) language, with French no longer used because it is so tainted by its history in Morocco. She is then "throw[n] ... for a loop" when a Moroccan woman insists on speaking French ("the language of Morocco's former colonizer") although perfectly capable of speaking Darija. As a consequence of this ethnographic lesson on the cultural meaning of language use and realizing that psychiatric professionals frequently use French in their practice, van den Hout is pushed to position herself with respect to these various languages and to construct her presence in this light, using Darija in her role as anthropologist and French as a student of psychology, employing both languages as a sign of her double identity.

Rignall, who already has some experience in Morocco managing a community development organization, is embarking on her first fieldwork as an anthropologist. Coming to Kelaa Mgouna, a town situated south of the High Atlas Mountains, she is accompanied by her husband and two children and intends to position herself as someone who will extend into Morocco a strict separation of work and life—a separation that she believes will facilitate her research and that she sees as characterizing U.S. culture as a whole. Constructing herself as someone who will control her fieldwork situation in this way, who will compartmentalize her roles as anthropologist (work) and as wife and mother (life), she finds her initial expectations challenged and her life orientation reworked. As she confronts the problematic relationship between work and life that arises in the course of her fieldwork, she questions her neat dichotomy and is drawn into the more fluid, interpenetrating conception of work and life she sees in Morocco: her children begin to accompany her on field visits, they adjust well to their new role as participants, the time she considers wasted (in bureaucratic procedures, for example) Moroccans view as simply an inevitable part of their lives. She realizes she can learn much from "an unplanned trip to the market to get provisions for a wedding and an afternoon spent accompanying a neighbor to a government office." As a result, she discovers that behaviorally and intellectually she requires a flexible approach rather than one oriented toward control and concludes that her initial assumption that "I do not live where I work . . . turned out to be wrong. I do live where I work."

Crawford, already an established anthropologist with a book on Morocco to his credit, returns to an Amazigh mountain community with his wife and two children and confronts the meaning of fatherhood and how it contributes to the construction of the person. As Crawford's status has shifted from unmarried adult (a status so different from their normal pattern that the villagers find it difficult to comprehend) to husband and father, he compares and contrasts his views of fatherhood and family with those of his Moroccan counterparts and provides a commentary on a theme that runs through many of this volume's chapters and that I will return to later—the theme of resemblance and difference.

In bringing his family to the field, Crawford faces a number of psychological and anthropological challenges that he admits to being unaware of beforehand. He mentions the almost tragic outcome of an earlier family visit—an experience he admits he was "not emotionally prepared" for (2008, xv)—that convinced him he would never again take his family to the field. In his chapter in this volume we learn that, as the memory of this experience fades, Crawford reconsiders and returns to the field with his family in 2009 (disarmingly, he titles a section in this chapter "Our Last Fieldwork," and we can only hope he means "most recent" or, if not, that again he reconsiders).

In this chapter we see moments of high parental satisfaction, even elation, but we also witness his daughter unwittingly bringing great embarrassment to the anthropologist and his Moroccan host. The counsel of Moroccans who have experienced parenting over much longer periods than Crawford has, that "children are *the* important thing," provides one of the chapter's key lessons; another is that Crawford, reflecting on experiences that have both traumatic and uplifting moments, finds himself forced to "rethink my relationship to Morocco, anthropology, and more" (with "more" no doubt referring to his family and to his life overall).

Both van den Hout and Rignall present their experiences to us in a matter-of-fact, conversational style. Each opens her paper by skillfully posing the main issues, van den Hout using a vignette that touches on the seemingly vital issue of religious freedom but veers—for the anthropologist, though not for the participants—to the question of language use, and Rignall opening her first paragraph with a challenge to the usual "arrival narrative" that re-interprets the often serendipitous choice of field site so that it appears, in retrospect, as "inevitable, even foreordained," and ending the paragraph with a down-to-earth closing sentence: "My choice of field sites had more to do with day care than serendipity."

In Crawford's essay—which displays a certain freshness in showing a male anthropologist seriously engaged with babies, children, and childhood—the author's strong first-person voice dominates throughout, winning the reader over with a fine blend of humor, sensitivity, and discernment. Crawford's children also play key roles and all the family roles are delicately balanced with those of members of the Tagharghist community he is closest to, so that we come to appreciate a complex, rich interplay among people from different societies.

David McMurray, Jamila Bargach:
The Uncertain Utility of Views from the West

McMurray, working in the northern Moroccan city of Nador and seeing himself as a Westerner trying to grapple with his view of Nadoris as exotic, shows an intense concern for how he situates himself with regard to Morocco and Nador and for how Nadoris view him, and experiences a tension between his desire to fit in and his wish to distinguish himself as having achieved a certain level of academic prestige. This tension comes to a head in a seemingly mundane incident, when a local barber questions McMurray's wearing socks with his sandals.

This incident spurs McMurray to explore the signs and meanings of status and prestige by wondering whether concepts used by some major Western thinkers to understand these aspects of their own societies might be useful in understanding Nadoris, a question that is intimately tied to that of how Nadoris may or may not be different from the populations that concerned these Western thinkers. This basic problematic—to see how Western ideas can help McMurray understand Nador—is something of an allegory for his own presence in Nador, as a Westerner trying to understand Nadoris. To move forward, he examines the different Western theoretical approaches of Thorstein Veblen, Jean Baudrillard, Pierre Bourdieu, and Paul Pascon (as an instance of Marxist analysis) to explore how they may help us understand the construction of status and prestige. McMurray finds Bourdieu particularly useful, not only because Bourdieu encourages a productive analytical dialectic between the similar and the different, and between resemblance and distinction (a theme we encounter frequently in these essays and that we will return to below), but also because Bourdieu's approach pushes McMurray to re-examine the meaning of his own dress and his own construction of self, as they may have appeared to the barber and perhaps other Nadoris as well.

Bargach faces challenges not dissimilar to those facing McMurray, among them one on the level of values, and another on that of method. Representing a Western funding agency (a German one), she has the task of using their "indicators and indices" to judge and evaluate a Moroccan institution, a nongovernmental organization (NGO) called Solidarité Féminine (SolFem for short), that seeks to provide support and counseling for unwed mothers and abandoned children. Yet her anthropological training in the United States has provided her with what she calls a "reflexive tool kit" that stresses relativism and that disputes the utility of both the scientific method and quantitative data. This training would seem to call into question not only the aim of judging but also the quantitative methodology she is required to employ—which, among its other deficiencies, seems to call for evaluating a charity with criteria applied to businesses and to neglect systematic differences in aims, constituencies, and values. Facing these tensions pushes Bargach to call her own self into question—how she has constructed it and what its implications are—in the course of which she recognizes that as a Moroccan woman of middle-class origins from a family with a "grandiose" past, as someone who has set "internal freedom" as her goal, she finds freedom being "constantly profaned, if not shattered" and begins to wonder whether the freedom that is violently "shoved in front of the women" isn't a distortion of the concept. "Was it really freedom, then—did it deserve this label?" she asks. All these considerations taken together allow her to embrace, rather than be demoralized by, the feeling of being a "non-native even at home."

With regard to form, McMurray grabs our interest with a rather humorous opening vignette that plunges us immediately into the daily life of the community he is working in. McMurray's presence in Nador is presented naturally, self-deprecatingly, reflectively, and reflexively, and the incident that triggers his interest introduces us to a local barber's habitus (to borrow a concept from Bourdieu). Bargach also grabs our interest quickly, but in a different way—beginning with an evocative scene-setting description that helps us appreciate SolFem and the Casablanca neighborhood in which it is located.

In spite of their very different positions—McMurray coming to Nador and battling his inclination to see Nadoris as "exotic," and Bargach coming "home" and to an awareness of how much of a "non-native" she has become—both authors attain a kind of balance, however unstable, between their training, preconceptions, and proclivities on the one hand, and the pressures and forces the field situation imposes on them on the other hand.

Katherine Hoffman and Paul Silverstein: Suspicion and Competition, Control and Unintended Consequences

Hoffman—like Rignall but at a more advanced research stage—is becoming aware of the obstacles she faces—and constructs herself as seeking to gain control over her field situation, even as she realizes that many of the obstacles are beyond her capacity to surmount. Her discussion enriches some of the issues raised in her book, *We Share Walls* (2008b), and we learn how difficult it was for her to obtain information (in a sort of ne plus ultra of discouraging advice, she is told that questioning is not an acceptable way to obtain it), the various kinds of suspicion that surrounded her at different stages of her work—those that were rife in the community she was studying, those that the state and other institutional representatives had of research among Amazigh (Berber) populations—and of many efforts to inhibit her research or to derail it entirely.

Silverstein has as themes for research his relations to a group of "Berber activists" who pursue the quasi-anthropological aims of documenting and understanding Amazigh communities, as well as relations within that group and between it and other groups. He faces some problems similar to those that Hoffman articulates—how to navigate amid competition and hostility among members of the community, and how impossible it is for the anthropologist to manage such feelings, whether they are based on loyalties and hostilities existing in the community prior to and independent of the anthropologist's arrival or are consequences of his or her presence. Hoffman certainly would have liked to visit Bu Afus—one of the rare men she found who was willing to discuss history with her—but she finds it impossible to do so without angering her main informants, so she stifles this desire; and Silverstein would no doubt have preferred to maintain his close ties to his "friend" Brahim but finds himself obliged to end this relationship, allowing him to re-establish fruitful contact with those who contested Brahim.

Both essays thus raise the general question of a researcher's control over the research situation and over the research project as a whole. This is tied to a related issue, that of the unintended consequences of human action.[11] Silverstein gives us an eloquent example of an action—repatriating colonial archives from France to Morocco—that seems unproblematic on the surface, but that leads to the unexpected consequence of an activist's using these documents to increase his own power in the community. Another instance Silverstein provides, in which his research is appropriated by other activists, reminds me of an incident in my own fieldwork, when a Moroccan sociologist published our interviews well before I had the chance to do so, although in this case I was pleased with the outcome.

These rather ironic incidents point to some others that, while equally unintended, may have positive consequences, such as moments when we lose control over the research situation but where the outcome is favorable. One example of this is Hoffman's finding her main informant (and through her, a field site) among the students she contacts, even as she is forbidden to continue her work in the

Taroudant boarding school; another is when Silverstein realizes that although Brahim has probably been stealing from him on occasion, their "friendship" grew in part out of that pattern. We have already seen some incidents that highlight this lack of control in earlier essays; we will encounter this phenomenon again in the next group of essays; and we will come back to this issue in the conclusion of this chapter.

Hoffman and Silverstein structure their contributions similarly and in a somewhat classic manner—an initial statement of a general problem (in Hoffman's case, in the first paragraph, the problem of "suspicion," including secrecy and obfuscation, among other aspects; in Silverstein's, raising the question of the relationship between resemblance and difference). After these general formulations, the authors move on to present their own experiences.

Hoffman's essay concludes by noting that the situation had changed significantly when she returned in 2008–2009 and encountered little or none of the suspicion that had marked her earlier stays. Perhaps this was due to a wider acceptance in Moroccan society of the Amazigh movement or to a general lessening of suspicion under Mohammed VI, after he succeeded his father. Or maybe the discussion about and adoption of new personal status laws—the *Mudawwana*—had enhanced the status of women and made research on them more acceptable, no longer so questionable. Or perhaps all these considerations, or some combination of them, played a role.

Silverstein's paper is dotted with revelatory incidents that are comments both on the nature of his presence and the character of the society around him. These and some related issues lead him to consider the existential nature of the anthropologist's presence and how this affects research—how the transitory nature of that presence, and its particular origins abroad, inflect the interests of those who occupy a similar field in Morocco, and how these aspects may be instrumentalized by community members. Silverstein's conclusion, that "resemblance may ultimately prove more academically and psychically challenging than difference," is very apt and thought provoking. It is related to the problematic of friendship, which appears in many of the contributions to this volume, but nowhere more powerfully than the chapter by Spadola, in the next group of essays I will discuss.

Emilio Spadola, Rachel Newcomb, Deborah Kapchan:
"Going Native," Conversion, Searching for Home

The contributions of Spadola, Newcomb, and Kapchan go a long way, as do some of the other chapters in this volume, toward helping us understand the personal itinerary and character of the anthropologist prior to engaging with Morocco, thus enriching our appreciation of the engagement while countering the traditional view of the anthropologist as a sort of tabula rasa, a technician armed only with the discipline's supposedly well-tested methods.

However, they are distinct from the other essays in directly addressing the fundamental theme of identification with the other. In these essays, this theme is pushed close to its limits in a series of refreshing, provocative, and at times gripping events and experiences. For Spadola and Newcomb, the anthropologist's self-construction develops in relation to communities defined largely as Muslim; for Kapchan, the central motivation is a quest for a "home," in the sense of reaching some sort of equilibrium or equanimity between the many aspects of her personhood and individuality, on the one hand, and the variety of sociocultural contexts and human activities she encounters, on the other hand. Spadola works out this construction primarily through his complex relationship with his "friend" Mohammed, his overall commitment to believing, and his ambivalence regarding conversion to Islam; for Newcomb it is through her relationship to her Muslim family by marriage (showing her marriage to a Moroccan as central to her anthropological experience), her encounter with Sufi Islam via her visit to the shrines, and the tension she experiences over conversion to Islam; for Kapchan, it is in her struggle to come to terms with her variety of dispositions—with her ambivalent relationship to the country of her birth, with her emotions and her "sensate" self, with her varied vocational proclivities (music, language, and anthropology).

Spadola's and Newcomb's contributions can be conveniently paired because they both have the question of conversion as a central problematic. Spadola opens by placing his concerns in the context of anthropological discourse over "rapport," and he traces the path he, as Ibrahim, followed with Mohammed, a relationship that was decisive in his conversion to Islam. Newcomb faces two conflicts that are related to one another: an anthropological conflict between remaining true to one's vocation of seeking to understand other communities and the impulse to identify with those other communities, and a more personal one between remaining true to one's origins and becoming a member of the other community, "going native." These two conflicts are in a tight dialectical relationship to one another and betray, respectively, the tensions between objectivity and empathy, and between continuity and transformation. Both conflicts are joined in the question of conversion—Newcomb's loyalty to her Christian upbringing versus her inclination to convert to Islam.

In addition to their similar concerns, there is also a similarity in how Spadola and Newcomb structure their presentations. Spadola begins with a general formulation of the problems of rapport, the various ways of generating it, and the challenges to traditional views of rapport raised by Rabinow, Crapanzano, and me. He then plunges us into an entertaining and often deeply moving account of his own experience in this area, which he frames in conversation with Rabinow's and Crapanzano's books. Newcomb opens by raising the general question of belief, framing the narrative around how she developed an interest in Morocco and its Sufi aspects. Both authors face a similar crisis in their efforts to identify with and move toward the people they are associating with—Spadola's blunder while performing ablution is like Newcomb's admission, while in the saint's shrine, that she's a Christian—and in both instances a dramatic moment of rupture threatens to upend the research project.

Spadola echoes, in a number of ways, points we have seen earlier that relate to a researcher's "control" over the field situation. His encounter with Mohammed, an encounter that will lead to a fundamental transformation in his way of being in the world, occurs largely by accident, and Spadola—referring back to the Geertzes' "accidental" rapport-generating incident in Bali—writes: "precisely because it is 'not a very generalizable recipe'—not a formal element of fieldwork—the mistake may lead to deeper ethnographic intimacy: their 'accidental host,' writes Geertz, 'became one of my best informants'" (Spadola is quoting Geertz 1973, 416).

In addition to accident (fortuitous or otherwise), another sign of the researcher's lack of control is the "mistake," and Spadola and Newcomb commit several of these in the course of their experiences and show them to us in their essays. For Spadola, mistakes constitute a central ontological category, since they open the potential for redemption through forgiveness: "By their incalculable, accidental quality, mistakes are quintessential gifts. And they are recovered through the return, the act of forgiving. . . . Friendship is like fieldwork, a series of accidents [including mistakes] in search of return, of forgiveness."

Kapchan is concerned with many of these issues—one's relationship to one's upbringing, building "rapport," and "going native"—but she adds some new ones and comes at them from a rather different perspective. She begins with an interesting account of how she came to be in Morocco in the first place—something she had not chosen and that was even in some way against her will, but that was chosen for her, perhaps an example of "fate." But it was also, as she says, a consequence of "following her heart." We learn, almost immediately, that in Morocco she "found 'home,'" and this leads to the questions that dominate her essay (and perhaps her life): "Why is it that some places are home-like and others remain forever foreign? What is the alchemy of place and affect that spurs the ethnographic imagination?" To help us understand her evolution, Kapchan looks at her Moroccan experiences in the light of Rabinow's presentation of his experiences (2007 [1977]) and Bourdieu's essay on the Kabyle house (1990), although it is certainly Rabinow's that elicits her strongest emotions—even her ire.

It is important to note the use Kapchan makes of "affect" (which also appears as a section heading, "Affective Methodologies and the Law of Genre," in her chapter), a close synonym to "emotion" and "desire," since these are fundamental aspects of being in the world and appear in many of the essays in this volume, although not usually named as such. This use is also related to another aspect that appears explicitly in her essay, that of the "aesthetic." Kapchan expresses her desire "to inhabit a new aesthetic position" as "a sentient and not just a thinking being" and, once again showing her corporeal stance, commenting that "aesthetic style . . . is in the body." She wishes to be similar to those "exiles, like artists, [who] seek out new aesthetic systems and try to domesticate them—that is, to make them their own, part of their home." One thinks of artists such as Paul Bowles and Juan Goytisolo, among others, who exiled themselves to Morocco and found new "homes" there.

Although centered on the problematic of conversion, both Spadola's and Newcomb's essays largely elide the basic question of what they actually believe. Spadola has come to the question of belief in part through his prior experience with Buddhist meditation, while Newcomb has reached it through her encounters with Sufi practice in Turkey and her reading of Fatima Mernissi's work; for both, the question of conversion is a central existential matter. While Newcomb wrestles with some aspects (or certain interpretations) of Islam that she has difficulty internalizing and Spadola with the intricacies of his relationship with his friend Mohammed, for both the motivation to convert appears tied more to their complex relationships with particular groups of people and particular individuals within those groups than it is to their specific religious beliefs. Neither brings us closer to understanding the question of conversion as a transition or break between sets of beliefs (or between non-belief and belief). Perhaps this reluctance to convey what belief means from the inside has to do with the deeply felt, almost all-encompassing nature of belief and how difficult it is to express in everyday language. These elisions, then, could be taken as an instance of Clifford Geertz's argument (using Alfred Schutz's terminology) that, when viewed from a "common-sense perspective," "religious belief [is seen] as the pale, remembered reflection of that experience in the midst of everyday life," while from a "religious perspective . . . it engulfs the total person, transporting him . . . into another mode of existence" (C. Geertz 1966, 16).

Kapchan's essay also has elisions—here, despite the rhetorical force of the notion of "home," we do not get a sense of individual Moroccans playing an important role in her search for home or in the essay overall, nor do we visit strongly affective places or geographical settings, other than the brief excursion into "The Berber House" as Bourdieu and as tourists see it (which provides almost a counter-example to "home"). These elisions are perhaps a sign of how Kapchan's ethnographic imagination differs from Spadola's and Newcomb's, for while it is similar to theirs in the concern with identification and belonging and, to adapt Kapchan's fertile discussion of genre, in being very much a *"Bildungs-Essay,"* Kapchan's elisions are applied in areas different from Spadola's and Newcomb's. Yet these elisions may also be seen as examples of the principle Geertz articulated: here the feature is not belief as seen from commonsense and religious perspectives but the private and intimate ("home," husband, child, divorce), shown as "pale . . . reflection[s]" when formulated in this public-publication perspective, but that might appear as "engulf[ing] . . . transporting," were this a private communication.

ANTHROPOLOGY, MOROCCO AND MOROCCANS, ANTHROPOLOGISTS AMONG MOROCCANS

Looking over all the essays in this book, we see that, in their variety and vividness, they provide examples of current, sometimes novel, concerns in anthropology; they give us insights into the diversity within Morocco and among Moroccans; and they present some of the emotional, behavioral, and cultural intricacies that arise when anthropologists are among Moroccans, as they try to live and work together.

Anthropology

In general we can see that the concerns that began to be expressed by a number of anthropologists writing on Morocco in the second half of the 1970s and into the 1980s are now central to anthropologists working on Morocco, a strong sample of whom are represented in this book, and that these concerns may now also be central to the discipline as a whole. The essays we have been discussing display a deep internalization of these concerns and move the discipline in some new directions.

In the first place, we see clearly the strong legacy of the challenge that "reflexive" approaches posed, in the 1970s and early 1980s, to traditional anthropology and how this challenge becomes, in these essays, integral to presenting anthropological experience and argument. No longer do we find reflections on the anthropologist's role limited to a section on "the significance and aims of the study," with perhaps a subsection set aside for "a note on field method,"[12] where we might find little more than a presentation of the fieldwork's timing, a recounting of its logistical difficulties, and a perfunctory remark or two on the nature of participant observation. Rather, we see reflexivity doing much heavier duty here, with extended discussions of the place and stance of the researcher and insights into the sensibility of the person through whose lens the reader views the community and into how the experience has transformed the researcher, his or her view of the discipline—and, sometimes, of life as well. Yet all this is deeply embedded in the life of the community being studied, so the interplay among these various actors provides us with a more profound understanding of the complexity of human behavior and belief.

This greater reflexivity has several implications. One is that it pushes the anthropologist to confront directly a number of epistemological questions, although not necessarily to come up with unambiguous answers to them. For example, what are the appropriate methods for anthropological research, and what criteria should be relevant in choosing among them (Rignall, Bargach); what is the utility of Western epistemologies in reaching an understanding of other communities (McMurray, Bargach); how should we weigh and decide among views of various community members and what seems important for the anthropologist (Hoffman); how should we deal with the tensions between judging, scientific evaluation, and a "relativist" understanding of a situation, or with the value conflict between treating women as victims and treating them as human subjects whose needs and situations should be seen as primary (Bargach); how should we reconcile the desire to convert, to find a new "home," or even the much-derided option of "going native" with the elemental loyalty to one's upbringing (Spadola, Newcomb, Kapchan)?

The lack of epistemological certainty, or even of a sure methodological procedure other than attempting to engage deeply with a community, is one of the many characteristics of the fieldwork situations appearing in these essays. Another, one of the most basic characteristics, is how the fieldwork experience calls into question the anthropologist's individual identity. Whatever conceptions of self the researcher may have had going into the field, some of these will certainly be challenged by the experience. In most of these contributions the authors, true to the reflexive impulse, make the situated "I" (that is, an "I" located in the field situation or within a personal itinerary, rather than a rhetorical "I" of the form "in this paper I will examine...") central to their chapters, and it appears, with but a couple of exceptions, on the first page, in the first paragraph, or even as the first word, of these essays.[13] This "I" is not abstract but one that, whatever its initial character, is shaped by the fieldwork situation; by the people the author encounters; and, we infer, by the people the author addresses in writing. In these essays we see anthropologists exploring how the language community they confront pushes them to use language to define and situate themselves (van den Hout, Bargach); how categories such as "U.S.," "Western," "Christian," and "Moroccan" are employed in changing ways to indicate identity (McMurray, Spadola, Newcomb); and how anthropologists, in interactions with community members, are increasingly offering their heritage, family relationships, and marriages as identity markers (this is central to the essays of Rignall, Spadola, Newcomb, Kapchan, and Crawford).

Another aspect that emerges clearly and that was often emphasized in the innovative works on Morocco of the 1970s and early 1980s is that, contrary to the received view that the anthropologist is in control and determines the nature of fieldwork, the fieldwork experience for both anthropologist and community members is a complex product of forces that include not only the anthropologist's will (especially as this is likely to change direction many times in the course of the experience) but also the plans, projects, and intentions (all of which are also subject to shifts) of people in the community the anthropologist is attempting to engage. Silverstein writes: "Fieldwork experiences are unpredictable, challenging, and—quite frankly—usually beyond the anthropologist's control." The impact of accident, serendipitous or otherwise, is very apparent in these chapters, sometimes in the choice of field site even before the fieldwork starts—a choice that is often the result of an extremely unlikely concatenation of events, as Rignall and Kapchan point out in their opening paragraphs—and Kapchan wonders whether her encounter with Morocco "may have been fate."

Escaping the anthropologist's control in countless ways, the fieldwork experience is likely to take on a shape quite different from what was imagined at the outset. We have seen many instances of this in the contributions to this volume: Rignall's realization that time she considered wasted was often quite productive, and that "some of my most important analytic insights have come from these daily encounters," from the apparently mundane aspects of "the rhythm of daily life"; Crawford's children's various mishaps and near calamities, which offer new experiences and possibilities for growth; McMurray's having his attire questioned by the Nadori barber, being "called . . . out" and having his "little white lie" challenged, pushing him to reflect on his own position and, more generally, on status and prestige in Morocco and elsewhere; Bargach's wondering why she took on a job—evaluating an NGO for a Western funding agency—so opposed to her anthropological training; Kapchan's chance encounter with a possessed woman leading her to further investigate and then publish a book on the Gnawa; Spadola's life-changing encounter with Mohammed.

Admitting this lack of control is one thing; perhaps even more importantly, many of these authors consciously bear witness to it. One sign of this lies in their portrayal of the emotional impact of these experiences. We are not shown the distanced behavior of participant observers efficiently collecting data, but rather anthropologists in the grip of deep and strong emotions—van den Hout writes of being "throw[n] ... for a loop" and Hoffman of being "scared"; Spadola is "frightened . . . unnerved . . . struggling . . . shaken . . . cry[ing] out"; Newcomb feels "shaken," as though someone was "ripping out [her] soul"; Silverstein undergoes "psychologically extremely painful" emotions; Bargach feels "impotence and frustration" and suffers "psychological turmoil"; Crawford experiences "one of the happiest moments of our parenting lives," which is soon followed by an incident in which his child "deeply embarrassed" his Moroccan friend and "embarrassed" him as well; Kapchan speaks of having "fallen in love," of having "the very core of my world rocked" in Morocco, of being "riveted" and "hooked."

Here anthropologists testify again and again to their inherent vulnerability, an issue I wrote about in *Moroccan Dialogues*: "In confronting the Other in so direct a manner; in seeking . . . to define and give form to experience; in questioning other people again and again to refine and articulate their experience: in all this the Self confronts an Other who parries, extends, and reworks the questions, who counters the Self's view of the experience, who may even refuse to continue the direct confrontation. Now, the very power of the Self is called into question and the fundamental problem of the Self's 'vulnerability' in the face of the Other is raised" (1982, xviii). The authors of these essays—in their openness to their own emotions and in testifying to them before the reader, in eschewing the somewhat stale distancing and contemplative techniques of conventional anthropological writing that worked to hide this vulnerability—push the quality and awareness of vulnerability to new levels and, in re-flexively putting the anthropologist in the action as a human subject, portray both anthropologist and community members with excep-tional density and vitality.

Another aspect of fieldwork that contributes to structuring human relationships is its transitory nature, an aspect that Silverstein refers to at some length. For the community members, the anthropologist is always a temporary visitor, perhaps someone who has provided some pleasure, perhaps a focus of complex emotions like those con-veyed to me toward the end of my first fieldwork in Morocco when I was told, in a voice that expressed both affection and regret, "You are like a pigeon—we raise you for a time and then you fly away." So the contrast is striking between what is for the anthropologist a deep personal and professional experience—a prolonged, intense encounter with other people that inevitably leads to a questioning of the self and the self's society, and that professionally is equivalent to an obligatory rite of passage and a distinguishing trait of the disci-pline of anthropology—and what may be for community members a relatively brief encounter, full of ambivalence, leading to a diver-sity of responses on departure and, should it ever actually occur, on return as well.[14]

The greater reflexivity now characterizing the discipline also has implications for matters of form and style. These essays are all delib-erately *written;* none is meant to express a "zero-degree" writing style or to present a distanced, objective picture. Instead, they are con-structed to reveal real people in often difficult situations. To accom-plish their ends, the authors employ a number of rhetorical strategies, ranging from the microstructural (vocabulary, sentence structure, and continuity) and medium structural (descriptions, actions, vi-gnettes, conversations, disputes, conflict, and social dramas) to the macrostructural (the overall construction of the essay, how the ar-gument or presentation of the experience develops, the point of view of the writer, the tone and mood, and the explicit or implicit vision of the audience being addressed). To examine these matters would take an essay in itself (or more), so I would like to focus narrowly on the existence of vignettes and episodes, where the presence of the anthropologist often gives these vignettes undeniable intensity.

There are a number of very dramatic, emotional episodes in these essays. Here we think immediately of the movement from elation to embarrassment stemming from the behavior of Crawford's daughter, the conflict Hoffman faces in whether or not to visit Bu Afus, Silverstein's attempt to have the French archives repatriated to Morocco, Newcomb's tense moments in the shrine, and the series of episodes in Spadola's relationship with Mohammed. But in addition to these very dramatic episodes, there are also a number of smaller ones in almost every paper that, in their own way, bring the reader into the world of the anthropologist and the community: a few examples are Nadia's appearance and reappearance in van den Hout's essay; the tense encounters Bargach has with SolFem's staff and beneficiaries; and McMurray's jousting with the Nadori barber.[15]

These episodes serve different purposes: to introduce the main topic (McMurray), provide a continuous thread throughout the paper (Bargach, Silverstein, Newcomb), make a particular point or move the paper in a new direction (Kapchan), furnish a climax (Hoffman, Crawford), or weave a rich and complex tapestry (Spadola). Some of them involve behavior by the anthropologist while others are more observational; some make abstract, theoretical points while others put the anthropologist in a delicate position and pose knotty ethical problems (this last aspect is also worth an essay of its own). But all contribute to the power of these essays in very effectively conveying complicated and often difficult situations and arguments.

Morocco and Moroccans

The Morocco—perhaps I should say the Moroccos—we encounter in these pages is a varied mixture of geographical, ethnic, societal, institutional, and class settings, and we see Moroccans as family members (parents, children, in-laws), patients, counselors, friends, activists, religious figures, and more. We witness events that span a period from the 1980s (McMurray) up through 2010, with most being located in the late 1990s or afterward. We see experiences taking place in densely populated urban settings (McMurray in Nador, Bargach in Casablanca, van den Hout in Salé, Spadola and Newcomb in Fes), in several smaller urban agglomerations (Hoffman in Taroudant, Silverstein in Goulmima), and in a number of rural ones (the High Atlas Mountains [Crawford], the Anti-Atlas Mountains [Hoffman]), sometimes with more than one setting in the same essay (Rignall is in the small urban setting of Kelaa Mgouna but makes many references to the rural community on which her research focuses; Kapchan evokes both densely urban Marrakesh and High Atlas village contexts). And we see situations in which Amazigh, Darija, Fusha, and/or French languages are used. Finally, we see behavior along a number of dimensions—competition, suspicion, friendship, empathy, hostility, and so forth. Yet even with all this variety, I am sure none of the authors in this book would argue that the volume as a whole can be construed as comprehensive, a point that Crawford and Newcomb make in their introductory remarks. In any event, Moroccan variety—or, as some have called it, the Moroccan mosaic—far outstrips the capacity of a small group of anthropologists to convey it.

What, then, can we say in a general way about Morocco and Moroccans, recognizing that the search for a Moroccan essence will inevitably fail but also that there is a legitimate need for some broader characterizations that go beyond simply repeating the particular and individual, however stimulating, entertaining, and edifying these may be?

In a number of these essays, we are made aware of significant aspects of civil society, with van den Hout bringing us inside a psychiatric hospital, Bargach inside an NGO providing support for unwed mothers and abandoned children, and Hoffman inside a girls' school in Taroudant, while Silverstein puts us among Amazigh activists, Spadola adds to our awareness of charity and doing good among Moroccans in everyday life, and Newcomb shows us the inside of religious institutions widely viewed as heterodox. And many of these essays, focusing on professionals, middle-class groups, and intellectuals, expand our awareness of social classes not usually treated in traditional anthropological research on villages, farmers, and illiterates. For example, we see psychiatrists (van den Hout), counselors (Bargach), teachers and school administrators (Hoffman), activists who are often middle-class professionals in their working lives (Silverstein), and religious professionals and intellectuals (Newcomb).

Almost all these contributions show Moroccans in relationships beyond the confines of local communities. Van den Hout discusses the use of language and how this expresses the complexities of relationships among various Moroccan communities and between Moroccans and France; McMurray shows us how returning emigrants affect symbols of status and prestige; Bargach explores the relationship between international funding agencies and Moroccan NGOs; Hoffman addresses inter-village relationships; Silverstein discusses the international aspects and awareness of local activists; Spadola focuses on internalizing the ties between his belief orientations and his multi-national, multi-ethnic heritage, on the one hand, and his impulse to convert on the other hand; Newcomb addresses the relationship between Sufi practices in Morocco and those elsewhere; and Kapchan discusses the relationship between migration and the tourism sector as well as the problems of finding a home in the world.

However, there are some significant gaps in what is presented here, which underlines how difficult—even impossible—it is in a small number of essays to encompass Moroccan variety. There is no treatment, for example, of important events in the life cycle of Moroccans, including births, weddings, sickness, old age, and deaths. Nor do authors discuss significant societal phenomena like the transition from Hassan II to Mohammed VI (although Hoffman makes some thought-provoking remarks in this regard), the impact of several "terrorist" attacks, and the new family code adopted in 2004.

Also, beginning in early 2011 and therefore outside the scope of this book, Morocco was the scene of significant agitation and unrest, following the popular uprising in Tunisia that deposed Zine el-Abidine Ben Ali, Tunisia's president since 1987, and that was followed by widespread upheaval throughout the Arab world that unseated rulers in Egypt, Libya, and Yemen; threatened others in Syria and Bahrain; and led to unrest in some other countries, including Jordan. In Mo-

rocco the unrest led King Mohammed VI to propose a new constitution, which was approved by referendum in July 2011 with over 98
percent of the vote, over 70 percent of eligible voters having turned
out. The unrest also led him to bring forward to November 2011 parliamentary elections scheduled for 2012 (in these elections the Islami-
cally oriented *Parti de la justice et du développement* [PJD] won the
most seats and, in line with the new constitution, provided the prime
minister). However, this did not stop the main protesting group—
known as the 20th February movement from the date of its first demonstrations in 2011—and other groups from continuing to demonstrate.

It would not be fair to expect the contributions to this volume
to foresee or foreshadow the uprisings throughout the region that
began in December 2010, but we do see in a number of these essays
conflicts that, as we trace them into the present, help us understand
some sources of tension in Morocco and, more specifically, what lies
behind two of the main changes introduced into Morocco's new constitution. These changes involve placing gender rights and Amazigh
language and culture at the center of Moroccan society.[16]

In an assessment of these changes, the Moroccan academic Fatima
Sadiqi, an astute observer of and participant in Moroccan societal
movements, has pointed out that "the new reforms in the constitution institutionalize Berber as an official language (alongside Arabic)
and reinforce the presence of this language in education and media.
The constitution also institutionalizes gender equality by encourag-
ing the creation of women's rights organizations and giving women
more legal rights—including the right to sue for divorce and to maintain custody over their children even if they remarry." But Sadiqi goes
on to argue that "all that is needed now is the political will to enact
these gender and language reforms," and she also cautions that, in
the area of women's rights, "the slowness of the implementation of
these reforms is largely due to a high rate of female illiteracy, poverty, and pervasive patriarchy, all of which constitute serious barriers to women's position rising in society and their understanding of
the reforms." The situation is similar in the area of Amazigh culture
and language where, although "the Royal Institute for Amazigh [Ber-

ber] Culture (IRCAM) and other Berber NGOs have largely contributed to pushing the Berber issue in constitutional debates," it is also true that "the ministries of education and communication have been slow to respond" (Sadiqi 2011).

In the contributions to this volume, we have seen a complex presentation of situations in these two domains, reinforcing both Sadiqi's optimism and her cautions (van den Hout, Bargach, Hoffman, and Newcomb, regarding the roles of women; Hoffman and Silverstein with regard to the situation of Amazigh communities).

Anthropologists among Moroccans: Living and Working Together

Hostility, Friendship; Difference, Resemblance

One of the key areas explored in many of these essays concerns the relationship between the anthropologist and community members, and this is often referred to directly using notions of hostility or friendship, or indirectly using ideas of resemblance or difference. It should be clear that, with regard to hostility and friendship on the one hand, and resemblance and difference on the other hand, we are not talking about simple, precise concepts, but about complicated ones that may have many dimensions each. Even a reading of these concepts that puts them in pairs as extremes on a continuum, from difference to resemblance or from hostility to friendship, is certainly a drastic oversimplification.

Let us look at friendship first, related as it is to the basic anthropological aim of building rapport. For many of the authors, the problematic of rapport is at the forefront: for some it is an essential structuring element (Bargach, Crawford, Kapchan), for others it is right at the center (Spadola, Newcomb). While ranking rapport from negative to positive may seem obvious, we also might rank it on intensity, running from mutually beneficial but not transformative relations of exchange (as we see them in van den Hout and Rignall) to the more intense forms of hostility and rejection (Hoffman's relationship with the head of the Taroudant girls' school) as well as competition (Hoffman's difficulties with the "lay folklorist" and Silverstein's with the

Berber activists), the broader self-questioning brought on by rela-tionships (Bargach, Silverstein, Crawford), and finally to the deeper, very complicated, and often transformative relations of friendship, devotion, and marriage (Spadola, Newcomb).

But any such scheme runs up against the rather fluid use and pol-ysemy of the terms "friend" and "friendship" that we find in these essays. We easily see that McMurray's rather generic use of "school-teacher friends" and Crawford's similar uses of "my rural friends," "my [Tagharghist] friends," and the "old friend" (with whom he has a short conversation) are quite different from Silverstein's unmasking, retrospective use of "my key informant and apparently close friend," who "led me to believe that we had achieved some equilibrium in mutual expected reciprocity" whereas the "friendship" may actually have been based on Brahim's occasionally stealing money from him, which "forc[ed] me to rethink my own understanding of local con-cepts of friendship, trust, and interestedness." And all of these are radically distinct from Spadola's rich exploration of the term with regard to his complex relationship with "my dearest friend, Moham-med." With the question of the relationship between friendship and interests always answered only partially, if at all, we need to ask how, and whether, the notion of "friendship" can be applied to situations deeply characterized by the "structured inequality" I have talked about above.

I believe we would find something similar if we unpacked the uses of the terms "resemblance" and "difference" (and terms related to these) as they occur in the course of these essays. Silverstein, after a nuanced exploration of his relationships with a community of Ber-ber activists who have many interests that overlap his, concludes: "Anthropologists and activists are mutually 'good to think'" (quot-ing Lévi-Strauss [1963, 89]), and that, with the similarities between them in mind, "resemblance may ultimately prove more academi-cally and psychically challenging than difference."[17] This phrase has echoes in other essays as well, when van den Hout wonders how she fits into the psychiatric hospital community; Crawford explores how his experiences and views of fatherhood compare to those of his Moroccan counterparts; Bargach asks herself whether she has come so far from her Moroccan origins that she has become, paradoxically, a "non-native even at home"; Spadola and Newcomb wrestle with whether they wish to identify themselves religiously with Moroccans; and Kapchan finds a new "home" to house her particular aesthetic, affective, and corporeal dispositions. Silverstein's notion also resonates strongly for a reason I have mentioned before: a growing number of works on Morocco (and elsewhere) focus on populations that are urban and middle-class and therefore have much in common with many researchers.[18]

Perhaps this discussion does not advance us very far in our effort to reach generalizing statements regarding the complexity of human relationships between researchers and Moroccans, but we can always return to the specific portrayals of complicated relationships such as those we find in Spadola's essay—which is exemplary in this regard—and many of the other essays in this volume. Some might say that the singularity of these essays reduces our appreciation of the general nature of human relationships; I would argue, on the contrary, that each in its own way enriches our appreciation.

Living and Working Together: From the Exotic to the Everyday

There is also an ontological aspect to the relationship between anthropologist and community members, between self and other. I am talking not only about relationships between individuals but also about how these are embedded in, provide commentaries on, and perhaps even challenge the relationship between the societies of which the various actors are members. As we look at this issue in the ethnographies on Morocco over the past four decades and in this book's essays, I believe we can see a subtle but significant shift of perspective. In the first decade or so of U.S. anthropological writing on Morocco, Morocco was seen as strange, exotic, foreign, and different, with anthropologists constructing versions of the strange and the different in domains such as religion (Crapanzano 1973, Eickelman 1976), institutions (C. Geertz 1979), family ties (H. Geertz 1979), interpersonal behavior (Rosen 1979 and 1984), psychology (Crapanzano

1980), and gender (D. Dwyer 1978, S. Davis 1983), perhaps epitomized in Rabinow's reification of a Moroccan "fundamental Otherness" (2007 [1977], 162).[19] But on his way to the "fundamental Otherness," Rabinow also related much in the way of the everyday. This change in register was central to my *Moroccan Dialogues* (K. Dwyer 1982), which dealt with a series of events in the normal, daily lives of particular, individual Moroccans. Then, increasingly, as we move toward the present, this perspective is deepened, as we find Moroccans seen by U.S. anthropologists less and less as exotic and more as adjusting rationally and naturally to the strangeness of the globalizing world around them. Several of the many ethnographies that adopt this perspective are by authors in this book (McMurray's 2001 study of migrants and smugglers in Nador, and Crawford's [2008] and Hoffman's [2008b] work on male and female Berber villagers respectively), and almost all the essays here adopt this perspective as well.

Taken together, I believe these considerations have led many anthropologists, including most of those writing in this volume, to abandon viewing "the field" and "home" as strictly separate from one another, a view that dominated classic anthropological writings and even the work of Clifford Geertz—for whom, as I have argued elsewhere, there is a "radical disjunction" between the two (K. Dwyer 2009, 408).[20] Certainly in the essays of Bargach, Spadola, Newcomb, and Kapchan, such a strict separation is not tenable. And this is arguably also the case for Rignall, who is no longer able to adhere to her initial hard-and-fast distinction between work and life; for Silverstein, who says, "Anthropologists do not control their destinies in the field any more than they do at home"; and for Crawford, who finds—in an interesting reversal—that it is his family life and structure that deeply interact with his vision of research in the field. This recalls an argument I made as I was working through the implications of my own first fieldwork in Morocco, when I suggested that, in our effort to imagine new forms of anthropology, "the solipsistic identity of the self has been destroyed . . . we have both left ourselves afield, and returned with the other" (K. Dwyer 1977, 150). It is interesting to see how this point and many others made by those of us working in Morocco in the 1970s have been extended, deepened, enriched, and taken in many new directions by the authors in this collection.

I have found the essays in this collection intellectually stimulating as well as extremely useful in helping us understand both Morocco and anthropology. In addition, many of the chapters elicit strong emotional responses, and I found them moving, exciting, and even exhilarating at times. As I finished reading them and realized how strongly I felt, of course I began to wonder, self-reflexively (again!), why I felt this way. No doubt it was partly a consequence of imagining myself back in Morocco and being reminded of some of the difficulties, obstacles, surprises, and mistakes in my own numerous fieldwork experiences in the country. But there is another reason, as well. Kurt Vonnegut Jr.—who had a direct, if ambivalent, relationship to anthropology, seeing himself as a "mediocrity [as a graduate student] in the anthropology department of the University of Chicago" (1981, 74)—argued that "newspaper reporters and technical writers are trained to reveal almost nothing about themselves in their writings . . . [but] almost all of the other ink-stained wretches in that world [of writers] reveal a lot of themselves to their readers. We call these revelations, accidental and intentional, elements of literary style. These revelations are fascinating to us as readers. They tell us what sort of person it is with whom we are spending time." He goes on to offer this advice to writers: "Find a subject you care about and which in your heart you feel others should care about. It is this genuine caring, and not your games with language, which will be the most seductive element in your style" (ibid., 77). This book's contributors unfailingly display this "genuine caring" and—in providing the reader with an anthropologist as central character, as human subject, in intense, prolonged, intricate, and sometimes bewildering relationships with other human subjects and with other places, and in enabling the reader to share these experiences—carry the reader along with a winning combination of sincerity, self-questioning, and openness to the other, offering essays that I believe will appeal not only to anthropologists but to a much broader public.[21]

NOTES

1. The heading of this section is a glancing reference to the subtitle of Clifford Geertz's *After The Fact: Two Countries, Four Decades, One Anthropologist* (1996) and should be taken as suggesting both the extent and limits of Geertz's influence on U.S. anthropological writings on Morocco, a subject I will deal with below.

2. I am excluding monographs written by non-anthropologists, even works that resemble ethnographies (among these are the historian Ken Brown's study of Salé [1976], Elizabeth Fernea's work on Marrakesh [1975], the geographer James Miller's study of a High Atlas community [1984], Will Swearingen's work on agricultural development [1987], and Cynthia Becker's study of Amazigh women's artistic work [2006]), as well as anthropology doctoral dissertations that deserved to be published but for one reason or another never were (such as Thomas Dichter's study [1976]). I also exclude works by Moroccans (or people of other nationalities) who are working in U.S. institutions but were trained outside the United States, or who were trained in U.S. institutions but have spent their entire careers working in Morocco (Abdellah Hammoudi [1993, 1997] comes immediately to mind in the first category, and Fatima Mernissi [1975, 1988, 1995, and many others] in the second). I do include Jamila Bargach, an anthropologist of Moroccan origin, since her anthropological training and a good part of her career took place in the United States (although she currently works in Morocco)—and besides, she is one of the contributors to this volume.

3. "What is certain is that these [anthropological] texts [on Morocco] are part of the recent history of American thinking about the Arab world, have been especially influential, and are part of what Moroccans themselves grapple with and respond to in contemporary cultural and intellectual production" (Edwards 2005, 268–69).

4. Geertz's comparative and mostly historical study of Islam in Morocco and Indonesia, *Islam Observed* (C. Geertz 1968), may be taken as the starting point of deep U.S. anthropological interest in Morocco. It is revealing that the only U.S. anthropological work treating Morocco that Geertz cites in this book is Carleton Coon's study (1962 [1951]), although Geertz does refer to the works of U.S. political scientists and historians. For a discussion of many aspects of Geertz's work on Morocco, see Slyomovics 2010.

5. This is an abbreviated version of the comments on Crapanzano's and Rabinow's work I offered in *Moroccan Dialogues* (K. Dwyer 1982, 277–80).

6. Geertz's views on placing the anthropologist in the text evolved from opposition to acceptance and even support, very much in line with the general trend in anthropology. In his *Works and Lives* (C. Geertz 1988) he was quite criti-

cal of such texts, specifically, of Rabinow's, Crapanzano's, and mine, although his arguments against each were different. Later, however, he reconsidered: "In *Works and Lives* I have some sardonic things to say about some attempts in that direction [of reflexivity], though I think it's the direction to move . . . we are part of what we study, in a way, we're there. . . . Now, I've never done it. Well, . . . once in a while I've done it. But I've never really thoroughly done it, and I've written a lot of books which are written from the moon—the view from nowhere. I am persuaded that at least for some works, for a lot of works, we've really got to get ourselves back into the text, to have ourselves truly represented in the text. . . . In the book I'm writing now, *After the Fact* [1996], that's what I'm trying to do. It's not confessional anthropology, and it's not about what I was feeling or something of that sort; it's trying to describe the work I've been doing with myself in the picture" (quoted in Olson 1991, 203–204).

7. In Hoffman, even though the focus is on women in a Berber village, they are seen in part as women who are "staying put" (2008b, 3), left behind by their emigrating men.

8. Crawford offers a somewhat different reading of shifts in subject, distilling "three main veins of scholarly writing" on Morocco: "First, there are the writings on the mountains that focus on lineages and egalitarianism [Ernest Gellner and David Hart]. . . . Second, there is an interpretivist literature . . . that focuses on culture as a kind of text that begs translation and interpretation [Clifford Geertz and Lawrence Rosen]. . . . Finally, [there is] a more contemporary set of writings . . . that emphasizes the power of the state, and a cultural emphasis on authoritarianism, writings that are in some ways the precise opposite of the egalitarian emphasis of the earlier tribal work [Rahma Bourqia and Susan Gilson Miller, Elaine Combs-Schilling, and Abdellah Hammoudi]" (2008, 142).

9. There were some throwbacks during this period to the "classic" anthropological monograph, as in Hart 1976—a work that, while traditional in its form, calls forth admiration for its generosity of spirit and attempt at comprehensiveness.

10. I use the term "confront" not in the sense of opposition and hostility, but in the meaning Hans-Georg Gadamer gives it: "Every experience is a confrontation. Because every experience sets something new against something old and in every case it remains open in principle whether the new will prevail, i.e. will truly become experience, or whether the old, accustomed, predictable will be confirmed in the end" (Gadamer 1975, 6). I would simply question his either-or formulation here.

11. Unintended consequences are closely tied to what I have called elsewhere the "wager" nature of the anthropological project and, indeed, of all human ac-

tion: "Its constituent elements are not neutrality, objectivity, and distance but rather, as in all human action, 'risk, possibility of failure, hope of success and the synthesis of these three in the form of a faith which is a wager'" (K. Dwyer 1982, 272–73, quoting Goldman 1964, 301). That the project may fail, that its "success is inevitably tied to social forces beyond the anthropologist's control" (K. Dwyer 1979, 214), is one way of conceiving such unintended consequences.

12. I have taken these section titles from Hart's excellent 1976 study.

13. Only in Bargach and Silverstein does the situated "I" appear much later, but this doesn't mean it plays a less important role than in the other essays.

14. Rabinow seems to have found a way to avoid the dilemmas and ambivalence of return by constructing his first fieldwork as a journey toward "fundamental Otherness" (2007 [1977], 162). Reaching this endpoint, Rabinow has no choice but to return home and, one might add, no need to do further fieldwork in Morocco—which, in fact, he never did. Spadola makes a similar argument against Rabinow's vision: "But just as mistakes are not the end of friendship, neither is friendship (contra Rabinow) the end of fieldwork, a magical path to cultural essence beyond which nothing more need be said."

15. The only essay that does not have such an episode is Rignall's.

16. Some of the other significant changes in the new Moroccan constitution include a much-expanded and more pluralistic notion of Moroccan identity and stipulations that the person of the king is no longer sacred, that the king's roles as head of state and Commander of the Faithful are clearly distinguished, and that the king must choose the prime minister from the political party that gains the most seats in the parliamentary Assembly of Representatives (Majlis al-nuwwab). There are also reinforced habeas corpus provisions, among other important, if not radical, changes.

17. Silverstein's formulation, "That anthropologists and activists are mutually good to think . . . ," which he used when he presented his paper at the MESA panel in the fall of 2009, constituted a very timely homage to Claude Levi-Strauss, who had recently died.

18. Silverstein's emphasis on resemblance has echoes, too, in my work on Morocco. In my second and third books, I focused on people who were mostly urban and middle-class and engaged in activities that can be termed "intellectual"— Arab Voices on people involved in articulating and spreading human rights notions (K. Dwyer 1991) and in Beyond Casablanca on Moroccan filmmakers creating and spreading their ideas and visions (K. Dwyer 2004).

19. Here are three examples that give the flavor of this approach and show the emphasis on difference, often with the aid of some rather sweeping generalizations: "One of the most striking features of social life in the Sefrou region . . . is the great emphasis placed on the individual. All societies, of course, are com-

posed of individuals, but in Sefrou the cultural stress and repercussions of individual action—the free play of personality—determine, to an extraordinarily high degree, the shape and operation of everyday social life" (Rosen 1979, 20); "[In Morocco] all three—family, friendship, and patronage—are ordered by the same cultural principles. In American culture the three are viewed as contrasting or even conflicting forms of personal relationships. . . . For many Moroccans, however, the social ties of friendship and patronage intergrade with family and many of the same norms apply to any of them" (H. Geertz 1979, 315–16); "in the details of bazaar life [in Morocco] something of the spirit that animates that society—an odd mixture of restlessness, practicality, contentiousness, eloquence, inclemency, and moralism—can be seen with a particular and revelatory vividness" (C. Geertz 1979, 235). And Kapchan, in her essay in this volume, highlights generalizations of this sort in Rabinow 2007 [1977].

20. Again, Kapchan's essay makes this point about Rabinow 2007 [1977].

21. I would like to thank Kirin Narayan for introducing me to Vonnegut's remarks.

REFERENCES

Abu-Lughod, Lila. 1986. *Veiled Sentiments.* Berkeley: University of California Press.

———. 1990. Romancing Resistance: Tracing Transformations of Power through Bedouin Women. *American Ethnologist* 17 (1): 41–55.

———. 1991. Writing against Culture. In *Recapturing Anthropology: Working in the Present,* edited by Richard Fox, 137–62. Santa Fe, N.M.: School of American Research Press.

———. 1993. *Writing Women's Worlds: Bedouin Stories.* Berkeley: University of California Press.

Ahmad, Irfan. 2005. Between Moderation and Radicalization: Transnational Interactions of Jamaat-e-Islami of India. *Global Networks* 5 (3): 279–99.

———. 2008. "The Society of Suspicion" and Anthropological Ethics. *ASA Globalog,* 4 February. http://blog.theasa.org/?p=49.

Amrouche, Jean. 1988 [1938]. *Chants berbères de Kabylie.* Paris: Harmattan.

Apffel-Marglin, Frédérique. 2008. *Rhythms of Life: Enacting the World with the Goddesses of Orissa.* New York: Oxford University Press.

Asad, Talal. 1993. *Genealogies of Religion.* Baltimore: Johns Hopkins University Press.

Bakhtin, Mikhail, and Pavel Medvedev. 1985. *The Formal Method in Literary Scholarship: A Critical Introduction to Sociological Poetics.* Translated by Albert J. Wehrle. Cambridge: Harvard University Press.

Bargach, Jamila. 2002. *Orphans of Islam: Family, Abandonment and Secret Adoption in Morocco.* Lanham, Md: Rowman and Littlefield.

Baudrillard, Jean. 1988. System of Objects. In *Jean Baudrillard: Selected Writings,* edited by Mark Poster and translated by Jacques Mourrain, 1–28. Stanford: Stanford University Press.

———. 1995. *The Gulf War Did Not Take Place.* Translated by Paul Patton. Bloomington: Indiana University Press.

———. 2002. *The Spirit of Terrorism.* Translated by Chris Turner. London: Verso.

Becker, Cynthia. 2006. *Amazigh Arts in Morocco: Women Shaping Berber Identity.* Austin: University of Texas Press.

Behar, Ruth, and Deborah A. Gordon. 1995. *Women Writing Culture.* Berkeley: University of California Press.

Bellah, Robert. 2007 [1977]. Preface. In Reflections on Fieldwork in Morocco, by Paul Rabinow, xxxi. 30th anniversary ed. Berkeley: University of California Press.

Ben-Layashi, Samir. 2007. Secularism in the Moroccan Amazigh Discourse. *Journal of North African Studies* 12 (2): 153–72.

Berry, Sara. 1993. *No Condition Is Permanent: The Social Dynamics of Agrarian Change in Sub-Saharan Africa.* Madison: University of Wisconsin Press.

Bidwell, Robin. 1973. *Morocco under Colonial Rule: French Administration of Tribal Areas, 1912–1956.* London: Frank Cass.

Borneman, John. 2007. *Syrian Episodes: Sons, Fathers, and an Anthropologist in Aleppo.* Princeton: Princeton University Press.

Boum, Aomar. 2007a. A Berber Heresy in the Arabo-Islamic Borderlands. Paper presented at the annual meeting of the Western Jewish Studies Association, Portland, 18 March.

———. 2007b. Dancing for the Moroccan State: Berber Folkdances and the Production of National Hybridity. In *North African Mosaic: A Cultural Reappraisal of Ethnic and Religious Minorities,* edited by Nabil Boudraa and Joseph Krause, 214–37. Cambridge: Cambridge Scholars Publishing.

Bourdieu, Pierre. 1970. La maison kabyle, ou le monde renversé. In *Echanges et communications: Mélanges offerts à Claude Lévi-Strauss,* edited by Jean Pouillon and Pierre Maranda, 739–58. Paris: Mouton.

———. 1984. *Distinction: A Social Critique of the Judgment of Taste.* Cambridge: Harvard University Press.

———. 1990. *The Logic of Practice.* Translated by Richard Nice. Stanford: Stanford University Press.

———. 2003a. Entre amis. *Awal* 27–28: 83–88.

———. 2003b. Participant Objectification. Translated by Loïc Wacquant. *Journal of the Royal Anthropological Institute* 9 (2): 281–94.

———. 2004. Algerian Landing. Translated by Loïc Wacquant. *Ethnography* 5 (4): 415–44.

———. 2007 [1977]. Afterword. In Reflections on Fieldwork in Morocco, by Paul Rabinow, 166–67. 30th anniversary ed. Berkeley: University of California Press.

———. 2008. *Esquisses algériennes.* Edited by Tassadit Yacine. Paris: Seuil.

Brennan, Teresa. 2004. *The Transmission of Affect.* Ithaca: Cornell University Press.

Brown, Ken. 1976. *People of Salé: Tradition and Change in a Moroccan City.* Manchester, U.K.: Manchester University Press.

Burke, Edmund, III. 1972. The Image of the Moroccan State in French Ethnological Literature: A New Look at the Origin of Lyatuey's Berber Policy. In *Arabs and Berbers: From Tribe to Nation in North Africa,* edited by Ernest Gellner and Charles Micaud, 175–200. London: Duckworth.

———. 2007. The Creation of the Moroccan Colonial Archive, 1880–1930. *History and Anthropology* 18 (1): 1–9.

Clifford, James. 1986. Introduction: Partial Truths. In *Writing Culture: The Poetics and Politics of Ethnography,* edited by James Clifford and George E. Marcus, 1–26. Berkeley: University of California Press.

———. 1988. *The Predicament of Culture: Twentieth-Century Ethnography, Literature and Art.* Cambridge: Harvard University Press.

Clifford, James, and George E. Marcus, eds. 1986. *Writing Culture: The Poetics and Politics of Ethnography.* Berkeley: University of California Press.

Cohen, Shana. 2004. *Searching for a Different Future: The Rise of a Global Middle Class in Morocco.* Durham: Duke University Press.

Combs-Schilling, Elaine. 1989. *Sacred Performances: Islam, Sexuality, and Sacrifice.* New York: Columbia University Press.

Coon, Carleton. 1962 [1951]. *Caravan: The Story of the Middle East.* New York: Holt, Rinehart, and Winston.

Crapanzano, Vincent. 1973. *The Hamadsha: A Study in Moroccan Ethnopsychiatry.* Berkeley: University of California Press.

———. 1980. *Tuhami: Portrait of a Moroccan.* Chicago: University of Chicago Press.

———. 1992. *Hermes' Dilemma and Hamlet's Desire: On the Epistemology of Interpretation.* Cambridge: Harvard University Press.

———. 2004. *Imaginative Horizons: An Essay in Literary-Philosophical Anthropology.* Chicago: University of Chicago Press.

Crawford, David. 2007. Making Imazighen: Rural Berber Women, Household Organization, and the Production of Free Men. In *North African Mosaic: A Cultural Reappraisal of Ethnic and Religious Minorities,* edited by Nabil Boudraa and Joseph Krause, 329–46. Cambridge: Cambridge Scholars.

———. 2008. *Moroccan Households in the World Economy: Labor and Inequality in a Berber Village.* Baton Rouge: Louisiana State University Press.

Crawford, David, and Hillary Haldane. 2010. What Lula Lacks: Grappling with the Discourse of Autism at Home and in the Field. *Anthropology Today* 26 (3): 24–26.

Csordas, Thomas. 1993. Somatic Modes of Attention. *Cultural Anthropology* 8 (2): 135–56.

Davis, Diana K. 2007. *Resurrecting the Granary of Rome: Environmental History and French Colonial Expansion in North Africa.* Athens: Ohio University Press.

Davis, Susan Shaefer. 1983. *Patience and Power: Women's Lives in a Moroccan Village.* Cambridge, Mass.: Schenkman.

Davis, Susan Schaefer, and Douglas A. Davis. 1989. *Adolescence in a Moroccan Town: Making Social Sense.* New Brunswick, N.J.: Rutgers University Press.

De Certeau, Michel. 1984. *The Practice of Everyday Life.* Berkeley: University of California Press.

Derrida, Jacques. 1980. The Law of Genre. Translated by Avital Ronell. *Critical Inquiry* 7 (1): 55–81.

Dichter, Thomas W. 1976. The Problem of How to Act on an Undefined Stage: An Exploration of Culture, Change, and Individual Consciousness in the Moroccan Town of Sefrou—with a Focus on Three Modern Schools. PhD diss., University of Chicago.

Dumont, Jean-Paul. 1979. *The Headman and I.* Austin: University of Texas Press.

Dwyer, Daisy Hilse. 1978. *Images and Self-Images: Male and Female in Morocco.* New York: Columbia University Press.

Dwyer, Kevin. 1977. The Dialogic of Fieldwork. *Dialectical Anthropology* 2 (2): 143–51.

———. 1979. The Dialogic of Ethnology. *Dialectical Anthropology* 4 (3): 205–24.

———. 1982. *Moroccan Dialogues: Anthropology in Question.* Baltimore: Johns Hopkins University Press.

———. 1991. *Arab Voices: The Human Rights Debate in the Middle East.* London: Routledge.

———. 2004. *Beyond Casablanca: M. A. Tazi and the Adventure of Moroccan Cinema.* Bloomington: Indiana University Press.

———. 2009. Geertz, Humour and Morocco. *Journal of North African Studies* 14 (3–4): 397–415.

Edwards, Brian T. 2005. *Morocco Bound: Disorienting America's Maghreb from Casablanca to the Marrakech Express.* Durham: Duke University Press.

Eickelman, Dale F. 1976. *Moroccan Islam: Tradition and Society in a Pilgrimage Center.* Austin: University of Texas Press.

———. 1985. *Knowledge and Power in Morocco: The Education of a Twentieth-Century Notable.* Princeton: Princeton University Press.

Ennaji, Moha. 2005. *Multilingualism, Cultural Identity, and Education in Morocco.* New York: Springer.

Ewing, Katherine. 1994. Dreams from a Saint: Anthropological Atheism and the Tendency to Believe. *American Anthropologist* 96 (3): 571–83.

Fabian, Johannes. 1992. *Time and the Work of Anthropology: Critical Essays 1971–1991*. Amstreldijk, the Netherlands: Harwood Academic.

———. 2002 [1983]. *Time and the Other: How Anthropology Makes Its Object.* New York: Columbia University Press.

Fanon, Frantz. 1963. *The Wretched of the Earth.* Translated by Constance Farrington. New York: Grove.

———. 1965. *A Dying Colonialism.* Translated by Haakon Chevalier. New York: Grove.

———. 2008. *Black Skin, White Masks.* Translated by Richard Philcox. New York: Grove.

Favret-Saada, Jeanne. 1981. *Deadly Words: Witchcraft in the Bocage.* Cambridge: Cambridge University Press.

Featherstone, Michael. 1982. The Body in Consumer Culture. *Theory, Culture and Society* 1 (2): 18–33.

Fernea, Elizabeth. 1975. *A Street in Marrakech.* Garden City, N.Y.: Doubleday.

———. 1998. *In Search of Islamic Feminism: One Woman's Global Journey.* New York: Doubleday.

Foster, Susan Leigh. 2011. *Choreographing Empathy: Kinesthesia in Performance.* New York: Routledge.

Foucault, Michel. 1988. Technologies of the Self. In *Technologies of the Self: A Seminar with Michel Foucault,* edited by Luther H. Martin, Huck Gutman, and Patrick H. Hutton, 16–49. London: Tavistock.

———. 2006. *Psychiatric Power: Lectures at the Collège de France, 1973–1974.* Translated by Graham Burchell. New York: Picador.

Fussell, Paul. 1983. *Class, a Guide through the American Status System.* New York: Summit.

Gadamer, Hans-Georg. 1975. The Problem of Historical Consciousness. *Graduate Faculty Philosophy Journal (New School for Social Research)* 5 (1): 1–51.

Geertz, Clifford. 1966. Religion as a Cultural System. In *Anthropological Approaches to the Study of Religion,* edited by Michael P. Banton, 1–46. London: Tavistock.

———. 1968. *Islam Observed: Religious Development in Morocco and Indonesia.* Chicago: University of Chicago Press.

———. 1973. *The Interpretation of Cultures.* New York: Basic.

———. 1979. Suq: The Bazaar Economy in Sefrou. In Clifford Geertz, Hildred Geertz, and Lawrence Rosen, *Meaning and Order in Moroccan Society: Three Essays in Cultural Analysis,* 123–313. Cambridge: Cambridge University Press.

———. 1983. From the Native's Point of View. In Clifford Geertz, *Local Knowledge: Further Essays in Interpretive Anthropology,* 55–70. New York: Basic.

———. 1988. *Works and Lives: The Anthropologist as Author*. Stanford: Stanford University Press.

———. 1996. *After the Fact: Two Countries, Four Decades, One Anthropologist*. Cambridge: Harvard University Press.

Geertz, Clifford, Hildred Geertz, and Lawrence Rosen. 1979. *Meaning and Order in Moroccan Society: Three Essays in Cultural Analysis*. Cambridge: Cambridge University Press.

Geertz, Hildred. 1979. The Meaning of Family Ties. In Clifford Geertz, Hildred Geertz, and Lawrence Rosen, *Meaning and Order in Moroccan Society: Three Essays in Cultural Analysis*, 315–91. Cambridge: Cambridge University Press.

Gellner, Ernest. 1969. *Saints of the Atlas*. Chicago: University of Chicago Press.

Goldman, Lucien. 1964. *The Hidden God*. New York: Humanities.

Goodman, Jane E. 2005. *Berber Culture on the World Stage: From Village to Video*. Bloomington: Indiana University Press.

Goodman, Jane E., and Paul A. Silverstein, eds. 2009. *Bourdieu in Algeria: Colonial Politics, Ethnographic Practices, Theoretical Developments*. Lincoln: University of Nebraska Press.

Grosz, Elizabeth. 2008. *Chaos, Territory, Art: Deleuze and the Framing of the Earth*. New York: Columbia University Press.

Guerts, Kathryn Linn. 2002. *Culture and the Senses: Bodily Ways of Knowing in an African Community*. Berkeley: University of California Press.

Guyer, Jane I. 1992. Small Change, Individual Farm Work and Collective Life in a Western Nigerian Savanna Town, 1969–1988. *Africa* 62 (4): 465–89.

———. 2004. *Marginal Gains: Monetary Transactions in Atlantic Africa*. Chicago: University of Chicago Press.

———. 2007. Prophecy and the Near Future: Thoughts on Macroeconomic, Evangelical, and Punctuated Time. *American Ethnologist* 34 (3): 409–21.

Hammoudi, Abdellah. 1993. *The Victim and Its Masks: An Essay on Sacrifice and Masquerade in the Maghreb*. Translated by Paula Wissing. Chicago: University of Chicago Press.

———. 1997. *Master and Disciple: The Cultural Foundations of Moroccan Authoritarianism*. Chicago: University of Chicago Press.

———. 2006. *A Season in Mecca: Narrative of a Pilgrimage*. New York: Hill and Wang.

Hart, David. 1976. *The Aith Waryaghar of the Moroccan Rif: An Ethnography and History*. Tucson: University of Arizona Press.

Harvey, David. 1990. *The Condition of Postmodernity: An Enquiry into the Origins of Cultural Change*. Cambridge, Mass: Blackwell.

Herzfeld, Michael. 1997. *Cultural Intimacy: Social Poetics in the Nation State*. New York: Routledge.

Hirsch, Marianne. 1979. The Novel of Formation as Genre: Between Great Expectations and Lost Illusions. *Genre* 12 (Fall): 293–311.

Hirschfeld, Lawrence. 2002. Why Don't Anthropologists Like Children? *American Anthropologist* 104 (2): 611–27.

Hoffman, Katherine E. 2000. Administering Identities: State Decentralization and Local Identification in Morocco. *Journal of North African Studies* 5 (3): 185–200.

———. 2002. Generational Change in Berber Women's Song of the Anti-Atlas Mountains, Morocco. *Ethnomusicology* 46 (3): 510–40.

———. 2008a. Purity and Contamination: Language Ideologies in French Colonial Native Policy in Morocco. *Comparative Studies of Society and History* 50 (3): 724–52.

———. 2008b. *We Share Walls: Language, Land, and Gender in Berber Morocco.* Hoboken, N.J.: Wiley-Blackwell.

Holmes, Douglas R., and George E. Marcus. 2005. Cultures of Expertise and the Management of Globalization: Toward the Re-Functioning of Ethnography. In *Global Assemblages,* edited by Aihwa Ong and Stephen J. Collier, 235–52. Oxford: Blackwell.

———. 2012. Collaborative Imperatives: A Manifesto, of Sorts, for the Reimagination of the Classic Scene of the Fieldwork Encounter. In *Collaborators Collaborating: Counterparts in Anthropological Knowledge and International Research Relations,* edited by Monica Konrad, 126–44. Oxford: Berghahn.

Hood, Mantle. 1960. The Challenge of Bi-Musicality. *Ethnomusicology* 4 (2): 55–59.

Howe, Marvine. 2005. *Morocco: The Islamist Awakening and Other Challenges.* Oxford: Oxford University Press.

Howes, David. 2003. *Sensual Relations: Engaging the Senses in Culture and Social Theory.* Ann Arbor: University of Michigan Press.

———. 2004. *Empire of the Senses: The Sensual Culture Reader.* Oxford: Berg.

Ilahiane, Hsain. 2004. *The Political Ecology of a Moroccan Oasis: Ethnicities, Community Making, and Agrarian Change.* Lanham, Md.: University Press of America.

Jackson, Michael D. 1996. *Things As They Are: New Directions in Phenomenological Anthropology.* Bloomington: Indiana University Press.

———. 1998. *Minima Ethnographica: Intersubjectivity and the Anthropological Project.* Chicago: University of Chicago Press.

Jameson, Fredric. 1972. *The Prison-House of Language: A Critical Account of Structuralism and Russian Formalism.* Princeton: Princeton University Press.

Jamous, Raymond. 1981. *Honneur et baraka: Les structures sociales traditionnelles dans le Rif.* Paris: La Maison des Sciences de l'Homme.

Jones, Tobias. 2005. *The Dark Heart of Italy*. New York: North Point.

Kapchan, Deborah. 1996. *Gender on the Market: Moroccan Women and the Revoicing of Tradition*. Philadelphia: University of Pennsylvania Press.

———. 2007a. A Colonial Relation Not My Own: Coming Home to Morocco and France. *Ethnologia Europaea* 37 (1–2): 115–17.

———. 2007b. *Traveling Spirit Masters: Moroccan Gnawa Trance and Music in the Global Marketplace*. Middletown, Conn.: Wesleyan University Press.

Keller, Richard C. 2007. *Colonial Madness: Psychiatry in French North Africa*. Chicago: University of Chicago Press.

Kirshenblatt-Gimblett, Barbara. 1998. *Destination Culture: Tourism, Museums and Heritage*. Berkeley: University of California Press.

Kulick, Don, and Margaret Wilson. 1995. *Taboo: Sex, Identity, and Erotic Subjectivity in Fieldwork*. New York: Routledge.

Laoust, Emile. 1930. *Mots et choses berbères*. Paris: A. Challemel.

Leamer, Laurence. 2001. *The Kennedy Men: 1901–1963*. New York: Harper-Collins.

Leguil, Alphonse. 1985. *Contes berbères du Haut Atlas*. Paris: Harmattan.

Lévi-Strauss, Claude. 1963. *Totemism*. Translated by Rodney Needham. Boston: Beacon.

Maher, Vanessa. 1974. *Women and Property in Morocco: Their Changing Relation to the Process of Social Stratification in the Middle Atlas*. Cambridge: Cambridge University Press.

Mahmood, Saba. 2005. *Politics of Piety: The Islamic Revival and the Feminist Subject*. Princeton: Princeton University Press.

Malinowski, Bronislaw. 1984 [1922]. *Argonauts of the Western Pacific*. Prospect Heights, Ill.: Waveland.

Mammeri, Mouloud. 1980. *Contes berbères de Kabylie*. Paris: Bordas.

Mansouri, Abdelmouneim. 1997. Code-switching et représentation des langues en contact au Maroc. In *Plurilinguisme et identité au Maghreb*, edited by Foued Laroussi, 81–92. Rouen, France: Presses Universitaires de Rouen.

Marcus, George E. 1995. Ethnography in/of the World System: The Emergence of Multi-Sited Ethnography. *Annual Review of Anthropology* 24: 95–117.

Marcus, George E., and Michael M. J. Fischer. 1986. *Anthropology as Cultural Critique: An Experimental Moment in the Human Sciences*. Chicago: University of Chicago Press.

Mauss, Marcel. 1990 [1950]. *The Gift: The Form and Reason for Exchange in Archaic Societies*. Translated by W. D. Halls. New York: W. W. Norton.

McMurray, David A. 2001. *In and Out of Morocco: Smuggling and Migration in a Frontier Boomtown*. Minneapolis: University of Minnesota Press.

Mernissi, Fatima. 1975. *Beyond the Veil: Male-Female Dynamics in a Modern Muslim Society.* Cambridge, Mass.: Schenkman.

———. 1977. Women, Saints, and Sanctuaries. *Signs* 3 (1): 101–12.

———. 1988. *Chahrazad n'est pas Marocaine: autrement, elle serait salariée!* Casablanca: Editions Le Fennec.

———. 1995. *Dreams of Trespass: Tales of a Harem Girlhood.* New York: Perseus.

Messick, Brinkley. 1993. *The Calligraphic State: Textual Domination and History in a Muslim Society.* Berkeley: University of California Press.

Metcalf, Peter. 2002. *They Lie, We Lie: Getting on with Anthropology.* London: Routledge.

Miller, James. 1984. *Imlil: Moroccan Mountain Community in Change.* Boulder, Colo.: Westview.

Mitchell, Timothy. 2002. *Rule of Experts: Egypt, Techno-Experts, Modernity.* Berkeley: University of California Press.

Moretti, Franco. 1987. *The Way of the World: The Bildungsroman in European Culture.* London: Verso.

Munson, Henry. 1991. *The House of Si Abd Allah: The Oral History of a Moroccan Family.* New Haven: Yale University Press.

———. 1993. *Religion and Power in Morocco.* New Haven: Yale University Press.

Newcomb, Rachel. 2009. *Women of Fes: Ambiguities of Urban Life in Morocco.* Philadelphia: University of Pennsylvania Press.

Obdeijn, Herman, Paolo de Mas, and Philip Hermans. 2002. *Geschiedenis van Marokko.* Amsterdam: Bulaaq.

Olson, Gary A. 1991. The Social Scientist as Author: Clifford Geertz on Ethnography and Social Construction. In *(Inter)Views: Cross-Disciplinary Perspectives on Rhetoric and Literacy,* edited by Gary A. Olson and Irene Gale, 187–210. Carbondale: Southern Illinois University Press.

Ong, Aiwha. 2006. *Neoliberalism as Exception: Mutations of Citizenship and Sovereignty.* Durham: Duke University Press.

Ossman, Susan. 1994. *Picturing Casablanca: Portraits of Power in a Modern City.* Berkeley: University of California Press.

———. 2002. *Three Faces of Beauty: Casablanca, Paris, Cairo.* Durham: Duke University Press.

Ouariachi, Kaïs Marzouk. 1980. Le Rif oriental: Transformations sociales et réalité urbaine. PhD diss., École des Hautes Études en Sciences Sociales, Paris.

Pandolfo, Stefania. 1997. *Impasse of the Angels: Scenes from a Moroccan Space of Memory.* Chicago: University of Chicago Press.

Pascon, Paul. 1986. *Capitalism and Agriculture in the Haouz of Marrakesh.* Translated by C. Edward Vaughn and Veronique Ingman. London: Methuen.

Pennell, C. R. 2000. *Morocco since 1830: A History.* New York: New York University Press.

———. 2003. *Morocco: From Empire to Independence.* Oxford: Oneworld.

Rabinow, Paul. 1975. *Symbolic Domination: Cultural Form and Historical Change in Morocco.* Chicago: University of Chicago Press.

———. 2007 [1977]. *Reflections on Fieldwork in Morocco.* 30th anniversary ed. Berkeley: University of California Press.

———. 2008. *Marking Time: On the Anthropology of the Contemporary.* Durham: Duke University Press.

Rabinow, Paul, George E. Marcus, James D. Faubion, and Tobias Rees. 2008. *Designs for an Anthropology of the Contemporary.* Durham: Duke University Press.

Rachik, Hassan. 2012. *Le proche et le lointain: Un siècle d'anthropologie au maroc.* Marseille: Editions parenthèses.

Rosen, Lawrence. 1979. Social Identity and Points of Attachment: Approaches to Social Organization. In Clifford Geertz, Hildred Geertz, and Lawrence Rosen, *Meaning and Order in Moroccan Society: Three Essays in Cultural Analysis,* 19–122. Cambridge: Cambridge University Press.

———. 1984. *Bargaining for Reality: The Construction of Social Relations in a Muslim Community.* Chicago: University of Chicago Press.

Sadiqi, Fatima. 2002. *Women, Gender, and Language in Morocco.* Leiden: Brill Academic.

———. 2011. Gender at Heart of New Constitution. MoroccoNewsBoard, 6 September. http://www.moroccoboard.com/news/5414-morocco-gender-at-heart-of-new-constitution.

Sahlins, Marshall. 1993. Goodbye to *Tristes Tropes:* Ethnography in the Context of Modern World History. *Journal of Modern History* 65 (1): 1–25.

Sennett, Richard. 1977. *The Fall of Public Man.* New York: Knopf.

Shammas, Anton. 1987. Kitsch 22. *Tikkun* 2 (4): 22–26.

Sharman, Russell Leigh. 2007. Style Matters: Ethnography as Method and Genre. *Anthropology and Humanism* 32 (2): 117–29.

Shyrock, Andrew. 1997. *Nationalism and the Genealogical Imagination: Oral History and Textual Authority in Tribal Jordan.* Berkeley: University of California Press.

Siegel, James T. 1986. *Solo in the New Order: Language and Hierarchy in an Indonesian City.* Princeton: Princeton University Press.

Silverstein, Paul A. 2004a. *Algeria in France: Transpolitics, Race and Nation.* Bloomington: Indiana University Press.

———. 2004b. On Rooting and Uprooting: Kabyle *Habitus,* Domesticity, and Structural Nostalgia. *Ethnography* 5 (4): 553–78.

———. 2010. The Local Dimensions of Transnational Berberism: Racial Politics, Land Rights, and Cultural Activism in Southeastern Morocco. In *Berbers and Others: Beyond Tribe and Nation in the Maghrib*, edited by Katherine E. Hoffman and Susan Gilson Miller, 83–102. Bloomington: Indiana University Press.

———. 2011. Masquerade Politics: Race, Islam, and the Scales of Amazigh Activism in Southeastern Morocco. *Nations and Nationalism* 17 (1): 65–84.

Sklar, Deirdre. 1994. Can Bodylore Be Brought to Its Senses? *Journal of American Folklore* 107 (423): 9–22.

Slyomovics, Susan. 2005. *The Performance of Human Rights in Morocco*. Philadelphia: University of Pennsylvania Press.

———, ed. 2010. *Clifford Geertz in Morocco*. London: Routledge.

Stewart, Katie. 2009. *Ordinary Affects*. Durham: Duke University Press.

Stewart, Robert Scott, and Michael Manson. 2009. Growing Up through the Ages: Autonomy and Socialization in *Tom Jones, Great Expectations,* and *I Am Charlotte Simmons*. *Janus Head* 11 (2): 257–86.

Stoller, Paul. 1989. *The Taste of Ethnographic Things: The Senses in Anthropology*. Philadelphia: University of Pennsylvania Press.

Stoller, Paul, and Cheryl Olkes. 1989. *In Sorcery's Shadow: A Memoir of Apprenticeship among the Songhay of Niger*. Chicago: University of Chicago Press.

Susman, Warren. 1973. *Culture as History: The Transformation of American Society in the Twentieth Century*. Washington: Smithsonian Institution Press.

Swearingen, Will D. 1987. *Moroccan Mirages: Agrarian Dreams and Deceptions, 1912–1986*. Princeton: Princeton University Press.

Taussig, Michael. 1993. *Mimesis and Alterity: A Particular History of the Senses*. New York: Routledge.

Trencher, Susan. 2000. *Mirrored Images: American Anthropology and American Culture, 1960–1980*. Westport, Conn.: Bergin and Garvey.

Tsing, Anna Lowenhaupt. 2005. *Friction: An Ethnography of Global Connection*. Princeton: Princeton University Press.

Veblen, Thorstein. 1899. *The Theory of the Leisure Class*. New York: Macmillan.

Vonnegut, Kurt, Jr. 1981. Triage. In Kurt Vonnegut Jr., *Palm Sunday: An Autobiographical Collage*, 73–81. New York: Delacorte.

Wagner, Daniel. 1993. *Culture, Literacy and Development: Becoming Literate in Morocco*. Cambridge: Cambridge University Press.

Warner, W. Lloyd, Marsha Meeker, and Kenneth Eells. 1949. *Social Class in America, a Manual of Procedure for the Measurement of Social Status*. Chicago: Science Research Associates.

Waterbury, John. 1970. *The Commander of the Faithful: A Study in Segmented Politics*. New York: Columbia University Press.

Weber, Max. 1978 [1968]. *Economy and Society*. Translated by Ephraim Fischoff et al. Berkeley: University of California Press.

Wehr, Hans. 1993. *Arabic-English Dictionary: The Hans Wehr Dictionary of Modern Written Arabic*. Urbana, Ill.: Spoken Language Services.

Westermarck, Edward. 1926. *Ritual and Belief in Morocco*. London: Macmillan.

Winegar, Jessica. 2006. *Creative Reckonings: The Politics of Art and Culture in Contemporary Egypt*. Stanford: Stanford University Press.

Yacine-Titouh, Tassadit. 2001. *Chacal ou la ruse des dominés*. Paris: La Découverte.

CONTRIBUTORS

JAMILA BARGACH is the secretary general of the Association Dar Si Hmad, in Sidi Ifni, Morocco. Her most recent book is *Orphans of Islam: Family, Abandonment, and Secret Adoption in Morocco.*

DAVID CRAWFORD is an associate professor and chair of the Sociology and Anthropology Department at Fairfield University. He is the author of *Moroccan Households in the World Economy*, winner of the American Anthropological Association's Julian Steward Award in 2009.

KEVIN DWYER has carried out anthropological research in Morocco, Tunisia, and Egypt and is the author of *Moroccan Dialogues: Anthropology in Question, Arab Voices: The Human Rights Debate in the Middle East,* and *Beyond Casablanca: M. A. Tazi and the Adventure of Moroccan Cinema* (IUP, 2004). He was most recently professor of anthropology at the American University in Cairo and a visiting professor at Columbia University.

KATHERINE E. HOFFMAN is an associate professor of anthropology at Northwestern University. She is the author of *We Share Walls: Language, Land, and Gender in Berber Morocco* and co-editor, with Susan Gilson Miller, of *Berbers and Others: Beyond Tribe and Nation in the Maghrib* (IUP, 2010).

DEBORAH KAPCHAN is an associate professor of performance studies at New York University. She is the author of *Gender on the Market: Moroccan Women and the Revoicing of Tradition* and *Traveling Spirit Masters: Moroccan Gnawa Trance and Music in the Global Marketplace.*

DAVID A. MCMURRAY is an associate professor of anthropology at Oregon State University. He is the author of *In and Out of Morocco: Smuggling and Migration in a Frontier Boomtown.*

RACHEL NEWCOMB is an associate professor and chair of the Anthropology Department at Rollins College. She is the author of *Women of Fes: Ambiguities of Life in Urban Morocco.*

KAREN RIGNALL is the 2012–13 Qatar Postdoctoral Fellow at the Center for Contemporary Arab Studies at Georgetown University.

PAUL A. SILVERSTEIN is an associate professor of anthropology at Reed College. He is the author of *Algeria in France: Transpolitics, Race, and Nation* (IUP, 2004) and co-editor, with Ussama Makdisi, of *Memory and Violence in the Middle East and North Africa* (IUP, 2006).

EMILIO SPADOLA is an assistant professor of anthropology at Colgate University.

CHARLOTTE E. VAN DEN HOUT is a PhD candidate in medical anthropology at the University of California, San Diego.

167–68, 178–87; in genres of ethnography and memoir, 168; Kapchan on finding home (belonging)
in Morocco, 167–68, 189, 234, 236,
238, 242; learning to inhabit a new
aesthetic position, 187–89, 193n41,
237; and Rabinow in Morocco, 187;
radical disjunctions between the
field and, 251–52; role of the household in cultural transmission and
personal transformation, 211–12. See
also ethnographic imagination and
the performance of everyday life;
"going native"
Hood, Mantle, 194n43
hospitality in Moroccan culture, 173.
See also friendship (rapport) and
fieldwork
hostility. See suspicion and hostility
Hurston, Zora Neale, 4

identity and the anthropologist: attire /
social status questioned by a Moroccan, 56–60, 229, 241; being
seen as outsider, 58–60, 133, 135–38,
200–201; conceptions of the self/
identity (the "I"), 240–41; control
and the fieldwork situation, 232–
33, 241–43, 254n11; ethnography as
anthropological bildungsroman,
176–78, 194n44; fieldwork and personal transformation, 6–7; finding "home" (belonging), 167–68,
189, 234, 236, 238, 242; and friendship (rapport), 12, 77–98, 235–36,
248–49, 255n14; inhabiting a new
aesthetic position, 187–89, 193n41,
237; and language abilities, 28–29,
132–33; local salience of the anthropologist's marital and family status,
208–209, 222; and the "native" an-

thropologist, 13–14, 151–54, 163–64,
230–31; new ontological conceptions of self ("I") and Other, 240–
41, 250–51, 255n19; parenthood and
the ontological shift, 195–97, 208–
10, 228; and religious conversion,
86–87, 90–96, 138–45, 234–35, 237;
resemblance/difference between
anthropologists and informants,
118–22, 233–34, 249–51, 255nn17–19;
shock of encountering difference /
fundamental Otherness, 41–43,
169–70, 187, 251, 255n14. See also
reflexivity / reflexive ethnographies
informants and anthropologists:
activist-informants, 13, 116–30,
231–34; Bourdieu on, 116–17, 118;
differing views of participant observation, 104–105, 106–107; the
"doubling of self-consciousness"
demanded of, 117–18; expectations
of reciprocity, 125–28; interrogations
of the anthropologist, 121–22; resem-
blance/difference between, 118–22,
233–34, 249–51, 255nn17–19; secrecy,
suspicion, and obfuscation, 12–13,
99–115, 231–34; self-reflection and
cultural objectification required
of, 118; the semi-commodified relationship, 125–26, 129n4; the term
"informant," 222; and "testing" of
the anthropologist, 82, 125–26. See
also Amazigh (Berber) activists and
the anthropologist-informant relationship; friendship (rapport) and
fieldwork
Islam, Moroccan: middle-class Moroccans' little interest in secondary
aspects of, 132; and Modern Standard Arabic (Fusha), 39n12; practicing salat (prayer), 86, 91–95, 97;

Milton Keynes UK
Ingram Content Group UK Ltd.
UKHW031959310124
437050UK00014B/1009

9 780253 009111